Chicken Soup for the Soul®

Parenthood

D0044080

Chicken Soup for the Soul: Parenthood
101 Heartwarming and Humorous Stories about the Joys of Raising Children of All Ages
Jack Canfield, Mark Victor Hansen, Amy Newmark
Published by Chicken Soup for the Soul Publishing, LLC www.chickensoup.com

The publisher gratefully acknowledges the many publishers and individuals who granted Chicken Soup for the Soul permission to reprint the cited material.

Front cover photo courtesy of iStockphoto.com/ivanastar. Back cover photo courtesy of iStockphoto.com/DNY59. Interior photo courtesy of iStockphoto.com/BanksPhotos, Vetta Collection.

Cover and Interior Design & Layout by Pneuma Books, LLC

Distributed to the booktrade by Simon & Schuster. SAN: 200-2442

Publisher's Cataloging-in-Publication Data
(Prepared by The Donohue Group)

Chicken soup for the soul : parenthood : 101 heartwarming and humorous
  stories about the joys of raising children of all ages / [compiled by]
  Jack Canfield, Mark Victor Hansen, [and] Amy Newmark.

  p. : ill. ; cm.

  ISBN: 978-1-61159-907-7

  1. Parenthood--Literary collections. 2. Parent and child--Literary collections. 3.
Parenthood--Anecdotes. 4. Parent and child--Anecdotes. 5. Anecdotes. I. Canfield,
Jack, 1944- II. Title: Parenthood : 101 heartwarming and humorous stories about the
joys of raising children of all ages

PN6071.P28 C45 2013
810.8/02/03525   2012954879

PRINTED IN THE UNITED STATES OF AMERICA
on acid∞free paper

22 21 20 19 18 17 16 15 14   03 04 05 06 07 08 09 10

Parenthood

101 Heartwarming and
Humorous Stories about the
Joys of Raising Children of All Ages

Jack Canfield
Mark Victor Hansen
Amy Newmark

Chicken Soup for the Soul Publishing, LLC
Cos Cob, CT

Chicken Soup for the Soul

www.chickensoup.com

for the Soul

Contents

❶
~Becoming a Family~

❷
~All in a Day's Work~

❸
~Is There a Manual for This?~

❹
~Parenting Faux Pas~

❺
~Stop and Smell the Roses~

❻

~Learning from Each Other~

❼

~Treasured Moments~

8
~From the Mouths of Babes~

9
~What Goes Around Comes Around~

10
~Love Conquers All~

⑪

~Saying Thank You~

⑫

~Giving Them Wings to Fly~

Chapter
1

Parenthood

Becoming a Family

Call it a clan,
call it a network,
call it a tribe,
call it a family.
Whatever you call it,
whoever you are, you need one.

~Jane Howard

Our Sunrise

What greater thing is there for human souls than to feel that they are joined for life — to be with each other in silent unspeakable memories.

~George Eliot

The only light in my hospital room came from the hall outside my door, yet I couldn't sleep. Across the room, the nurses had set my husband up in a bed of his own, but I didn't hear his usual snores.

"Are you asleep?" I asked.

"No," he replied. "I can't sleep a wink!"

With that, I scooted my enormous body to the edge of my bed, as best I could.

"Come on over," I said. "It's almost morning."

As he climbed in with me, we were silent. Both of our minds were racing with thoughts of what had brought us to this point, what this day would bring, and what our futures would hold, depending upon this very day's outcome!

We did not have to speak of the six years of infertility, all the procedures, the disappointments, the devastation of being told that we would never have a child of our own, and finding the strength to keep trying anyway. There were no words to describe the miraculous day when we found out we were finally pregnant via a payphone in a restaurant lobby. We both fell to our knees, sobbing. Weeks later we saw the three heartbeats on the monitor!

Triplets!

We did not discuss the crazy, fragile pregnancy we had endured, the emergency room trip when I went in to premature labor, nor the eighty-five-day hospital stay that had brought us to this very moment. We just lay there together, lost in our thoughts, with me remembering my husband as the annoying little schoolmate who had become much more interesting in seventh grade. We'd been together since we were thirteen years old and this wonderful man had stuck with me through so much.

Now, the lump in my throat closed off the words of gratitude and love I wanted to share with him on this last morning we would share alone. As the sun began to come up outside, it bathed the hospital room in a subtle, beautiful pinkish, orange light, seeping slowly through the slats of the window blinds, and quiet tears began to slide down my cheek as he held me close and rubbed my belly.

"Do you realize this is the last morning we will ever wake up as just Tommy and Julie?" he whispered.

"When the sun comes up tomorrow morning, we will be 'Mommy and Daddy,' and there will be three brand new human beings on this earth, all because of you and me."

"I was just thinking the same thing," I smiled.

"I know," he said. And, he did, because he could read my mind.

At that point, Tom got out of bed, walked over to the big window, and opened the blinds.

"This is our sunrise," he said, as he climbed back in beside me.

And, then, we watched it magically float up toward the cloudy winter day that would change our lives forever. It was one of the most beautiful moments of our lives.

Six hours later, with our family and friends down the hall, along with nineteen nurses, doctors, and various hospital staff in the delivery room, we watched three tiny miracles take their first breaths of life, as Emily Hope, Katie Beth, and Cari Marie entered the world—living, breathing proof that doctors don't know everything, good things come to those who keep believing, and love can make miracles happen.

The sun has risen and set many times since that perfect, glorious day seventeen years ago. And parenting triplets has brought us many days of ups and downs, laughter and tears, doubts and fears, memories and unimaginable joys and pains. We had no idea what was in store for us that morning.

From the very first day we brought our babies home, there has never been a "dull moment." From the feedings that came every fifteen minutes in the beginning and the thirty diaper changes per day, to the school days, packed lunches, house packed with teenagers, all the way to junior prom, there are days Tom and I find we've barely had time to talk to each other.

It is a busy, crazy, wonderful life in our home, very different from the quiet life the two of us had for the first six years of our marriage, when we chased our dream of parenthood so fiercely.

There are still times though, when we find a private moment together, when the two of us remember that moment, so long ago, when time stood still and the sun rose just for us. That day, our minds took a photograph of all we were as a couple right then, all we had been in the past, and all we hoped to be in our new role as parents, in the future.

And, we knew, in that moment, no matter what happened, we would always have our sunrise, and we would always have each other.

~Julie Speece

Sleepless Nights

*If you have a mom, there is nowhere you are likely to go
where a prayer has not already been.*
~Robert Brault, www.robertbrault.com

om wasted no time returning my phone call. "Don't put the baby on eBay," she urged. "I'll be over in an hour to give you a break." She showed up in a few minutes and removed my screaming newborn from my arms. She proceeded to rock her grandchild and sing to him while I went upstairs for a nap.

It was a well-deserved rest. I had gone without a good night's sleep for the first four weeks of my child's life. While everyone else in the world counted sheep, I counted down the minutes until the baby's next feeding. That was when the room would finally be peaceful again. Then, in the early morning hours, I burped, changed, and rocked my baby as the sun rose on a new day.

There were times when my fatigue caused me to be a bit short tempered with my mom—a very silly thing to do when someone is offering you help. "You are not the only new mother who has ever felt stressed and overwhelmed," she reminded me. "We've all been there."

My mom told me about spending late nights and early mornings in the rocking chair. "There were times when I tried everything to get you to stop fussing. I was at the end of my rope. But those days passed quickly for me. They will for you too."

I knew she was right. It would pass quickly—too quickly—and then there would be other reasons for staying up all hours of the night: driver's licenses, proms, dates, etc.

I remember coming home a bit late from a date when I was a teenager. I slid my key in the lock, quietly turned the door handle and closed the door behind me. I tiptoed past the squeaky floorboards in the dining room and headed towards my room. Then, a light flicked on and there sat my mother, waiting for me in the living room.

"Where have you been?" she demanded. "You were supposed to be home at eleven o'clock."

"It's only midnight," I argued. "What difference does an hour make?"

My mom grounded me for arguing with her and for breaking my curfew. She tried to make me understand that she was only angry with me because she was worried. I thought she was mean and unfair. It would take me years to realize otherwise.

There were several other occasions when my mom went without sleep because of me. She tossed and turned when I moved two states away and she undoubtedly paced the halls when I announced that I had withdrawn from college. I kept her awake with the kind of worry that only a mother can feel.

It's four o'clock on a Wednesday morning and my baby and I are wide awake. He has eaten and has been changed but he will not stop fussing unless I hold him. So together we sway in the rocking chair, his tiny head against my chest and my head drooping from exhaustion.

Years from now, I will be awake for other reasons. He will be late for curfew, driving for the first time, or going away to college. I will wonder where he is and whether or not he is okay. I will long for the late nights and early mornings that we spent together in the rocking chair. Then, when the sun rises and the rest of the world is awake again, I will call my mother. She will understand.

~Melissa Face

Reprinted by permission of Mark Parisi
and Off the Mark ©1994.

Outside My Reach

However motherhood comes to you, it's a miracle.
~Author Unknown

y friend Mandy fashioned her black hair into a lovely bun at the nape of her neck for the special day. After all, she'd been asked to present each mother of the congregation with a delicate rose. When she greeted the women entering the church, her cheeks flushed with pride—until she turned to me. The moment remains like a stubborn stain that cannot be removed. "Oh," she said with a glance, "you don't get a rose. You're not a mom."

Being childless for many is a respite, a relief from worry and responsibility, but for me it was an aching emptiness that could not be filled with anything material or spiritual. Infertility was a psychological mind-bender, a riddle of fate, or chance, or providence. At age thirty, after several years of marriage and infertile for no known reason, I never thought I'd be a mother.

When children didn't come into my marriage, I went back to finish my college degree. I threw myself into my studies and found a deep satisfaction in learning, but it was never a substitute for the ache of childlessness. I reasoned that with my husband in graduate school, me finishing a degree, and both of us working that it wasn't convenient to have children.

My community service in our neighborhood, however, threw cold water on my patience. The day I visited sixteen-year-old Gina, who was pregnant with her second child, I decided I'd had enough waiting and life was cruel like that.

A summer internship for my husband in another state became available, so we welcomed a change of surroundings. After three short months in the small town, one domino fell on the next until it changed my heart forever.

"I know an unwed mother who is willing to place her baby with you," a friend confided one day. Hopes, prayers, and arrangements ensued for the next seven months. She delivered early, so a blur of activity sent me on an airplane immediately, while my husband arranged to follow.

I wept in the hospital elevator after seeing the pink bundle through the maternity window. I wrapped her tiny fingers around mine in the back seat of the car while my friend drove us to her home. And in the morning, even before my husband arrived, the birth mother changed her mind.

To visit my older sister during a school break, I stepped over a bulging plastic lawn mower and nearly tripped on an array of balls, stuffed zoo animals, and a princess wand before tumbling into her sticky, cereal-laden kitchen. Kids. The footprints and fingerprints of her daily life was a cruel reminder that I was the sister who had none.

When I unbolted my door each day to go out, I realized that the only way to keep my sanity was to wear blinders to all the unwed teens and abusive parents who mauled and killed their children and the women who conceived as easily as breathing.

"You don't make enough money," the woman on the telephone at the adoption agency said. My mouth went dry and my brain numb, groping for a response. The list of adoption agencies that considered us worthy parents diminished with each phone call.

Finally, at our two-seater kitchen table in a dilapidated duplex on the east side of Dallas, my husband and I held hands and set a serious goal to bring children into our lives. We calculated the exorbitant cost of an adoption in light of our meager income and changed our perspective. After all, we were young and able, in a time when jobs could be had.

My husband worked from three in the morning to sun up delivering newspapers, attended graduate school in the daytime, built swimming pools until sundown and studied at night. In between those hours he washed windows on mansions at the far end of town. I added a secretarial job to my home-based calligraphy business while finishing my bachelor's degree.

Within four weeks, the phone rang. "You're invited to a baby shower for Jane!" the lady said. "Haven't you heard? They adopted a baby girl this week!" I slammed down the phone and refused to talk to anyone for days.

However, Jane's speedy adoption turned out to be the answer to our quest for an agency. Her agency told us, "We care more about your character than your income." I did a cartwheel in our cramped duplex.

My husband and I continued to work hard and resisted spending our hard-earned money on new wardrobes and excursions. We ate beans and rice, watched PBS movies with homemade popcorn and dreamed about the fruit of our labors. By the end of the summer we had saved enough to cover adoption fees.

The same phone that was wept over, slammed down, and cursed rang at the beginning of November. "It's a boy," Rhonda from the agency said. I repeated it over and over until I realized it wasn't a dream or a bad joke or a miscarriage, but the birth of our son.

Mandy peeked through the screen door to see me rocking a squirmy newborn and smiled. She brought me an offering of flowers from her garden to celebrate my new life—motherhood.

More than one well-meaning friend told me that as soon as we adopted, my womb would open and I would be pregnant. It was not to be. Instead, over the next ten years we were blessed with the adoption of another son and eventually twin daughters. Each adoption came to us through sacrifice and perseverance, the lessons I learned from wanting something outside my reach.

~Krisan Murphy

Baby Steps

In the eyes of a child... there is joy, there is laughter... there is hope,
there is trust, a chance to shape the future...
~Air Supply

knew things had changed the moment I stopped a lady on the street and complimented her—on her stroller.

My old driver's education teacher once said you don't really learn to drive until after you get licensed. I've heard a professor say you don't really learn how to work until you leave school and join the workforce. I have another universal truth to add to the collection—you don't learn about parenting until after the little bundle of joy is already in your house, screaming like there's no tomorrow.

Ironically, I really thought I was prepared. I watched episodes of *A Baby Story* over my wife's shoulder. I practiced disciplining my nieces. I watched (and judged) other parents in public settings. I even spent three Saturdays in baby classes at the local hospital. I thought I was ready. I was wrong.

The moment when I realized I was in way over my head will be forever etched in my memory. In the midst of yet another sleepless night, I arose to perform a diaper change. After reaching the changing table, I was confused by my inability to get my son to lie flat on the table. His legs seemed oddly strong for a seven-day-old. I turned the light on to discover that I had picked up my cat instead of my son. I knew it was time to get some sleep, or to get some therapy. Or maybe both.

Those newborn days were nearly a year ago, but in many ways they feel like just yesterday. Those first few months were the hardest for my wife and me, but somehow I already miss them. For weeks and weeks, you love and care for the baby and ask nothing in return. Then, one day, it happens—an awkward, toothless smile emerges that warms your heart in an instant and make all the troubles of the world seem insignificant. No matter how bad my day is, that smile never fails to instantly melt the troubles away.

As much as my son has changed over his first year, I think I've changed even more. While I was never really a daredevil, I nevertheless find myself taking more care with my physical well-being, whether it means locking the doors, eating healthier, or deciding I really don't need to hit fifty miles per hour on a downhill run on my mountain bike. Let's just say I don't want to miss what lies ahead for us if I can help it.

I've tried to augment my new parent eyes by trying to see life from my son's perspective. Strange as it sounds, I even got down on all fours and followed him around for a bit. I suddenly understood his fascination. The sofas really are like giant, soft cliffs. The edge of the bed is an endless abyss, but one worth exploring. A trip to the mailbox is like circumventing the earth, with a broad array of unfamiliar sounds, smells, and sights.

My son has recently begun to pull himself up to a standing position, though he doesn't know how to walk, nor does he know how to sit back down again. The pattern is as consistent as it is comical—he'll get to his feet, look around with a beaming smile as if to say "look what I just did," then he'll start to cry when he realizes he doesn't know what to do next. Sometimes he'll eventually sit back down with a thud, sometimes we'll help him. Either way, he'll try to stand again immediately.

Somehow I think we could all learn an important lesson from our children. How many of us have timidly shied away from a new goal or objective because we feared the unknown that followed. How many of us have focused so much on possible future problems that we failed to recognize the joy of standing up. It's a good thing these "adult" sensibilities aren't developed until later in life — otherwise, we'd all still be crawling on the floor.

More and more, my son impresses me. I'm impressed by his joyful approach to a world of mystery. I'm impressed by his total lack of fear and shame. I'm impressed that he has no self-doubt, despite the first haircut we saddled him with. I'm impressed by his ability to inspect a new toy with the same concentration as though he were doing calculus or disarming a bomb. I'm impressed by his understanding of what really matters — family, joy, food, fun, sleep, and love. Mostly, I'm impressed that he continues to stand up, even though he doesn't yet know what's next.

So, as we march blindly into year two, I have two goals. First, I will try to live my life with the same wonderment and sense of adventure as he does. Second, and most importantly, I will do everything in my power to ensure the next seventeen years don't go by as quickly as the first.

~Rob L. Berry

Our Sunshine

You are my sonshine.
~Author Unknown

I shook the hand of the seven-year-old boy in the church foyer after his foster mother introduced him to my husband Barry and me. "Someone ran into me today with a swing," he tried to say as he held out the front tooth that had been prematurely knocked out, but the sound came out all "ethes." Even so, his smile stretched from one side of his face to the other. His ears peeked out from both sides of his head like cautious mice on either side of his buzzed blond hair, and he wore cargo shorts and a striped green and blue T-shirt.

"Nice to meet you, Zackery," I said, and then I quickly excused myself and ran to the bathroom, where I leaned against the door to steady myself. Something about that boy tugged at me. Why was he with that foster mom? He should have been mine. Yes, that was it: it felt as if he were my son. How was that possible?

When I came out, Barry leaned over with concern. "Are you okay?" I nodded yes. How could I talk about this? It made no sense, this connection I felt, and yet, ultimately, it did. In just a few short months his placement disrupted and we were asked to take him. We said yes immediately, and "Sunshine," as I privately called him, moved in.

Though Zack was charming, as a younger boy he had been mistreated by a couple of women in his life and consequently did not like women. I tried everything to get him to like and trust me, but he remained distant, preferring to trail around after Barry and sit on his lap. As pleased as I was for the bond the two were forming, I felt jealous, too.

We didn't insist that he call us Mom and Dad—that was a mark of affection he would have to decide upon—if he ever did. Of course my heart ached just a bit when I registered him for school, calling myself his foster mother, only to have him call me "Drema" in front of the teacher. I blushed and explained that he was new to our home.

"Give him time," my husband said, and I knew he was right, but still it hurt to know Zack didn't trust me simply because I was a woman. When I bent to hug him goodnight and he flinched, I was hurt, but not only for me. What had happened to this poor boy? How could I show him he was safe here?

He had been so severely neglected in his early years, we were warned, that he didn't know how to care for anything, routinely destroying all of his toys. He didn't know how to play properly. The box of toys he brought with him really consisted of only parts of cars and trucks, tiny riderless horses, and headless action figures.

One gorgeous day soon after he came to us I asked him if he would like to go outside to play. "Why?" he asked. That's when I discovered that to him "go play" meant go outside and sit, maybe stare up at the sky. No one had ever taught him how to play! Well, maybe I could help with that.

"Let's play," I said, and I helped him gather some trucks. Once outside I helped him construct an obstacle course from tree limbs and bricks for his tiny trucks. I talked in funny voices and made the trucks race one another. Soon he was laughing and playing along, looking at me periodically to see if he was doing okay. I smiled and nodded a lot.

"What's that?" he asked as an ant scampered over a stick. "That's an ant," I said, and we trailed it all the way back to its home, a hole in the ground on our sidewalk.

After a while I sat on the porch with a magazine and watched Zack play. Now he was entering into the spirit of it, even making noises while sending the vehicles careening around sandy curves. Every now and then he would look up at me to be sure I was still there.

"When does Dad get home?" Zack asked, looking carefully at me. "In another hour," I said, pretending it wasn't a big deal that he had called Barry "Dad." It was a huge step for Zack. Yet a part of me so badly wanted him to call me "Mom." Patience…

After supper Zack brought me his stuffed dog, Fluffy. "Fluffy wants to play," Zack said. I smiled, remembering a birthday party my mother had helped me arrange for a favorite doll. "Isn't tomorrow Fluffy's birthday?" I asked. "I don't know," he said, his blue eyes looking troubled. "I think so," I said. "Why don't we bake Fluffy a cake and throw him a party?"

The next day we worked in the kitchen together, Zack gleefully icing the cake. I sang to him as we worked. Then we put a party hat on Fluffy and surrounded him with all of his stuffed pals. "What do we do now?" Zack asked. "Why don't we sing to him after we blow the candles out?" I suggested.

At bedtime Zack sat on my lap. "I liked throwing Fluffy a party. And I like ants," he said. He dropped his voice: "And I like you, Mom." I glanced at my husband through my tears as I hugged my son who, in a short year, would become our adoptive son. We smiled together, Barry and I, and though I don't think he knew why, Zack smiled too. Our Sunshine.

~Drema Sizemore Drudge

Breathing Easy

When you have brought up kids, there are memories you store directly in your tear ducts.

~Robert Brault, www.robertbrault.com

oments after our daughter was born, the doctor held her up and pronounced, "She's beautiful and perfect!" With her healthy cries ringing in my ears, I reached out and the nurse placed her in my arms. "Hello Summer," I whispered. "Welcome to the world." At my voice, her sobs quieted and she began to nurse. "Look at that," I said to my husband Fred and my best friend Marcie. "She's a natural!"

A heartbeat later, she turned blue.

The nurse's happy expression turned to one of concern. "Doctor," she said quietly. He looked over at the baby, frowned and in two strides was at my bedside. He observed her with concern for only a second or two before reaching out and gently lifting her from my arms, then turning to hand her to the nurse, who whisked her away to the bathing area across the room. Summer, upset at having her first meal so unceremoniously interrupted, began to wail again.

"Don't worry," the doctor told us. "We'll just suction her mouth and throat and clean her up a little. I'm sure she's fine." A few minutes later, the nurse called out, "Okay, all better now—pink and perky!" and having wrapped her in a soft blanket, brought her back to me to nurse. Once again, she stopped crying to latch on greedily. Once again, within seconds, she turned blue.

"What's happening?" I cried.

The doctor looked up from the chart he was writing in; his expression went from concerned to grave. In seconds he was at my bedside, taking her from me once more. "I think we'll just go run some tests," he said.

"What's wrong with her?" my husband asked him.

"Probably nothing serious, but we'll know more in a few minutes. Try not to worry, okay?" he told us. "See, she's already looking better." Summer was crying again and thankfully, turning pink as we all watched.

As he and the nurse left the room, Fred and Marcie and I all looked at one another with worried eyes. Reaching for my husband's hand, I said, "She's going to be okay, right?"

He nodded. "Sure. Of course." Marcie took my other hand silently and squeezed it. The three of us spent the next hour staring at the door through which the doctor and our baby had disappeared.

When the nurse came back into the room, her troubled expression spoke volumes. Marcie cried, "Is she okay?"

"The doctor will be in any minute now," said the nurse evasively. As predicted, the doctor came through the door and before we could ask, he said, "Well, I'm sorry to tell you this but your baby has a very rare birth defect; it's called a choanal atresia. It is a congenital disorder where the back of the nasal passage (the choana) is blocked, usually by abnormal bony or soft tissue formed during fetal development," he told us. "In other words, your daughter can't breathe through her nose at all. She needs to have surgery as soon as possible because babies don't breathe through their mouths when their nasal passages are blocked. They don't know how." He moved to my bedside and explained further, "That's why, when she was crying, she stayed pink—she was getting enough oxygen. But when she began to nurse—well, there was no air getting through her nostrils. She was suffocating."

"Surgery?" I whispered. I was trying to grasp the enormity of this nightmare.

He nodded. "Fortunately though, there is a surgeon up on the hill at Oregon Health Sciences University Hospital who has actually had several of these cases before. I've talked to him already and he'll be waiting to see her when she gets there." He laid a comforting hand on my shoulder. "He's very good. Try not to worry, okay?"

I blinked away tears and shook my head. How could I not worry?

"They're sending an ambulance team from OHSU to pick her up. They should be here within the hour."

"An hour? But she can't breathe!" my husband said. "How are you keeping her alive?"

"We have a tracheal tube in place; she's breathing fine for now. We'll bring her in to you so you can hold her before they take off, okay?"

We nodded our heads, too overcome to speak, questions racing though our minds. How could something like this happen? Would she survive the surgery?

When they brought Summer in barely an hour later, she had a tube down her throat keeping her airway open. Surgical tape across her cheeks held the tube in place. They laid her in my arms; I held her and cried while Fred and Marcie stroked her little hands and downy hair and fought back their own tears. Finally, after too short a time, one of the paramedics stepped forward and said, "I'm sorry, but we have to go now. The surgeon is waiting to examine her." As I handed my daughter to him, I had to turn my face away; I couldn't watch him take her out the door, knowing I might never see her again.

It was one of the longest nights of my life.

• • •

Three days later, Summer had the surgery. The surgeon drilled through the wall of bone at the floor of her nasal cavity, creating twin passageways for her to breathe through. When that was completed, he stitched clear plastic tubes, called stents into the passages to keep them open. "These will stay in place for three months," he told us.

We left the hospital with our daughter two days later. Before we were allowed to take her home, however, we were given CPR training, and outfitted with a heart monitor and a suction machine to keep the tubes cleared of mucus.

The coming days were nerve-racking, especially after the three months became six months; but we made it! When the tubes were ultimately removed, Summer could finally breathe easy; and so could we.

Today, our daughter is a beautiful, healthy, twenty-eight-year-old woman. I look at her and thank God for the precious gift she is. I think about how easily we could have lost her and I reflect on how going through all the worry surrounding her birth deepened my appreciation of being a parent. Mostly though, I simply think about how blessed we have been and are, and I'm grateful beyond measure.

~Tina Wagner Mattern

Reunion

To us, family means putting your arms around each other and being there.
~Barbara Bush

I barely heard my phone ring over the driving rain beating down on the windshield. "This is Andrea, how can I help you?"

"You don't know me, but my name is Cozette. Is this a good time for you?"

"Certainly Cozette, what can I do for you?"

With that I opened the floodgates as she poured out her life story. She had recently lost "another" baby she said, as she began to cry. She could not seem to carry one to full-term. She needed to know her medical history—but she had been adopted at birth. She related how she had finally found her birth mother three years ago but still had not found her father. I quietly listened. She talked for close to ten minutes and then suddenly she got very quiet. I asked, "Honey, are you all right?" What she said next made my heart skip a beat.

"Yes, but I have something to tell you and I need to know that you are going to be okay... are you driving? Can you pull over?"

"What?" What had I missed? Had she said anything about calling from a hospital? What was wrong?

"You know how I told you that I was adopted and looking for my biological father? Well, I think your husband may be my father." She began talking very fast trying to get it all out. My head was spinning and I was only catching snippets of her words now: "never told the father;" "unwed mothers home;" "birth certificate—Father:

Unknown." Once she realized I was not going to hang up she slowed down and filled in the blanks. Her birth mother had been reluctant to tell her who her father was at first but because of her medical issues she had finally agreed to help her find him.

I regained my composure and said, "Honey, I know you really want to find your biological father but I'm afraid you probably have the wrong person. I'm sorry, but we have been married quite a long time and I'm pretty sure it is not him. And what did you say your mother's name was?"

"Deborah," she quickly answered and then told me her last name. She was the last girl that my husband dated before we met. I remember the look of hurt and confusion as he told me the story when we started dating. They had been seeing each other about six months and shortly after Christmas she just disappeared. "Her mother told me she decided to go live with her grandmother in another city and attend school there. She never even said goodbye," he said. He and I married the following year and I had not heard her name in over twenty-five years!

I had married young and was divorced with three small children when we met. While he always assured me he was perfectly content being a father to my children, I knew he had always wanted a child of his own and for years I carried a lot of guilt because of that. Could this really be my husband's daughter—his only biological child? The magnitude of that began to sink in. She was babbling excitedly now—certain with that last bit of information that her lifelong quest was nearing an end. We talked the rest of my two-hour drive. She told me how she had contacted an agency to help her find her parents and had been coached on how to approach them. She said she knew that I might hang up on her or that her father might not want anything to do with her.

I remember thinking how silly that sounded. He had been waiting for her all of his life. I assured her he would call her as soon as he got home… and of course he did.

At fifty years old and after twenty-six years of marriage, we got our fourth child. She was an unexpected blessing who made our family truly complete. I remember assuring her at our first meeting that God works in mysterious ways and I truly believed that He used her prior health issues to bring our family together at last. I told her I had complete faith that she would now be able to carry and give birth to a healthy baby with no further problems.

That was eight years ago and not only did we get a new daughter but now two beautiful grandsons as well!

~Andrea Peebles

My New Family

*One good thing about Internet dating:
you're guaranteed to click with whomever you meet.*
~Mongo

When I was twenty-seven years old I did something very uncharacteristic for me. I answered a personal ad on the Internet.

Most of the ads that people had posted were the regular old stuff. None of them really caught my attention until I came to his. The ad said, "I have four kids and they need a mommy." Call me crazy, but there was just something about what he wrote that drew me in. I sat there for several minutes thinking about how I doubted he would be getting any responses with a headline like that. Most people wouldn't be interested in taking on someone else's family.

I sent him a message. We clicked right away. I worked first shift and he worked second shift, so I would eagerly wait up late at night for him to get home so we could chat. After talking via e-mail for a month, I learned his wife had abandoned him and the children and he was raising them on his own. That made me like him even more. I knew he was a responsible person to be raising four kids. We seemed to have so much in common and we got along so well that we agreed to meet in person.

On Sundays he took his children to the park close to his home and on this Sunday I was invited to join them. I very nervously drove the forty-five minutes from my home to the park. I parked my blue Dodge Neon and stepped out of my car, took a few steps onto the crunchy summer grass, turned around and got back into my car. I was too nervous to meet him. I thought to myself, "What if he doesn't like me? What if he thinks I am unattractive?" I didn't think I could handle the rejection.

Finally, I forced myself to go and meet him and the children. When I found him and introduced myself, we sat there for what seemed like a very long time, neither one of us having much to say. We were both very shy. We made small talk, talked about the ages of his children who were two, four, six and seven, and the hot June weather that day. The next thing I knew, a little girl came running by asking, "Who is that, Daddy?" She made a few more laps around us, checking me out, when she suddenly fell and skinned her knee, bursting into tears. I had a first aid kit in the trunk of my car, so we went and I cleaned out her wound, put a bandage on her knee and gave it a big kiss. The tears quickly dried and she asked, "Are you going to be our new mommy?" Caught by surprise I didn't know what to say, so I just smiled at her and said, "Uhhhhh..."

As it was getting to be evening, it was time to go home. The boys were off playing on the opposite side of the park so we went to gather them up. We found them playing and running around like active children do, and all of us walked back to our cars, marking the end of the day. Paul was putting the boys into their cars seats, so Melanie decided she would invite me over to their home. "We just live down the street," she said to me. I laughed at her, as she was very much the social butterfly, thanked her for inviting me, but told her we all had to go home for the evening.

After all the children were safely strapped in, Paul and I said goodbye. He held my hands for the longest time. I thought he was absolutely wonderful. I hoped he had liked me enough to want a second date. We said our goodbyes and went our separate ways.

People told me I was crazy to date a man with four small children. I heard everything from "there is no way I would do that" to "you don't want someone else's children, you want your own."

After only four months of dating, we eloped in October 2000 and I became the new mommy to four wonderful children. I had no doubts that I was doing the right thing and we have never looked back.

The kids are now fourteen, sixteen, eighteen and nineteen. I can't say there have never been bumps in the road, but they have been the best years of my life. I have loved every minute of being their mother and being Paul's wife. All four children have made us very proud as they have grown into responsible teenagers. At eighteen, Melanie is still the social butterfly, just like she was back when I met her at age six. Cody and Wyatt are still rambunctious and are growing into responsible young men. Ryder is a wonderful fourteen-year-old who still exhibits the same personality as the toddler that was sitting on his father's lap the day I met him. Paul has been the husband I always wanted. I couldn't love him any more than I do now.

There is one thing I know for sure. We are a family. I have not been raising someone else's children. I have always been raising my own.

~Karen Lynn Filek

Chapter
2

Parenthood

All in a Day's Work

Pleasure in the job puts perfection in the work.

~Aristotle

Juggler Extraordinaire

Our greatest danger in life is permitting the urgent things
to crowd out the important.
~Charles E. Hummel

"Play with me, Mom! Please! Come play *Memory* with me!" my daughter, Alicia, would plead.

When the kids were young and the house in a state of chaos, I would feel the pressure of divided loyalties—clearly both the house and my children needed my attention. When I made the choice to sit on the floor and play the *Memory* game with my daughter, I would comfort myself by saying, "No one is going to remember if on (fill in the date) your house was clean or not, but your kids will remember if you had time for them."

In those years when the kids were young I decided to go back to college and finish my degree. I became a juggler extraordinaire. We would pick a favorite park and, in between rescuing a child dangling from the monkey bars, I would work on my statistics homework. We would spend an afternoon at Chuck E. Cheese, a pizza parlor filled with noisy arcade games, where I would dole out tokens while grappling with a calculus problem. I would cheer my son around the baseball bases after a big hit and at the same time crack the books to cram for an exam.

Finishing my degree led to a corporate job, and more juggling. Over the years I did my best to divide my loyalties wisely. I wish I could say I always prioritized in favor of my children, but sometimes it wasn't possible. But I can say that I have never regretted the times I chose my children over other demands. It was a juggling act that I continued to practice even as the children grew into adulthood.

When Alicia graduated from college she took a job that required her to move across the country. "Mom, will you come out to D.C. with me? Could you stay with me that first week, Mom? I have so much to do!" Life was busy at home with our own business, but I knew when I looked back on that week in July of 2006 no one would remember what work I did, but my daughter would remember the time we spent together. How could we forget the drive from the airport in D.C. in the convertible rental car? It was so small that we had to drive with the top down and sit the luggage, the bulk of her belongings, upright in the back seat like two large, lifeless hitchhikers. Or the hours spent picking out work clothes to get her started in her new career with confidence. The week went by fast. She settled into her new job and soon weeks became a couple of years, and then I got the call.

"I think he's the one, Mom." I could tell from the sound of her voice that he was. I thought back over the years, the beaus that had come and gone. The drop-everything-I-need-your-help talks on the phone about heartache and healing. I thought about the juggling, the prioritizing, the wisdom, the growth and the love.

It was decided that the wedding would be in Georgia, where my daughter's fiancé was from. It was hard to be of much help planning a wedding from so far away. At a time when mother and daughter would normally tackle the task together, we were many miles apart.

"Mom, I'm going to e-mail you a link. I think we have found the place. It's absolutely beautiful! I wish you could see it!" She was right; it looked gorgeous. A Tuscan-themed winery, with the Georgia mountains as a backdrop, would make the perfect place for a wedding. Her words, "Mom, I wish you could see it…" echoed in my mind.

"I know you're busy, Mom, but what would you think about going with me to Georgia? You could meet Drew's folks and we could get stuff done for the wedding." You couldn't keep me away.

It was a week spent meeting new family and taking walks with the mother of the groom, who became a new friend. There was cake tasting and flower viewing. And then there was the drive to Dahlonega, a quaint town and home to Montaluce, the winery location for the big day. I was charmed the minute we drove onto the property. A gently winding road wove its way through what looked like a little Tuscan village. Villas dotted the hills and a congregation of homes in a little valley had me imagining that people lived there who spoke Italian with a southern twang.

At the end of the road stood the winery itself, and we walked inside to the balcony overlooking the vineyards.

"Down there is where they would do the ceremony, Mom." My eyes filled with tears. It was beautiful, almost as beautiful as my precious daughter standing next to me. I had to juggle things to be there that week, but it was all worth it. And I knew that as the wedding date drew near I would juggle some more to be there for her.

The wedding was a magical day, made even more memorable by the time spent with my daughter in preparation for the big event. In hindsight, I don't remember the things that didn't get done or the money that I didn't make during that time. I don't regret juggling some things so I could spend that special time with my daughter. In fact, I think the art of proper juggling has served me well. I expect to use it often when I hear my future grandchildren say, "Nana, will you play with me? Please?"

~Lynne Leite

I Don't Have to Be Super Momma

My cooking is so bad my kids thought
Thanksgiving was to commemorate Pearl Harbor.
~Phyllis Diller

t was my hope that I could, between Thanksgiving and Christmas, cook our meals at home. It would be healthier than picking up fast food. It would be more economical than heading out to the chips and salsa place every other night. As I made my Martha-Stewart-esque decision, I had visions of us sitting around the candlelit table using the Christmas dishes and laughing with each other right before we broke into "Silent Night" sung in three-part harmony. Idyllic to say the least...

For heaven's sake, why couldn't I pull off this "cooking at home" bit for a month?

Why couldn't I? Basketball, choir, play practice, Christmas parties, deliveries, shopping, groceries, play dates... But, that didn't stop me from trying.

I could have cooked ahead, but that requires more planning than I am capable of doing at this time of year with the family that I live with (which is my own family, by the way). I could have plugged in the Crock-Pot in the mornings and done some cooking, but the last three times I dumped a dish in the Crock-Pot, I came home to find that the dish had not cooked because I had not turned ON the Crock-Pot. Mornings are not my best time of day.

Despite all the pitfalls that seem to line my life's path on any given day, I decided that cooking at home would be completely and totally do-able. Nooo... I was not drunk when I made that decision. Not even tipsy!

It was one crazy evening where both of our daughters had basketball practice and we'd been up early to get to choir on time and we'd delivered dozens of pounds of pecans and still, in an effort to be economical and healthy, I attempted to cook dinner at home. It was ten minutes till seven and I was still chopping and mincing and boiling and sipping the sangria…. If I was going to be cooking this much, I was going to have to get in the right frame of mind.

I peeked around the corner of the kitchen to find my hubby snoozing in the recliner, my younger daughter doing cartwheels in the living room, and my first-born baby—God bless her precious heart—in the dining room making some sort of mess that I would clean up two days later. I was slaving in the kitchen preparing a healthy, economical meal for my family when a blue box of the cheesy goodness would have been met with more enthusiasm and would have taken half the time.

My older daughter snuck into the kitchen and cozied up to me with her arm around my waist. "Momma?" she began and I sucked in my breath. I just knew she'd ask me when dinner would be ready—the question that drives Mommas the whole world over to scream and throw food in their very own kitchens. Instead, she took a very deep breath and said, "Why are you trying to be Super Momma? Isn't it more important to be with your family than in the kitchen?"

My shoulders slumped. I squeezed her tight to me. A lump grew in my throat and tears pooled in my eyes. I loved my baby. She had helped me to see that even the best of intentions will rob us of the day's blessings. She spoke again, "Why don't you put this meal up and let's go out to eat?"

I kissed the top of her ever-growing head, nodded and said, "Sure, honey. Let's go...."

At which time, she broke free of my hold as if I were holding kryptonite to her Super Daughter act and hollered, "She caved, y'all! Let's go," and in a matter of SECONDS, my baby and my hubby had their coats on and the three of them were sitting in the van.

I quickly packed away my chopped and diced and minced foods for another night and as I stepped into the garage, my smarty-pants daughter rolled down her window and hollered, "Get a move on, Momma! We're starving out here!"

Why didn't Norman Rockwell ever paint pictures of THAT scene?

~Heather Davis

"Cooking is easy. You put stuff on the stove, burn it and then order pizza. My mom does it all the time."

Mama,
Will You Dry My Hair?

It's difficult to decide whether growing pains are something
teenagers have — or are.
Author Unknown

I remember the first time my daughter asked me that question. She was about five and it was obvious she was frustrated. She was fully immersed in her "I can do it myself" stage and had informed me just minutes earlier that she was going to dry her hair all by herself. Until that day, I had automatically pulled out the hair dryer with one hand, comb in the other, and groomed her long brown locks until each shiny strand was dry.

But today would be different. So, after plugging the dryer in the wall and showing her how to turn it on, I passed my five-year-old the dryer with a smile and a cheery "here you go." By the time I reached the bottom of the stairs, I heard her call in frustration, "Mama! Will you dry my hair?" Evidently the dryer was too heavy or maybe she had never noticed how long it actually took to dry her long hair, which hung almost to her waist.

For the next several years, I continued to dry her hair. Then when she was about ten, I decided she could handle the responsibility and she reluctantly took over the task. Being an avid reader, she soon discovered that if she asked me to blow dry her hair, then she could sit on my vanity stool to read one of her many books. So for a while, we took turns drying her hair. Sometimes she would do it, then other times she would appear with a damp towel wrapped around her head and a book in her hand. "Mama, will you dry my hair?" she would say with a smile. "Please?"

Then her teenage years hit, causing our days to be filled with her talking back, me lecturing, her rolling her eyes, me sending her to her room, and so on. On one particular occasion, my daughter approached me at 10:30 on a school night with the infamous question. It was late and I was tired. I had reminded her to take a shower three hours earlier. And on top of that, we had argued earlier that day and I didn't appreciate her rude tone of voice. Who was she to come ask me for a favor after the way she treated me earlier? I disapproved of her disrespectful behavior and I wanted to teach her a lesson.

"No," I simply said. "You'll have to dry your own hair."

Her mouth dropped open. "But..." she paused, "you always dry my hair."

"Not tonight." I stacked the placemats firmly on the counter, trying to look busy.

"But…" she pleaded. "You're not doing anything."

True. Nonetheless, I stood firm.

Over the next few weeks, she didn't ask me to dry her hair. I wondered if she had learned anything. If she now realized that as a family we should be kind and considerate to one another. If she understood the importance of showing respect to her parents. Then one night, she appeared from the bathroom, towel atop her head, and an innocent smile on her face.

"Mama, will you dry my hair?"

I paused for a brief moment. She sensed my hesitation, then offered these simple words.

"One day, I'll be gone and you will turn to Daddy and say, 'I wish she was still here so I could dry her hair.'"

"Ha, ha," I jokingly replied, hoping she didn't notice the truth of her words pierced right through my heart.

Tonight, I'm standing at the kitchen sink scrubbing baked-on lasagna from the dish. Overhead, I hear the drone of a hair dryer coming from my daughter's bathroom. I set the scrubber and dish aside, then quickly dry my hands. As a scurry up the stairs, my husband asks if something is wrong.

"I hope it's not too late," I call as I reach the top step.

After a humble knock on her door, I offer a faint whisper: "Can I dry your hair?"

~Deanna Ingalls

Tales from the Road

The phrase "working mother" is redundant.
~Jane Sellman

I pull out of the driveway feeling euphoric (and slightly guilty for feeling so). It's as if the absence of car seats in their usual places in my back seat has created an out-of-proportion buoyancy. I pull the Kindermusic CD out and replace it with a new audio book I've been dying to hear. I'm free!

I settle back into the car's seat to listen to my book and enjoy the drive to the airport for a semi-annual meeting. I blast the heater on this cool afternoon, without my eight-year-old son complaining, "Mom, I can't breathe in here!" I'm not used to battling the commuter traffic, but I've got my audio book, and I'm alone—gloriously alone.

The traffic is getting worse, and I glance at the clock to make sure I will make my flight. No problem. At least I only have one deadline to meet. My husband's the one who will have to worry about school pick-ups, soccer practice, and homework today.

Once inside the airport and through security, I relax again and enjoy my freedom. I have a half hour before boarding time—an entire thirty minutes to myself! I treat myself to a latte and a chocolate croissant—pure decadence. Settled in a tiny café table with my indulgences and a magazine (one from six months ago that I've never found time to read), I feel utterly pampered. It doesn't matter that this café table is on a busy airport concourse instead of a quaint city street—I already feel as if I'm a million miles away.

Once I arrive at my destination and check into the hotel, the fun really begins. I close the door to my room and grin like a crazed fool. The next twelve hours are mine. I have no responsibilities, and no one to take care of but myself.

I peruse the room service menu and choose things my kids would hate, along with a rich, chocolate dessert—something my kids would love that I won't have to share with anyone tonight. When my dinner arrives, I eat it propped up in bed with four pillows, watching old sitcoms on TV, not even glancing at Nickelodeon or Cartoon Network. After dinner, I sip my wine and enjoy some uninterrupted writing time.

After a while, I head back to the bed for an evening of mindless television, with no permission slips to sign or lunches to prepare. The huge bed seems a bit empty, but I have the remote control to myself. I flip through the channels recklessly, watching three shows at once (something that drives my husband crazy), and stay up way too late watching shows on HBO that I never see at home.

I'm awakened with a start by the jarring sound of the alarm clock. It's an unwelcome change from my usual wake-up call, when my sleepy four-year-old son crawls into bed with me and puts his warm arms around me. I groan at the early hour and curse all that late-night TV.

A shower and room service breakfast help perk me up, and I enjoy getting dressed in what another stay-at-home mom friend of mine refers to as grown-up clothes. Most mornings, the only clothing decision I face is whether to wear my "good" jeans or the ones with a hole in the knee. Today, I dress in a silk blouse, a seldom-worn suit, and real jewelry.

When I'm ready to leave the room, I glance in the mirror and am startled by my own reflection. I look good! It's amazing what a little make-up can do for my normally bare face. I can't even see the dark circles under my eyes.

The rest of my day proceeds smoothly as I attend my meeting.

To my surprise, it's kind of fun. People listen to me when I say something, ask for my opinion, and don't squabble over who gets to use the wipe board first.

By 3:00, I'm back at the airport, ready to begin the long travel process in reverse. After navigating through security, I look at my watch and see that I have an hour before boarding time. My husband is making his way to the school to pick up our older son right now, and I'm startled to realize that it's the first time all day that I've thought about the timetable that directs my life at home.

All I can find for dinner in the airport is a turkey sandwich, probably made two days ago. I munch on the tasteless sandwich while reading, but I'm distracted by the crowds of people around me. An adorable toddler squeals in delight as she runs away from her mother, and I smile reflexively at her antics.

I sit in an uncomfortable seat near the gate to wait for my flight, glancing at my watch for the tenth time in as many minutes. My husband is getting the kids ready to go to soccer practice by now. I wonder how Craig's Show & Tell went today at preschool and whether Jamie did well on his spelling test.

I try to lose myself in a magazine, but it has lost its appeal. I listen to the conversations around me—a couple on vacation, a mother talking to her son, two co-workers heading home together. My back is aching from trying to fit my five-foot one-inch frame into conference chairs and airline seats made for a six-foot man. I notice my feet are starting to hurt and yearn for my red fleece slippers, my usual choice of footwear.

My flight is called, and I follow the line of passengers onto the plane. After a fitful nap and a little more reading, I'm back at my home airport. It seems to take forever to steer through the crowds off the plane, through the endless concourse, and back to the airport parking lot. I'm finally in my own car. The thirty-five-minute drive home seems to take longer, as I yawn and flip back and forth between radio stations.

As I approach my neighborhood, I perk up in anticipation of the welcome I'll receive. The kids will be all ready for bed and will greet me with hugs and kisses, telling me how much they missed me. I pull into the garage and turn off the car with a sigh.

As I close the door and set down my briefcase, my four-year-old shouts, "Mom! Is that you?"

I call out in return, "It's me, sweetheart."

"Do you know where Biscuit is?" he asks as if I've never left, in his nightly quest to locate the tiny stuffed dog he drags everywhere with him.

"Mom!" yells my eight-year-old son. "Guess what? My school caught on fire today!"

I slide my feet into my slippers, find Biscuit on top of the dryer, and head upstairs to my boys. There's no place like home.

~Suzan L. Jackson

Priceless Art

Painting is just another way of keeping a diary.
~Pablo Picasso

"I'm bored," my five-year-old daughter Katie said. Her one-year-old sister stared out the window at the rain. Christmas was over. The anticipation more exciting than the aftermath: empty boxes, torn up wrapping paper, leftover cookies and broken candy canes. Even the joy of watching the tree and the moving ornaments had faded.

I was out of ideas. That morning, I'd already dressed them up in their rain gear—such as it was, and taken them into the rain. Timid at first, it didn't take long until they were running and splashing and stomping in the puddles, their umbrellas forgotten.

"Want to go back in the rain?"

Katie sighed. "And get all wet again." Then she brightened. "Can we have more hot chocolate?" That was part of the ritual: get wet and cold in the rain, come inside, change into dry clothes while Mom made cocoa, and then warm up from the inside out.

Two weeks off from kindergarten hadn't seemed very long at the beginning. The first week already was a blur. But now, with all the festivities over, the last few days dragged. Then I remembered the giant roll of white paper I'd bought in the midst of Christmas shopping. My initial plan had been to use it for wrapping. The girls could decorate it.

"What are we gonna do with that?" Katie asked as I dug the roll out from the closet.

"Go get a pencil and I'll show you." I unrolled the paper onto the floor. We had to use several shoes to hold down the corners. "Now, lie down on it and pick a pose."

"That tickles." She squirmed as I traced all the way around her body, including her long hair, splayed out in a ponytail across the paper.

"Me, me," Anna said the entire time.

"What do you think?" I asked when I was finished.

"Where's the crayons?"

There was room on the paper for Anna to lie down right next to Katie's drawing. Side by side they were, and we colored all afternoon.

They couldn't wait to show Dad. So we taped our work of art to the blank wall in the entryway where the front door opened. The life-size drawing of my daughters stayed up for the entire year.

The next year, Katie dragged the paper out of the closet herself. It wasn't raining, and she wasn't bored. But it had become an instant tradition. I carefully dated the first one, rolled it up and put a rubber band around it. We replaced it with the new one. As the girls grew, we needed more and more paper.

"Let's do it this way," Anna said and they lay down head to foot so that she spent the entire year upside down, hands reaching toward the floor.

One year, I bought brown paper instead, the kind people use to mail packages. I figured it was closer to their skin color. But all their other coloring faded into the brown, so we went back to white and kept using our "People Color" crayons.

As they grew older, they became more critical of their own art. Katie stared in the mirror, holding pencils, markers, and crayons next to her clothes. "Nothing matches."

"You know, the drawing doesn't have to match what you're wearing. Make your dream clothes instead."

She drew cartoon characters all over her shirt. "How's this?" she asked.

"Priceless," I told her.

The most challenging time was the year their baby brother was only seven months old, and they insisted on tracing him.

"Hold still," they giggled, knowing that he wouldn't listen.

It had started as an accident—a desperate attempt to find something creative and inexpensive to entertain my children. In the end, I had more than a tradition; I had many rolls of paper chronicling my children's growth, coloring skills, and artistic expression. And when all the holiday festivities were over, we still had something to look forward to.

~D.B. Zane

Monkey Soap

Accept everything about yourself—I mean everything. You are you and that
is the beginning and the end—no apologies, no regrets.
~Clark Moustakas

"And what is your skin care regimen?" my sister-in-law asks me at the Mary Kay party. My sister-in-law has just become a consultant, joining the ranks of my other stay-at-home-mom friends who have started home businesses selling products such as Pampered Chef and Discovery Toys.

"Um, well, the kids have this great new soap that foams when it dispenses," I start.

"No," she laughs, "what products do you use on YOUR face for cleansing and moisturizing?"

"Like I said," I continue, a little annoyed, "the new foaming soap with the monkeys on the front does quite nicely for my skincare."

"Oh, honey," she says. "You do need help. First you must start with a clarifying agent...." She starts a long speech about the ten steps of facial awareness. It's not that I'm opposed to spending twenty minutes a day cleaning my face; it's just that I can't see where I can fit it into the schedule with the kids. I decide to keep my mind open.

By the end of the party, I am equipped with facial cleanser, moisturizer, clarifier, lipstick, lip liner, lipgloss, foundation, concealer, two kinds of blush, four colors of eye shadow, as well as a host of other products. All for $250, with a promise to make me a new woman. I feel great. I can't wait to start my new life the next day.

I wake up early to spend a little extra time using my new products. I'm not even through with the seventh cleaning step when my four-year-old groggily appears downstairs. "Bunny milk," he mumbles. "Teletubbies." I turn on the television for him, get the requested milk, and continue to step eight.

I am proudly applying my new Pink Pout lip color when my three-year-old daughter joins him. "You lips funny Mommy," she says, and before I can move she swipes a hand over my mouth, smearing my Pink Pout all over my freshly applied foundation and two layers of blush.

"Dammit," I say under my breath. "Back to step one." Undeterred, I get her settled in front of the video and begin the process of putting together the new me.

It isn't five minutes later and both kids are in the bathroom with me. "Are these toys?" my son asks, climbing on the vanity, sending my applicators all over the floor.

"No, they are for Mommy," I say. "It's make-up."

"Put it on me!" my daughter shouts.

"No, this is special for Mommy." They both start whining and crying at the same time. I cave. "Okay, just a little." My daughter grabs the lipstick, opens it, and smashes it on her eyebrow, completely breaking it off. My son turns the fifty-dollar moisturizer over and spills half of it in the sink.

I lose it. "OUT! OUT!" I scream. My husband comes in. I mutter, "At this moment I am a danger to myself and to others. I need to be left alone in this bathroom for fifteen minutes." Knowing that look in my eyes, he backs out with the children, careful not to make any sudden movements. I'm alone, minus a few products, but I have enough to regroup and start over; the monkey soap sits in the corner of the vanity, mocking me.

Thirty minutes later, I emerge from the bathroom. "Wow!" my husband says. "Is that all the Mary Kay stuff you got at the party last night?"

"Yep," I say proudly. "I am a new woman."

"How much did all that stuff cost?" he asks, trying to sound nonchalant.

I give my usual answer. "Twenty-five dollars."

My beauty is wasted that day since we never leave the house. Soon it becomes clear that the emotional price of wearing Pink Pout and four types of eye make-up is too high.

I'm back to the monkey soap now, and life is easier, but every now and then, I don a Pink Pout face just to see the jealous looks of other women marveling at my perfection. My husband says they are staring and I need to "tone it down a bit," but I know they are marveling. Women can tell these things.

~Shannon McCarty

In Pursuit of Sleep

If evolution really works, how come mothers only have two hands?
~Milton Berle

It's 6:30 p.m. As I serve dinner, I announce, "Listen, guys. Mommy had a rough day today and I'm really tired. I'm going to bed early." Just saying it makes me feel better. Dinner proceeds as usual. A minor negotiation with eight-year-old Molly over how many carrots constitute the forkful I insist she eats. A squabble between ten-year-old Haley and five-year-old Hewson because he won't stop looking at her, and she keeps repeating everything he says and she wants him to know that she hates it when he breathes like that. Molly won't eat her potatoes because they touched her meat. I'm falling asleep in my pot roast. But I know I'll be in bed in a few minutes. Then there is another argument over whose night it is to clear the table.

"I did it last night!"

"No, you didn't!"

"Yes, I did!"

I give my husband David my most pitiful look. "Just go," he says. "I'll figure it out."

I prop myself against the kitchen counter. "What about baths?"

He points toward the bedroom. "I'll take care of it," he says. "Go to bed."

I'll take off my make-up, brush my teeth, and be under the covers in three minutes. On second thought, forget all that—I'm heading straight for bed. My hand's on the doorknob when Haley comes up behind me. "Mom, what about my book report? You promised you'd type it for me." I did? No problem. I can knock that out and still be in bed in ten minutes. "You talk and I'll type," I tell her. I type four pages in twenty minutes, and Haley is still talking. Is this a book report or a novella?

Molly finds me at the computer. "Mom, you said I could wear my new jumper tomorrow." The jumper that needs to be shortened. I leave Haley and grab the sewing kit, whip up a temporary hem, lay the dress on Molly's bed, gather the dirty clothes from her floor, and dump them in the washing machine. The cat rubs against my leg. I start the washer, feed the cat and the dog, toss a little fish food in the tank. The water needs changing, but I'll deal with that tomorrow. I can't keep my eyes open another minute.

It's 7:40 p.m. Molly waddles by, wrapped in a bath towel. "Mom, did you call Katie's mom to see if she can come over tomorrow?" Oops. I grab the phone. There are messages on the machine. Haley is still at the computer. I tell her to take a bath, and I call Katie's mom and return two calls while I scrub the pots from dinner and get the coffeepot ready for the morning. It's 8:00. I take three minutes to test Molly on her spelling words and tuck her into bed. Heading back to my room, I notice Haley at the computer again. The book report! I finish typing, check the spelling, print it out, stick it in Haley's backpack, kiss her good night, place the kids' backpacks and my briefcase by the front door. I'll worry about lunchboxes in the morning. I can barely put one foot in front of the other.

I shuffle toward the bedroom again, and here comes Hewson—naked, dripping water, screaming, with shampoo lather in his hair. "Daddy won't give me a washcloth to put over my eyes. I'm going to go blind."

I start telling him to explain it to Dad, then decide it would be faster to bathe him myself. I carry him back to the tub, rinse his hair, wrap him in a towel, put him in his pajamas, brush his teeth, read him a quick story, lay out his clothes for the next day, mop up the water on the bathroom floor, and finally make it to my bedroom. David, already in bed, says, "I thought you were going to bed early."

"I am."

I wash my face, brush my teeth, and notice that the washer has stopped. David is snoring as I walk past to toss the clothes in the dryer, grab an armload of dry cleaning and some overdue library books, lug them to the car, drag the trash cans out to the curb, jot "baby shampoo" on the grocery list, let the dog in and the cat out. I shove Haley's gym clothes into her backpack and check on the kids—sleeping like angels. I lay out my clothes for the next day and rinse out a pair of stockings. I desperately need a manicure but that's not happening. It's 10:45. As my head hits the pillow, I make myself a promise: "Tomorrow night, I'm definitely going to bed early!"

~Mimi Greenwood Knight

Reprinted by permission of Dan Reynolds
and Cartoon Resource ©2010.

No "Me" in Mommy

She never quite leaves her children at home,
even when she doesn't take them along.
~Margaret Culkin Banning

I didn't realize how selfish I was until my son was born last year. As it turns out, I really want to take a hot shower each day. I also like being able to drink an entire cup of coffee while it's still hot. And, every now and then, it's nice to get more than three consecutive hours of sleep. Who knew I was so self-centered?

There's nothing like having a child to remind you that you are no longer the center of your own universe. I understand that now. Evan's needs surpass mine on a daily basis. He eats first, he gets the first bath, and he decides when everyone else in the house will start the day.

Most days, being number two doesn't bother me a bit. But every now and then, I need to recharge with some "me" time.

That is exactly how I was feeling back in June when my mom and I booked an overnight trip to Dover, Delaware. We left on a Thursday afternoon, had a quick dinner on the road, and arrived in Delaware right after sunset. Mom and I settled into our hotel room and went downstairs to explore the casino. I found a slot machine that looked like fun and then I ordered myself a drink. I had taken two sips when I noticed my cell phone vibrating inside my purse. The call was from my husband.

"I'm so sorry to bother you," Craig said softly. "The baby is burning up and we are on the way to the hospital. He wouldn't drink his bottle and when I checked his temperature it was 102 degrees."

I didn't know how to reply. I was so desperate to get away, to take a break. And now, my baby was sick and I couldn't do a thing for him. The situation made me feel so helpless.

"I don't know what to do," I told him. "I'm five hours from home!"

"I know," my husband said. "You can't help that. I'll call you when I know what's wrong."

My husband and my father took the baby to the emergency room. Meanwhile, I searched the casino for my mom. Once I found her, we went to our hotel room and waited... and waited... for a phone call.

Over an hour later, Craig called to tell me that the baby had bronchitis. He was on an antibiotic and already seemed to be feeling better. He was going to be just fine.

After vowing to never go anywhere without the baby again, I got a couple hours of sleep so we would be prepared for the drive home the next morning.

When I returned home, the baby was already back to his typical, happy self. He was playing in his bounce seat and chewing on his toys. Still, I didn't leave his side for several days.

Ever since this incident, I have really struggled with the concept of "me" time. I tried to figure out why I needed a break from the child I wanted so badly and love so very much. Why did I need to get away from a baby who smiles when he sees me, laughs when I sing like Elmo, and turns his head toward my voice regardless of how many people are in the room?

Well, maybe it was because that same beautiful child demands my undivided attention, requires constant supervision, and sometimes renders me completely exhausted when he screams all night. Sometimes I need to feel like a person and not just a bottle making, diaper changing, bath giving, mommy machine.

In recent months, I have taken some "me" time in small doses. My mom has kept the baby so I could grocery shop, take a nap, and clean my house. On a couple of occasions, Craig and I went to dinner with friends. And this summer, I even managed to read an entire novel while the baby rested. It felt great to immerse myself in a different setting for a while.

I'm still not ready to leave the baby overnight again or travel a long distance without him. It's too soon and it makes me anxious. But I do give myself a break when I need it. It's good for both of us.

I remember when I first announced my pregnancy, a friend told me to do whatever I wanted while I could. "There is no 'me' in mommy," she said. Maybe there's not. But there is a "my." And for now, I'm taking "my" time, in small doses, when I can.

~Melissa Face

Mom's Night Out

By and large, mothers and housewives are the only workers who do not have regular time off. They are the great vacation-less class.
~Anne Morrow Lindbergh

othing can bother me today—not the mud tracked all over the carpet, not the half-hour search for my car keys, not the eternity spent on hold with the insurance company, not the crayon on the living room wall, not the toilet paper trailed down the hallway, not even the neighbor's dog flattening my flower bed... AGAIN. Tonight is Mom's Night Out, and that knowledge is all I need to get me through the day.

Tonight is the night when my mom friends and I leave the kids at home and get to act like kids ourselves. While the game of Pokeno is our excuse for getting together once a month, it's secondary to the support, encouragement, and friendship we offer each other.

At three o'clock, I call my husband David's office with a gentle reminder. He wouldn't forget anyway. He knows how important these nights are—not just to me—but to him and the kids too. Later, I breeze through dinner, hum through my shower, and jump into a favorite pair of jeans.

As I dry my hair, I've already begun the evening in my mind, thinking about which stories I'll tell about the kids' latest antics. I wonder who'll be there and what has changed in their lives since last month. The kids object as I start to leave, but David comes to the rescue with the promise of a pizza snack and a favorite video. He winks at me and, with kisses all around, I'm off.

In the car, I crank the radio to full volume. I feel like a teenager pulling out of the driveway in my mom's old, green station wagon. I can't stop smiling. To make the experience complete, I roll down the windows, throw my head back, and sing at the top of my lungs. Here we go! Mom's Night Out at last!

Ten minutes later, I'm pulling up to Lisa's house. I scan the mini-vans to determine who's arrived before me. There's Jane's van. Good, I have a box of maternity clothes to pass along to her. There's Lelia's. I wonder how her job interview went? As soon as I step inside, I hear bits of conversations in progress. Cheryl catches me at the door with a gift, a thank-you for watching her girls last month. We all take time to hug. Then, someone screams, and I look to see that she's hold-ing up Stephanie's hand, gleaming with a diamond engagement ring. More hugs! No one is surprised. We all suffered through Stephanie's divorce two years ago and have dated Jeff vicariously through her for the past several months. When she reminds us that he has two girls the same ages as her own two boys, we break into *The Brady Bunch* theme song.

What exactly is so therapeutic about Mom's Night Out? Everything!

Over the next four hours, we'll ask each other's advice on top-ics ranging from teething and potty training to romance and office politics. We'll relate experiences with our kids and our jobs that may have had us crying at the time, but about which we can laugh together now. Time management tips, new lunch box ideas, behav-ior charts that worked and homework incentives that didn't will be discussed. Arrangements to watch each other's kids will be made and recipes, jokes, paperbacks, and baby and maternity clothes will be exchanged.

We'll complain a bit about husbands and in-laws, jobs, caregiv-ers, and the kids' schools, and somehow we'll play a game or two of Pokeno as well. In the past eight years, we've seen each other through ten pregnancies, two miscarriages, two divorces, four job transfers and three deaths.

When it's time to go, we linger in the driveway for another half hour or so, not wanting the evening to come to an end. Driving home, radio not quite as loud, I have renewed energy and my positive outlook is back. I feel like I can take on the world. Bring on the neighbor's dog! Bring on the insurance company, the toilet paper comets and murals on the living room wall! I can handle it all!

I can't wait to get home and start being Mommy again. I'll kiss each little sleeping angel, pick up the clothes scattered across the bedroom floor, and read phonetically spelled love notes left on my pillow. Then I'll snuggle with David and tell him my new jokes, happy in the knowledge that whatever comes my way tomorrow, there's another Mom's Night Out and it's only a month away.

~Mimi Greenwood Knight

Chapter
3

Parenthood

Is There a Manual for This?

There is no such thing as a perfect parent so just be a real one.

~Sue Atkins

18

Guilt, Glory, and Google

Parents who are both conscientious and realistic discover sooner or later that they cannot do the job to their own complete satisfaction, much less to their children's complete satisfaction.

~Thomas Sowell

Ever since becoming a mom, I've been secretly worried that I'm doing it all wrong. Which is why the other day I found myself Googling "how to determine if you're a horrible parent." This came on the heels of my toddler sustaining bloody face injuries for the third day in a row.

Trevyn is my second child so you would think I'd have improved at this mothering thing by now. After all, I have nowhere to go but up. When my older son Kyler was an infant, I took him for a run around the neighborhood. When we returned, I parked the stroller a few feet from the garage, then went to punch in the door code. When I turned around moments later, I was horrified to see that the stroller had rolled down the ever-so-slight slope of my driveway and was now sitting in the middle of the street. As I raced down to get my son, his big brown eyes looked at me as if to say, "Really, Mom? Is that the best parenting job you can do?" I was asking myself the same question, especially when two days later I locked myself out of the house with Kyler still inside.

Kyler is now eight years old so I did successfully get him through his infant and toddler years—and without even one trip to the emergency room! The same can't be said for twenty-one-month-old

Trevyn. He was there today because I couldn't stop the blood gushing from his nose. Plus, earlier this week I called emergency personnel to my house when Trev did his impersonation of a flying squirrel and jumped off the couch. He landed hard and when he stood up, bright blood flowed from his mouth and nostrils.

When my husband returned home from work that afternoon, he could see the worry in my eyes. He pulled me close and said, "It's okay. He's fine." My husband's calm tone reassured me, and I finally relaxed and put Trevyn to bed, relieved that I no longer had to fret. Then I walked into the den and found Eric Googling "signs of concussions in toddlers."

"What?" I freaked. "I thought you said he was fine!"

"I'm sure he is," Eric said. "But still—we should be aware."

Aware of what, I wasn't sure. Because Googling medical advice as it relates to your child's wellbeing is bound to leave any parent perplexed, perturbed, and probably more anxious than ever.

Eric found a website that said to be concerned if your tot has a hard time sleeping. Another website stated that it's worrisome if a child sleeps too heavily. (But wait—this would mean he's not having a hard time sleeping. So that's a good thing, right?) A third site suggested watching for fussiness and irritability. Really! My toddler is simultaneously trying to grow teeth, learn how to communicate, and navigate the big, wide world with his short, stubby legs that cannot physically move as fast as his mind thinks they can. Every day he is fussy and irritable.

After two hours of researching the Internet, I didn't know whether I should sing Trevyn soothing lullabies or poke him throughout the night. Ultimately, I let him snooze. Was it the right thing to do? I have no clue. That's half the battle of parenting—trying to determine what's right.

Take yesterday. Was it a good idea to let Trevyn play on my bed while I made it? Clearly not, though it seemed harmless enough given that he had safely played up there many times before. How was I to know my kid was in a roly-poly mood on this day? You know what they say: It's all giggles and laughter until somebody rolls off the bed. Then it's thud, blood, and tears. At least it was at my house.

As I was cleaning the blood off my child's face for the third day straight, I was reminded, once again, why I value Mother's Day so much. I think the holiday supersedes the combined importance of birthday, Valentine's Day, and wedding anniversary. After all, I didn't have to work to grow older, fall in love, or say "I do." But I do have to consistently work at being a decent mommy. Of course, what qualifies as "decent" is debatable.

Despite doing all I can to keep my kids healthy and safe, every time one of them gets hurt physically or emotionally, I find myself asking, "Could I have done better?" I guess that's a pointless question. What's done is done. I try my best to learn from my mistakes and move forward. I try my best—period. I have to continually remind myself that falls and scars, scrapes and cuts, nose bleeds and split lips, even bruised egos and broken hearts, are all part of growing, learning, and living.

There are certainly days when I'm tempted to Google "how to determine if I can survive parenthood." But there's really no need for such a query. I know I can do it because I have my children to help me along the way (and a safety brake on the stroller—what a brilliant invention!).

~Christy Heitger-Ewing

The Talk

I think, at a child's birth, if a mother could ask a fairy godmother to endow it
with the most useful gift, that gift should be curiosity.
~Eleanor Roosevelt

ecently when my eight year old son Tyler asked me how babies were made, I did what I'd promised myself I'd never do: I ignored his question. I really didn't want to tell him this young.

Then again, I'd rather he hear it from me than another kid. But how do you delicately give them the information they want without overwhelming them with too much? I really didn't know. I was Tyler's age when I went to my mom with the very same question and I distinctly remember bellowing, "THAT IS DISGUSTING!"

Still, though, my mom hadn't avoided my question and that really counted for something. That's the kind of relationship we had, and have, and I want to have that with Tyler too. I want him to feel he can come to me with anything at any time. So I revisited the topic with him a few days later, asking if he still wanted to know.

"Yes," he said. "I mean do you just get lucky? Is that how you have a baby?"

Oh, that was my golden opportunity. I should have just ended it there and said, "Yes," adding a disclaimer, "the guy gets lucky and the girl gets pregnant." But I figured that was cheating and not really in the spirit of what I was trying to accomplish. That was more in line with the duck-and-dodge mode of parenting, which I've been known to employ.

So instead I sighed and said, "Well, first, you have a man and a woman who are married and in love..." Now, I know this isn't always true, but I really wasn't up for explaining all the variations that can make up a family.

"Mom, I know that! I mean, how are they made?"

At that point I decided it would be a good idea to borrow a line from one of the websites I'd Googled after he asked me the question the first time. "Well. The man gives love to the woman and then a baby grows in her belly and it comes out when it's ready."

Even to me it sounded vague and confusing.

"What? But how? I don't get it."

Tyler wasn't going to let me off the hook. So, finally, I just told him the real deal, plain and simple, careful not to give too much information, but using the correct terms.

Silence.

"I know it's confusing and it may sound weird, but it's a very beautiful thing," I added hopefully.

Tyler looked dubious.

"Are you confused?" I asked him.

"I don't know. But I know one thing."

"What's that?"

"Now I really don't want to get married!"

I guess you could say mission not accomplished.

Back to the drawing board and, maybe, the library.

~Christa Gala

A Gun in Every Gourd

Some parents say it is toy guns that make boys warlike. But give a boy a rubber duck and he will seize its neck like the butt of a pistol and shout "Bang!"
~George F. Will

"Cool!" said six-year-old Jamie, halting in front of a basket of decorative gourds I had just arranged as part of our Thanksgiving decorations. His two-year-old brother Craig ran up behind him and asked that perennial toddler question, "Whatzat?" Jamie grabbed a gourd with a thin, bent neck and proclaimed, "It's a gun!" This led to my crazed refutation, "That is NOT a gun! It's a gourd!" My boys were delighted in the response they evoked and continued to taunt me on a daily basis by picking up the gourd and pretending to shoot with it, just to hear that phrase.

Nobody prepared me for this part of child rearing, or more precisely, son-rearing. I grew up with one sister, a neighborhood full of girls, and a clan of almost all girl cousins. I had almost no experience with little boys until my first son was born.

Before we had children of our own, I had occasionally witnessed "wild boys" and was determined to bring up my own sons differently. I was firmly in the nurture camp of the nature versus nurture debate and believed it was all a matter of raising your child without gender stereotypes. You can stop laughing…. I realize now how naïve I was!

We strayed from the typical all-blue wardrobe of baby boys and dressed Jamie in bright primary colors. We provided all kinds of gender neutral, developmentally appropriate toys for him. One of his favorite toys was a play kitchen with plastic dishes. We got him a baby doll one Christmas. Our boy wasn't going to become obsessed with cars, sports, or superheroes. No way.

Then Jamie reached toddlerhood and began picking up little cars and making motor sounds with his mouth. He also developed an intense interest in dinosaurs and would growl menacingly when holding a plastic dino in his tiny hands. Where did he learn to make car and dinosaur sounds? He certainly hadn't observed my husband or me doing this. It was as if this innate masculine behavior just emerged from him.

The cars and dinosaurs I could handle, though. My real struggle has been with the unabashed fascination with all manner of weaponry and fighting. Nothing in my girl-centered childhood had prepared me for this.

As a preschooler, Jamie received some superhero action figures as gifts and was hooked. His favorite activity became "playing guys," which involved intricate fighting scenarios between action figures.

This was all foreign to me and left me perplexed. He'd never seen any of the TV shows but was still fascinated by Power Rangers, Batman, and other icons of maleness. His playtime was filled with growls, grunts, and weapon sounds. I stared at my sweet little boy in amazement and wondered where this all came from. He certainly had a vivid imagination, but would he grow up to be a serial killer?

Our younger son spent his infancy listening to his brother's imaginary battles. At three years old now, he's already well versed in superheroes, action figures, and playing guys. The two boys dress up and act out all sorts of scenes. Five years ago, if someone had told me we'd have plastic swords and rubber daggers in our house, I would have thought them insane.

Early on, I had decided that I didn't want my boys to play with toy guns, but as the boys grew older, I found that it didn't matter. Give them a bin full of Tinkertoys and they construct a weapon. Go on a hike through the woods and sticks become swords. Even feed them a piece of toast and it's chewed into a rough gun shape.

We must have two violent, wild boys in our family, right? That's what I would have thought before I had sons of my own. But our sons are loving, affectionate children with sweet dispositions. They just happen to be boys and thus fascinated by fighting.

In fact, they seem to perfectly understand the line between fantasy and real life. Once when my older son was playing guys and wanted me to join in, I said, "Mommy doesn't like fighting." He looked at me and patiently explained, "This isn't real fighting! In real fighting people get hurt. I'd never do that. This is just pretend."

I've learned to love our boys for who they are, and I try not to worry too much. I still encourage them to chase away the bad guys, rather than kill them, and they still humor my poor, limited imagination. We've managed so far to nurture their loving, caring sides while accepting their fascination with combat. Now I need to go rescue my gourd again.

~Suzan L. Jackson

A Christmas Eve Snack for Santa

*After today, I'll bet Santa takes a shovel to the reindeer stalls
to fill your stocking.*
~Bill Watterson

When our son Kenneth was about four years old, my husband David and I took him to the mall to see Santa. After Kenneth disclosed his Christmas wish list, Santa had a request for him. And even though we stood several feet away, we were able to overhear the following exchange:

"You know," said Santa, pulling thoughtfully at his thick white beard, "it just so happens that my stop at your house comes right in the middle of my Christmas Eve journey. Will you leave something out for me to eat?"

"Yes," my son replied. He said he would be happy to offer Santa some food that would help tide him over until he could get back to the North Pole and Mrs. Claus's home cooking.

"Oh? What will you leave me?" Santa asked. No doubt he expected some cookies and a nice tall glass of milk.

I waited to hear what Kenneth would say. He and Santa were not on the same wavelength. "Fish," Kenneth said.

I clapped a hand over my mouth to hide my grin.

"Fish?" Santa asked. He was clearly surprised by Kenneth's response. I half expected him to twist a finger in his ear to unblock his hearing. His next question revealed his curiosity. "What kind of fish?"

"A dead fish," said Kenneth in a matter-of-fact tone.

Santa was speechless. My husband and I were laughing so hard now we were wiping tears from our eyes.

Santa stared blankly into space as my son hopped off his lap and trotted toward us. Was Santa's stomach doing queasy flip-flops as he anticipated his mid-trip meal?

Later I asked Kenneth what he was thinking when he told Santa he'd set aside a dead fish.

"I don't know," Kenneth said with a shrug. "I don't know what kind of fish we eat."

In that he was wrong; he did know. In our house, we always eat dead fish!

~Susan Barclay

"But if we add to Santa's cholesterol we could be
ruining him for future generations."

22

Popular

Making the decision to have a child is momentous. It is to decide forever to have your heart go walking around outside your body.
~Elizabeth Stone

"**C**itadel," I say. "A fortress," my daughter Lilly says, then uses it in a sentence. "My room is a citadel." She moved into her own bedroom a month ago, when she turned twelve, and it became clear she could no longer share a room with her two younger sisters.

Lilly's room, once antique white, is now a blinding lime green, lit now by just one lamp. It is almost 11:00. Lilly, the oldest of my five children, is the only one still awake. Her hair smells like coconut shampoo. The still-wet strands, recently cut into layers, stick to her cheeks.

Lilly tucks the two textbooks into her backpack, then takes a second backpack from her closet. She stuffs her socks, soccer uniform and an outfit for Monday morning into the second bag. She squeezes the bulging pack between her thighs to get the zipper zipped. Tomorrow Lilly will sleep in a different bedroom, at her father's house.

Lilly is used to the every-other-weekend packing, but I'm not. The second backpack bothers me, a fat reminder that Lilly does not have the fairytale childhood I'd planned for her, that her father and I have been divorced for half of her life already.

"I'm not popular, Mom," Lilly says, as if randomly plucking the words out of the air. Lilly's back is to me; her oversized T-shirt comes well past her knees. She has always been small and tonight she seems even smaller, looking barely ten.

I pick up the Abercrombie jeans and toss them toward the wicker hamper. "What's popular?" I say trying to make time to find words that will fix everything all at once for Lilly, always my first instinct.

"Popular?" she repeats, with a look that says "Mom, you know this." "Popular girls sit at one lunch table. They're the pretty ones. They've all been asked out or are going out with one of the popular boys. They don't even talk to me, it's like I'm invisible."

Putting Lilly to bed used to be much easier. The words popular, citadel, Abercrombie, not yet part of her vocabulary. We used to read *The Paper Bag Princess*, her favorite story, where the princess, dressed in a paper bag, rebuffs Prince Charming. Like the Paper Bag Princess, Lilly, a diminutive dragon slayer herself, never cared what others said. Never gave a whit about what the prince thought.

I'm angry with these middle-school princesses. I put my arm around my oldest daughter, who has always been a source of comfort for me. The daughter who, at age six, seeing me in despair after her father moved out, took my hand, brought me out to the swings, and showed me how to kick clouds. I see her in my mind now, hopping off the swing, walking back towards the house, her shoulder blades like clothespins under her sundress.

"I don't think I'm invited to Rachel's party," Lilly says. I am quiet. I consider how I solved this when Lilly was in second grade. The year we moved to a new town after the divorce, and I dropped her in a class that already had its cliques: so-and-so played with so-and-so at recess. Lilly was left out. But I'd fixed it, inviting all the girls to our house to play, serving drippy ice cream in pastel bowls. Lilly shined, leading an excavation of old stones in our back yard, encouraging the girls to dig knee deep where the old barn had been. Lilly scooped the ice cream into five pastel bowls herself, and put toothpicks on top, one for each friend.

I could say, "Lilly you're the prettiest," the way my mother used to say to me, but that wouldn't work. Or, I consider my father's approach, his emphasis on perspective, when a party invite did not come or a friendship dissolved. "You won't even remember that girl's name a year from now."

"Remember your stuffed duck Daisy?" is what I say, thinking that a story where Lilly is the star may be what's needed. "You were three," I say. "You took an egg from the fridge, snuck it to your bedroom, and placed it under your pillow."

"I put Daisy the duck on top of the pillow," Lilly says and I'm relieved she's joining in and not rolling her eyes at me.

"And that night, when I tucked you into bed, gold yolk oozed onto the sheets."

"I thought the egg would hatch," Lilly says, and laughs. "I tried it again the next night."

"You always had your own ideas, Lilly," I say, sad that somewhere between when she was six and now twelve, Lilly stopped believing stuffed ducks could lay eggs.

I tuck her into bed, sheets to chin. "I wish to grow an inch," she says, a joke of ours since she wrote that in her letter to Santa in first grade. I push her hair back, and trace the freckles that stretch from one cheek to the other, a narrow trail over Lilly's small nose. When I was little I didn't like my freckles, but of course I love Lilly's.

I sit on the edge of the bed and turn off the lamp. I know Lilly is moving into a new phase where I can't solve everything with a Popsicle or play date. In this new place, Lilly has to believe in herself and I have to believe that in spite of the second backpack, the second house, my second marriage, Lilly will find her own way. Tomorrow, she'll get on the bus, weighed down with two backpacks and a violin. She'll sit at the popular lunch table. Or she will not. She'll be invited to Rachel's party. Or she will not.

"When I have a party Mom, I'm inviting everyone," Lilly says, turning towards sleep.

~Marcelle Soviero

23

About Face

Nothing in life is to be feared. It is only to be understood.
~Marie Curie

y son Josh didn't experience outdoor temperatures above seventy degrees until he was over three years old. He was born in Alaska where, even in summer, no one breaks a sweat. I, on the other hand, had lived most of my life in the Deep South, so I was unprepared for the adjustments he would need to make when we moved back to my hometown in November of the year he turned three.

Josh fell in love with New Orleans, especially the French Quarter. He enjoyed the lively music, interesting people, and the Mississippi River's constant parade of tugboats, barges, steamboats, tankers, and cruise ships. We soon began spending our Saturdays riding the streetcar to Canal Street, then walking to Jackson Square to watch the street performers. Afterwards, we'd walk along the levee until we reached a gate in the floodwall through which we could enter Dutch Alley. There we'd meet my parents by the outdoor stage, listen to whatever jazz band was performing that week, and end the day with French pastry at a nearby café. Our routine altered only when my parents stayed home.

On one of those occasions, a beautiful day in late spring, Josh and I began our weekly ramble with a ride on the Canal Street ferry. The early morning breeze on the river was brisk, masking the heat and humidity climbing rapidly in the paved city streets as spring segued into summer. Fascinated at seeing the river from a different viewpoint, we rode across and back twice. We finally disembarked, walking up Canal towards Chartres Street, which would lead us to Jackson Square. Josh trotted beside me, holding my hand and chatting happily about everything he'd seen. Suddenly he stopped and began crying.

I turned quickly and knelt facing him on the gritty sidewalk. "What's wrong, sweetie?" I brushed away the tears streaming down his cheeks, an action which only seemed to increase his anguished wails. Had something happened that I didn't understand? Was he in pain? "Please, Josh. Please tell Mommy what's wrong so I can fix it." I could hear the panic in my voice and hoped he didn't notice.

"My... my...." He choked on his sobs, unable to speak. I picked him up and looked around, fighting to stay calm while I decided what to do. Finally I spied a café in the lobby of a nearby hotel.

"Come on, let's go get something cool to drink so you can calm down and tell Mommy what's wrong. Okay?" He nodded, his agreement feeding my hope that whatever was wrong wasn't as bad as it seemed. Carrying him into the cool interior, I sat beside him at the counter and ordered two Cokes with plenty of ice. As we sipped, his sobs slowly subsided.

"Feeling better now?" I asked. His nods relieved my anxiety even though his sobs continued intermittently. Finally, he was quiet. I used a napkin to wipe away his tears, then fine-tuned my voice to soothe and comfort. "What happened, baby? Tell Mommy why you were crying."

He looked up at me, eyes large with fear. "My..." A sob caught in his throat, and I held my breath as he tried again. He rubbed his hand under his long silky bangs and held it out, but all I could see was moisture coating his fingers. His face crumpled again, but this time the words tumbled out. "My face is melting!"

I swallowed the laughter bubbling up inside even as my eyes filled with compassionate tears. Anxious to comfort him, I pulled him onto my lap and enveloped him in a bear hug. "Oh, sweetie, there's nothing to be afraid of. You're not melting. That's called sweat.

It's perfectly normal. Everybody sweats. Look." I wiped my own forehead and showed him the moisture coating my own hand. "I'm so sorry you got scared. Mommy completely forgot that you wouldn't know what sweat is. You need to sweat; it's how your body cools off when it's hot outside. I hate to tell you, but you're going to do a lot of sweating during the summer. But I promise, there's no reason for you to be afraid."

He studied my hand, then looked up at me. He didn't look convinced. "You sure?" he asked.

"Positive," I said in the most confident tone I could produce. "I grew up here, remember?" I did my best to reassure him as we talked about the effects of heat and summer, then we continued our walk to Jackson Square. Problem solved, or so I thought.

Even though I had managed to allay his immediate fear that day, Josh's aversion to sweating lasted a long time. He insisted on a buzz cut that summer and every year after until he reached his teens. Gone was my golden-haired toddler. He was now a little boy—a little boy with a mind of his own. He might have to sweat, but he didn't have to let it drip down his face.

~Barbara Hussey

The Comparison Monster

Don't forget that compared to a grownup person every baby is a genius.
Think of the capacity to learn! The freshness, the temperament,
the will of a baby a few months old!
~May Sarton

Most days, I believe my seventeen-month-old is doing just fine. He seems to be on track developmentally. He's discovering the freedom of walking, giggling at his mommy's silly songs, playing with his toys, and conversing with my husband and me in various consonants, diphthongs, and the occasional semblance of a word. He's growing taller, eating well, and thriving. In fact, all is well... until I take him to play group. In a room full of little people, I measure my son against his peers and feel the comparison monster emerge within me.

"Simon recognizes his letters," one parent's chest swells as little Simon-smarty-pants walks around the room saying cat, dog, mouse, house, and other cutesy English words. As I watch Simon, I wonder why the only recognizable word from my son is a repetitive "this, this" in the form of a question. This thought leads my mind on a spiral toward future reading remediation and speech therapy. I'd better drill the alphabet tomorrow and read the current research on how to teach your toddler to read.

As my eyes scan the play center, the comparison monster festers and digs his razor claws inside my mind. Across the room, Fanny-figure-out-all-toys stacks all the rings on a pole, puts puzzle pieces

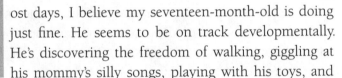

in the right places, and sorts all of the blocks—all within a matter of minutes. Meanwhile, my son repetitively bangs a stacking ring on the hardwood just to hear the loud sound. I watch as one ring flies across the floor and lands with a loud WHACK.

I'm now positive all eyes are on my boy and his improper use of this toy. Worse, all eyes are on me and my inability to teach. Or parent. I feel blood rush to my face. I wipe my palms against my pant legs.

"Put the ring on the pole," I tell my son in a taffy sweet voice, but inside I am upset. My son looks up and smiles, but instead of doing what he should, he shakes another ring in his hand and throws it down again. "Is that a crashing wooden ring or your son's future SAT score?" the monster jeers. I resolve to demonstrate how to use these toys properly.

As I continue to watch the other kids and hear parents describe their abilities, I feel the comparison monster taunting me. Soon I am measuring every kid against my son. Susie-sign-language says please, thank you, more, and all done with perfect gestures. Tony-throw-and-catch-the-ball runs around the room, while my son teeter totters around my leg, tripping and falling down many times.

Today I compare simple vocabulary and dexterity, but tomorrow I see reading levels and athletic ability. And so what if he can't stack blocks—he's still the cutest boy present—or is he? The list is endless, and soon my mind is a spinning top. In a matter of minutes, my son's future crumbles like the Roman Empire.

"Is he normal? Is he developing properly?" The comparison monster's voice is relentless. I go home and ask my husband, "Honey, is there something wrong with our son?"

After a few moments of silence, his answer surprises me. "We tend to focus on the capabilities of our children, but how often do we focus on character? Let's teach our son character—it's far more important." His gentle wisdom astounds me.

"Character versus capabilities," I whisper under my breath, and truth begins to fill my mind. Suddenly I remember these words from Proverbs, "train a child in the way he should go, and when he is old he will not turn from it." (22:6) I have a feeling this verse is not talking about counting to ten or singing the alphabet, but perhaps about teaching a child to obey his parents and ultimately his God. Perhaps it's about teaching him discipline, integrity, contentment, and love. As I let this truth sink into my heart, I feel the monster lose its grip.

My husband reminds me that by the time our son is eighteen he will most likely be able to talk, read, write, solve problems, run, and heck, even dance if he wants to, but what about his character? Will we have modeled love, joy, peace, patience, kindness, gentleness, and self-control? Will we have instilled in him a desire to give and serve? Perhaps asking these questions is the path toward training our son in the way he should go.

Later, I sit down to play with my son and he surprises me. He puts a puzzle piece in the correct spot. I jump up and down, clapping my hands and cheering him on. We play a game of "where is this or that," and he responds by pointing to the various things. As we interact, it dawns on me that my son has his own unique personality, special talents and gifts. He isn't a clone, or a machine, but he is a dynamic person, and he will learn at his own pace. I feel so blessed to be his mother, and once again I realize, that my son is growing well.

~Melanie N. Brasher

25

Running Home

I would not waste my life in friction when it could be turned into momentum.
~Frances Willard

hortly after my son turned ten, we moved to a new school district. Weeks passed and it seemed as though everyone in the family had made the transition well. After school, my son's only goal was to play outside with the neighbor kids. They all seemed to get along and have fun together. I found some comfort in knowing that he felt that he belonged. His new friends helped him blossom in a way that I had never noticed before. I told him one day that I thought his calling was to be a comedian. His eyes brightened and he beamed.

A few months after our move, my son walked in the door after school looking upset. I asked what was going on and he replied, "Nothing." I noticed as he passed that his brow was sweaty and his face looked a little flushed. With the cool weather outside, it seemed strange that he would build up a sweat walking from the bus stop to the house. I followed him into his room and asked him again if everything was all right. He seemed a little aggravated and said that he was fine, just tired. For a moment he seemed so mature for a ten-year-old. Still something seemed odd, but I decided to let it go.

The next afternoon I noticed the neighbor kids got home fifteen minutes before my son. I was beginning to get worried when he came in the door. He avoided my eyes as he passed and again I could see the sweat on his brow. I followed him into his room and tried to help him lift his backpack from his shoulder. He quickly pulled away. "What's going on?" I asked. I didn't know if he was fighting tears or trying to think up a story to tell me but he paused a few moments before answering.

Suddenly he stood up as tall as he could, looked me straight in the eye and said, "It's nothing, Mom. I can handle it." His maturity caught me by surprise, although my mother's intuition made me hesitate. I decided to back off and let him handle it for the time being.

The following afternoon I confronted the neighbor kids. Corralling the girl who professed to be his best friend, I asked if she knew where he was. She looked at her feet and managed to mumble something to the effect that I better ask him. I ran to the house to get my car keys and look for him. As I raced back to the car, keys in hand, I nearly stumbled over the neighbor girl. She was ready to confess and told me that my son had been getting off at the first bus stop eight blocks away. He would run home. She added that he wasn't doing anything wrong.

Then I saw my son walking slowly towards me. His head hung low and his shoulders where hunched. As he approached I could see tears on his cheeks. As soon as he saw me, he reached up quickly and wiped his eyes. I tried to act as though nothing were wrong. "Hey, did you decide to walk home?" I asked. He brushed past me and headed towards the house.

"What's going on?" I asked, when we were inside. He turned to me and dropped his backpack to the floor in a gesture of defiance.

"I didn't want to move here," he said quietly.

"Is there a problem at school?" I asked. "Is there something I need to know about?"

He let out a sigh of frustration, looked me straight in the eye and blurted out, "There's nothing you can do about this, Mom!"

"I could try," I offered.

"What could you do?" he cried. "This kid wants to beat me up and waits for me at the bus stop. If you call the school or anyone else he will just get even madder."

"Someone has to do something about a bully like that," I said. "I could talk to his parents."

"Mom, his parents don't care what he does. They cheer him on when he hits someone."

I was exasperated. I was devastated. I had taught my son never to hit anyone, to always try to talk things out, to resolve things peacefully. I felt completely useless as a parent. I sat down beside him. With a sigh of surrender, I said, "We can call the police."

Suddenly he sat up, turned to me and said, "Mom, I can take care of this. I'm not going to fight him. I can get off at the first bus stop and walk from there. It's no problem."

I was so angry at this bully and even more so at his parents. I wondered what kind of people would incite their son to bully other kids. I wanted to go to them and threaten them and give them a little of their own medicine. I just wanted to inflict the same fear and pain on them that their bullying son had inflicted on mine. But when I looked at my son, he actually looked sort of relaxed. His mouth turned up in his old familiar grin and he said, "Mom, it's going to be okay."

A few days later, my son was back to riding the bus home to the stop near our house. The bully had realized that my son was a comedian and had the ability to make even a bully laugh. Or maybe the kid realized that he needed fewer enemies; whatever the case, my son had reconciled their differences and resolved the problem peacefully.

It is amazing to me, as a parent, that my son was able to find a solution to such a big problem. He brings peace to situations where I would only create more chaos. Being a parent doesn't give us all the answers. Sometime the answers come in a simple form that only a kid can understand.

~Kim Ozment-Gold

26

The Butterfly

Not quite birds, as they were not quite flowers, mysterious
and fascinating as are all indeterminate creatures.
~Elizabeth Goudge

he's called The Butterfly for a reason. Butterflies are beautiful and full of life and energy. Just like our daughter. Just like our Butterfly.

Of course, we also know her as The Butterfly because of what Edward Lorenz taught us as part of Chaos Theory—the flap of a butterfly's wings in Brazil sets off a tornado in Texas.

It should be noted, for the record, that we do not live in Texas. However, we are still affected by the slightest changes in well, it seems, anything. It is impossible to know when there will be a tornado in The Butterfly's world.

As a result, my wife and I sometimes feel we are walking on egg shells. The Butterfly senses the shells trembling with each cautious step. At any time, these shells could break, and she could launch into full-fledged meltdown.

She's prone to mood swings. And tantrums. And crying fits. She's nearly nine years old as I write this. I was warned of the terrible twos. But, in all honesty, I could have lived without the tumultuous threes, the unfortunate fours, the frantic fives, the sickening sixes, the severe sevens, and the atrocious eights. In case you are wondering, I haven't chosen an adjective yet for the nines.

Our journey with Asperger's syndrome began when it became

apparent that something was not quite right with our little Butterfly. So my wife took her to a doctor, hoping for a magic pill to make all the troubles go away. Okay, we weren't really hoping for a pill, more like a diagnosis of mutual hypochondria affecting the parents of a wonderful Butterfly.

Sadly...

I was at O'Hare airport waiting on a delayed flight. Delayed because one of the toilets was broken on the plane. And my cell phone rang. It was the Dancing Queen ringtone—my darling wife. She usually called before I boarded flights—to see if I'd be on time or if I'd be late. Could I pick up milk on my way home? Could I take out the trash? Stuff like that.

But not today.

She said she had something to tell me, but she didn't want to do it over the phone. It was, therefore, my duty to drag it out of her. So, she dropped the A bomb on me. The Butterfly had been diagnosed with Asperger's syndrome.

I was speechless. Surely, this could not be true. The Butterfly did have some quirks, of course. She cried easily. She emptied the clothes from her drawers during her finest tantrums. She did not like crowds, loud noises, or sudden changes in plans. The Butterfly could throw a fit with the best of them—once refusing to get on a subway car because "trains were evil."

Maybe there was something to this.

Asperger's syndrome is apparently very difficult to diagnose in girls. Like The Butterfly, Aspie girls often have difficulty in social settings. The Butterfly covers her ears and cries in noisy restaurants. Crowds scare her, making her feel "small."

Asperger's syndrome and The Butterfly do not always match up one-for-one. Her empathy is without bounds. At the Book Fair, I insisted she buy good books—no Dora or Wiggles or anything Barbie. I helped her choose *Puff the Magic Dragon*. She was devastated at the end—when Puff ceased his mighty roar and was left alone. Jackie Paper abandons Magic Dragons; Butterflies do not. She slept with the book in her bed for over a month.

The constant mood swings and the corresponding meltdowns take their toll. The Butterfly can look me in the eye and say, "I hate you, Daddy." My wife's heart broke the first time The Butterfly said, "I wish I was dead." This led to her first psychiatric appointment in which The Butterfly didn't speak a word. And those magic pills I'd mentioned before—they don't work.

The Bean is The Butterfly's older sister. The Bean and The Butterfly were the stars of a reasonably successful blog I was writing called "Daddy I Want." Much of my content drew from our experiences with The Butterfly's tantrums. "Trains are evil?" You can't make that stuff up. Readers loved it. However, after the diagnosis, it didn't seem very funny anymore. And the blog went the way of the dinosaurs.

The Bean, incidentally, may be the only reason my wife and I feel we are not terrible parents. She is two years older, inquisitive and always very loving, especially to me. The Butterfly is still very Mommy-centric and takes up most of my wife's time. The Bean is almost mine by default, as there is little room in Mommy's life with such a jealous Butterfly abound.

Now Gigi rocks. Gigi is The Butterfly's cat. Gigi snuggles with The Butterfly when her moods turn bad or mad or sad. Whenever she crawls inside a dark place, her cat is with her, purring and offering "kitty comfort." I swear when she retreats to her room for some special "Gigi love time," she emerges a much happier Butterfly.

And what a happy Butterfly she can be! When her mood is good, there is no one happier, more loving, or just plain sweeter. She has a twinkle in her beautiful blue eyes and a smile from one cheek to the other.

I don't know what the future will hold for The Butterfly and our family. Will there be nasty nines? Will there be noticeably nicer nines? What of ten, eleven, twelve, and so on? All I can say is I love her and I can't wait to find out.

~Stu Blandford

Do Angels Wear Glasses?

If we were all like angels, the world would be a heavenly place.
~Author Unknown

"Do angels wear glasses?" she asked me, with unshed tears glistening in her dark brown eyes. My five-year-old daughter Carmen had just come out of the auditorium after participating in the final rehearsal of the Christmas pageant at our church. The dress rehearsal saw all the children made up, costumed and ready to present the Christmas Story in the splendor that goes along with a children's pageant. Carmen was one of the Christmas angels and another sweet little "angel" had pointed at Carmen midway through the practice and declared loudly, "Angels don't wear glasses!"

Up until that moment, Carmen had been the true essence of "angel-ness." She was resplendent in her white, floor length robe, with the gold wings pinned a little crookedly to the back and a tinsel halo encircling her fine, blond hair. Truly she looked the part. I had always thought my child "angelic" even if at times she didn't behave that way, but on this occasion, Carmen imagined herself an angel in every way. She swooped through the auditorium, spreading out her wings and pretending to fly. She touched the halo with a kind of wonder and cruised in her flowing robe for all to see her magnificence. And then just as suddenly, her demeanor changed, when with one callous comment her fantasy world evaporated. She hung her head and took off her glasses.

It had been quite by accident that we discovered Carmen was legally blind in her right eye at the age of four. I had taken my other two children to see the optometrist just before school started, and almost as an afterthought I suggested the doctor check Carmen out "if she'll sit still long enough." The doctor gave a "thumbs-up" to both Brett and Laurelle, but he looked serious and concerned when he evaluated Carmen. "I think she should see a specialist," he suggested.

Over the next year and a half, Carmen was forced to wear an eye patch to correct the "lazy eye," wearing the patch five to six hours a day on her "good" eye to force the other eye to focus. She also needed to wear glasses.

I prayed she would respond well to this treatment, and she did. She got used to wearing the glasses, and although she didn't like wearing the patch much she still accepted it with little complaining. Wearing glasses gave her a whole new persona. Having a cherub face to begin with, the glasses only seemed to give Carmen an even more precious look, not to mention the fact that her vision improved dramatically over that period of time. But now my angel was holding her glasses with tears glistening in her long eyelashes, and the question remained unanswered: "Do angels wear glasses?"

I enfolded her in my arms and her tiny body curled in close to mine as I hugged her close and tilted her chin so I could look at her pretty face. "Of course angels wear glasses!" I said loudly, so all her doubting friends could hear, and so that she knew I was passionate about my answer.

She somehow became lighter there on my lap. The angel wings were beginning to flutter about her again. I wiped a tiny tear away and kissed her lightly on her forehead. She smiled. Hers was (and still is) a smile that lights up an entire room. She was soaring again, borne on those imaginary wings that were pinned to her robe. She jumped from my lap, put her glasses back on, adjusted her halo and then flew away to enjoy cookies and juice.

As I watched her, I marveled at her accepting nature. I didn't need to explain myself to her. She was content with my answer, truly a wonderful attribute for a five-year-old! Certainly over the ensuing years she has questioned me quite a bit on a variety of topics and I'll admit, I've bluffed my way through sometimes. I've floundered to give her a reasonable answer to one of her most pressing issues of the day, and I've watched her roll her eyes at me and walk away with that look that says, "You have no idea what you're talking about." But I feel pretty confident that my response to her when she was five years old will stand the test of time.

You see, I'm convinced that angels not only wear glasses, but they wear back braces, and leg braces, and braces on their teeth too. They sometimes have prosthetics for legs and arms, and wigs to cover bald heads after chemotherapy. They sometimes "fly" with the aid of crutches and wheelchairs. They come in different colours, sizes and shapes. They have crooked smiles, dimpled cheeks, and runny noses. They are loud, they are quiet, they cry, they whine, and they laugh, but to their mothers they are in every sense of the word... angels!

Angels do wear glasses, it's only the truly blind that don't see that!

~Lynn Dove

Chapter
4

Parenthood

Parenting Faux Pas

To an adolescent, there is nothing in the world more embarrassing than a parent.

~Dave Barry

Kindergarten Exposé

Children seldom misquote you. In fact,
they usually repeat word for word what you shouldn't have said.
~Author Unknown

've heard the FBI holds extensive files on every American citizen—the good, the bad and the ugly. As the mother of a chatty, never-met-a-stranger five-year-old about to start kindergarten, my concerns are much more immediate. To be perfectly honest, I am petrified to think what and how much my son's kindergarten teacher is about to learn about me and mine.

My first three kids were a little on the quiet side, apt to speak only when they were spoken to. But my late-in-life child, Jonah, would talk to a post. The teacher seems like a nice enough lady. But I know my son. And I can't shake the image of her escorting him into the teachers' lounge one day, instructing him to, "Go ahead. Tell the other teachers what you were just telling me about your mommy." I shudder at the possibility.

It's not like there's anything that juicy in our family closet—or family tree, for that matter. I'm just worried about the way it might come out of Jonah's mouth. You know, like, "Guess what! We got to have cupcakes for breakfast because Mom's on deadline." (Eggs, milk, flour—aren't those breakfast foods?) Or, "You know, it's the thing you serve punch with, plus Mama uses it to scoop dead fish out of the fish tank."

That's actually mild for Jonah. This is the child who told the lady at the ball field as she was unfolding her ballpark chair, "Don't you think you're a little FAT for that?" and, after a half dozen lectures about not making such comments, hollered to me across a crowded church hall, "Don't worry, Mom. I'm not going to ask you why he's so FAT until we get in the car." My fears are not unfounded.

What Jonah thinks, Jonah says. And I'm not being paranoid when I imagine his teacher will be hearing things like:

- "Here. This is for you. Aunt Gail gave it to Mommy, but she didn't like it."
- "Then Mom said she'd KILL the next person who left dirty dishes in her office." (It's a figure of speech.)
- "Mommy thinks Daddy's made-out-of-money and Daddy thinks Mommy was born-to-wait-on-him."
- "But that's what Mommy called the man in the truck who honked at her."
- "I don't have to go to the bathroom. When we were stuck in a traffic jam, I just used a coffee cup." (Once! I let him do that once!)
- "If you open the bathroom door in a restaurant when my mom's on the toilet, she'll slam it on your arm."
- "Mom said it was okay to eat my hotdog after we cut off the part the cat licked."
- "My Mom says you're 'no-spring-chicken.' What does that mean?"
- "Mom couldn't find her running shorts 'cause they were under that gi-AN-tic pile in the laundry room." (I wouldn't exactly call it "gi-AN-tic.")

My strategy with this kindergarten teacher will be the same as with the three before her—ply her with baked goods and flowers from the yard, pamper her at Christmas and Teacher Appreciation time, extol her virtues to the principal, and hope beyond hope she has her own little blabbermouth at home and understands to take anything Jonah says with a grain of salt. Really!

~Mimi Greenwood Knight

Bad Hair Day

Parents are embarrassed when their children tell lies,
and even more embarrassed when they tell the truth.
~Author Unknown

t was a typical Thursday morning: Crazy, naturally, but not unusual. Luckily, my daughters decided to take matters into their own hands—they did their own hair and picked out their own clothes and lied about brushing their teeth without any grumbling. My younger daughter asked to borrow something of mine. I nodded my approval as I tossed a still-frozen strudel at each girl. Breakfast was done, and we were out the door!

With only moments to spare, I pulled into their school and slowed the van down as they jumped out the side door. My younger daughter turned to blow me a kiss; her little side ponytail was starting to fall but she looked cute, nonetheless. I was so proud of her for doing her own hair. It's not every seven-year-old that can create her own side ponytail, you know! That kid was going to go places. I got weepy thinking about how much I loved that independent little world-changer.

That afternoon, however, the school sent home an entirely different kid.

As she crawled into the van, she cried out, "Momma, your leopard ponytail holder is CRAP. Absolute CRAP!"

"Excuse me?" I countered, hoping that my tone and word choice would indicate that I didn't appreciate such language coming from the mouth of my seven-year-old daughter, future CEO of some major international, multi-galactic corporation and caregiver of her tired and aged momma.

"You heard me — it's CRAP!" she continued, failing to notice that her audience (me) was completely lost.

"It was hard enough getting it to work right the first time, but then it came out in the middle of reading. So, I had to put my hair back up without a mirror because my teacher wouldn't let me go to the bathroom even though it wasn't my turn to read. Then it came out again when we were going to centers and I asked Bobby to help me, but he was NO help. He said he didn't even know how to put in a regular ponytail holder. He really couldn't do a complicated pony-tail holder like yours. Then my teacher said she'd help me, but she didn't know how to work that ponytail holder either and she made me put it in my backpack. She said I couldn't wear it to school ever again. Thanks, Momma. Thanks for buying a leopard, stupid, no-good ponytail holder that's CRAP!"

Oh for heaven's sake! I had no idea what she was talking about. I didn't even have a leopard ponytail holder.... The only leopard print thing I owned was...

Oh geez.

Oh... well, she was right: Oh CRAP.

I felt all the blood rush to my face; I recalled the only leopard-print thing I owned.

I saw my innocent baby girl's second-grade teacher smile and wave really big as I drove by. I was mortified. From the back seat, my frustrated daughter pulled my leopard-print thong from her back-pack and threw it into the front seat. "Here!" she huffed. "I will never wear that again!"

You and me both, baby.

~Heather Davis

Reprinted by permission of Mark Parisi and
Off the Mark ©2010.

Chasing Perfection

*Memory is a way of holding onto the things you love, the things you are,
the things you never want to lose.*
~From the television show The Wonder Years

y husband stood at the changing table carefully removing the diaper of our two-week-old daughter, Tami. "Isn't she amazing?" I cooed, my heart swelling with tenderness as I watched them. I'd never imagined an infant could be so beautiful. A torrent of love washed over me the first moment I saw her, astounded by the wonder of her ten tiny fingers and toes, each with a delicate nail, her bright eyes, her rosebud mouth, the softness of her cheek. My firstborn, she deserved nothing less than a perfect mother and I vowed to be just that.

"What's this?" Bob took something from her diaper and held it toward me, chuckling.

I gasped at the sight of a tube of diaper rash ointment in his hand. "That was in her diaper?" I wasn't laughing. I had been the last to change her. Perfect mothers, or even pretty good mothers, didn't leave tubes of medication in their daughters' diapers.

Never mind that I hadn't slept ninety minutes in a row for the last fourteen days, responding immediately to Tami's slightest whimper. Or that I kissed the top of her head so often hair might never grow there. I'd been careless with our precious treasure.

In the next months, pursuing the art and science of perfect mothering, I read book after book on child development as I nursed Tami.

During her naps I made baby food from scratch and set up play dates with friends so she would have plenty of socialization. Perfection still eluded me. Sometimes her wispy blond hair needed a trim for weeks before I got around to it, or I failed to notice a stain on her dress when I took her to a birthday party. Occasionally my patience grew thin. But in general I was getting the hang of this parenting thing and groping my way toward perfection.

As she grew into toddlerhood I carefully gave Tami a truck with every doll and dressed her in blue as well as pink. I didn't want her exposed to any gender stereotypes. To my dismay, as soon as she could express an opinion she insisted on wearing only long dresses, never pants of any sort.

"Look at these cute jeans," I said one morning to my blond, blue-eyed two-year-old. "See the hearts on the pockets? Your friend Ashley has a pair like them."

"This one." Tami reached for her ankle-length blue dress with lace around the collar, cap sleeves, and hem. "Me."

"Okay, my love." I slipped the dress over her head and she held the skirt wide, twirling with pleasure. She looked like Cinderella going to meet her Prince Charming, as she called him, and turned my determined heart into mush. Maybe another day I could expand her vision of fashion.

"You have a play date with Jade," I said the following week. "What about these cute brown pants and the pink shirt with a teddy bear? You love pink and pants will be good at the park." Perfect mothers dressed their children appropriately.

Tami shook her head. "This one," she insisted as she pulled her long red dress out of a drawer and struggled to pull it over her head.

"Fine," I sighed, as I helped her with the dress and adjusted the belt with the glittering rhinestones.

Her eyes shone as she stroked the pleated skirt that hung gracefully to the ground.

I reminded myself that clothes didn't make the child. And maybe they weren't an indicator of adequate parenting after all. Tami's sweet personality would gain her admittance anywhere, and she could learn from our family values to approach all kinds of people and careers with an open mind.

When Tami started preschool I began writing and teaching about the subject that had become my passion and my life. At four, she was a bright, cheerful, cooperative child. I must be doing something right.

One day as I happily nursed her new little brother Benjamin, the pleasures of motherhood filling me with contentment, the phone jangled. Ben and I both jumped. Cradling my son in one arm, I answered it. Tami's trembling voice on the other end of the line pierced my heart. "Mommy, preschool is over. Are you going to pick me up?"

Gasping, I checked the clock. I was twenty minutes late. Shame clutched at my chest, stealing my breath. What kind of mother forgot her own child?

"I'll be right there, sweetie. I'm sorry you had to wait." I buckled Ben into his car seat and hurried to the school, an image burned in my mind of Tami sitting in the principal's office, her blond head bowed, her pale cheeks wet with tears. Surely I'd traumatized her and she would have abandonment issues forever.

I vowed this would be my last mistake.

Yet a year later, as I pawed through a table of cute children's sweaters on sale at JCPenney, Ben napping in a Snugli secure against my chest, I heard a voice over the intercom. "Samantha Waltz. Samantha Waltz. Your daughter is waiting for you at the security desk."

Security desk? Heat rose in my face as I hurried to get Tami. I knelt and put my arms around her. She wasn't crying, but her eyes lacked their usual sparkle as she explained, "I went to look for the toys and then I lost you."

The security guard glared at me, and I knew stories of every mall kidnapping in the last ten years were running through his mind, as they were through mine. I'd just that morning given a keynote address at a local early childhood conference on the emotional development of young children "Really, I kept my eye on her every moment," I stammered. "I don't know how she wandered off."

"Not every moment, obviously." Disgust thickened his voice. I imagined his hand itched to dial Child Services.

As my beloved daughter grew older, perfection continued to elude me, but she and I were close anyway. One day, when I was driving her to a friend's house to work on a school project, I asked her what she remembered from the time she was little. She didn't mention the morning I was supposed to be the mother helper at her nursery school and absent-mindedly went to a plant nursery to buy flowers for our garden instead. Or the afternoon I let go of her bicycle too soon when she was learning to ride a two-wheeler. Instead, she replied, "I remember making sugar cookies at Christmas and getting powdered sugar all over my dress. And I remember the time you made Ben and me Raggedy Ann and Andy dolls with all their clothes. I'd never seen you sew before."

"What about all the things I did wrong?"

"You always made me feel loved, Mama," she said and lifted her face to kiss my cheek. "Isn't that what matters?"

~Samantha Ducloux Waltz

Tact and Diplomacy

Pretty much all the honest truth telling there is in the world
is done by children.
~Oliver Wendell Holmes

y son William had the standard vocabulary: "Dada," "Mama," and even "Book!" (He always exclaimed that last word.) But he'd also learned some other words.

Being exactly one year old, William was toddling around the house unsurely and blabbering gibberish. The electrician was finally there to fix the outlet in our bathroom. He was a large man, muscular, for sure, but with an enormous belly, about which he seemed not the least self-conscious—he actually played with his belly button a little when he first examined the outlet.

As the electrician began drilling away, I was on baby patrol, following my son William around the house and keeping him from tipping over stools and chairs, or standing with both feet in the dog's water dish, a favorite pastime of his. I followed William to the bathroom door, and when he saw the electrician in there for the first time he let out a delighted giggle.

The electrician ceased running his electric screwdriver and turned. "Hi little fella!" he said warmly.

William pointed at the electrician. "Fat!" he announced.

Standing behind William, I laughed nervously. "He loves the kitty," I said. "Won't stop saying 'cat.'"

The electrician smiled, unconvinced. "That what he said?"

"Fat!" announced William again, jabbing his finger toward the electrician.

"Okay baby, okay," I said, picking up William and carrying him away from the door. "Fat fat fat fat!" he called as I carried him into the kitchen, out of the electrician's hearing.

A half hour later the electrician was all packed up, and passing through the kitchen, he said, "We'll send you the bill." Then he stopped. "You guys even own a cat?"

I shook my head, and he laughed.

~Ron Kaiser, Jr.

The Art of Parenting

Don't worry that children never listen to you;
worry that they are always watching you.
~Robert Fulghum

o one teaches us the art of parenting. Why aren't classes required? Why aren't we required to pass some kind of test to get a license to be parents? Certainly I wasn't prepared for this most important of all jobs.

After four children, though, I felt like I had a handle on it.

Or I did, until our nine-year-old son Robbie needed to complete a cultural arts requirement to earn an arrow point for Cub Scouts.

To appreciate the enormity of this, one needs to understand our family. We are not cultural arts people. My husband and three older children breathe sports. Football. Baseball. Soccer. Planning a cultural arts excursion for my crew took creativity and a large dose of courage.

After I presented Robbie with several possibilities, he decided to visit the local museum.

I loaded our four children in the car, placing the one-year-old in his car seat and strapping the other children in seatbelts.

"Remember," I told Robbie, "in order for me to sign off on this, you need to look at every exhibit. No slacking."

"Do we all have to go?" our daughter whined.

"Yes," I answered in my best mother-of-the-year voice. "This is supposed to be a family activity."

We arrived at the museum, and I congratulated myself on arranging this field trip, a nice alternative to the many sporting events we normally attended. I paid the entrance fees and walked in with four children in tow.

My heart dropped to my stomach, which was already doing an uneasy roll, as I gazed around the room.

I had neglected to find out what the museum was currently displaying: nudes. Of all kinds. In every shape and size. Oil nudes. Watercolor nudes. Clay nudes. Porcelain nudes. Bronze nudes.

One painting of a woman, with an improbable third breast placed in the center of the belly, caught Robbie's attention.

"Mom, is that her belly button?" Robbie whispered.

I could only shake my head helplessly.

True to my edict, we gazed at every exhibit.

An hour and forty-five minutes later, we trooped back to the car, where we repeated the process of car seats and seatbelts.

At home, I put the baby down for a nap, gave everyone a snack, and turned to Robbie. "Bring me your Cub Scout book and I'll sign off on the requirement."

Later that night, I recounted the adventure to my husband. "Nudes," I said. "Hundreds of nudes. Fat nudes. Skinny nudes. And we looked at all of them. Every single one."

"You're a good mother," he said. Wisely, he turned what sounded like laughter into a cough, but I caught the twinkle in his eyes.

I threw a pillow at him but decided he was right. I was a good mother.

Parenting. Definitely an art, not a science.

~Jane M. Choate

With a Song and a Prayer

Stress should be a powerful driving force, not an obstacle.
~Bill Phillips

One morning, back when my daughter Gigi was two and my only child, I was doing dishes in a cloud of self-pity and exhaustion, while thinking about what it takes to be a Great Mom. I had no close friends in town, since we had just moved recently, and I was lonely.

I was in dreamland about this new life until one of those thoughts, seemingly out of nowhere, zapped through my fog.

Gigi's preschool parent-teacher conference. It was today. It was this morning. It was in twenty minutes.

I looked at my watch and then the clock on the wall, hoping one of them was wrong. I had two thoughts: I am never going to get there. I have to get there.

The facts weren't good. Gigi wasn't allowed to be at the conference, and I had no babysitter.

I called my mom who lived nearby. No answer.

I called my best friend from high school who lived twenty minutes away. After her machine answered I hung up. She lived too far away.

I stared out my window, desperate for an answer.

I was still in the getting-to-know-you phase with the other preschool moms. And I didn't know our neighbors.

As my eyes focused, I saw Mister Song, the kind Vietnamese

man who mowed our lawn who we also knew through church. The same church where Gigi's preschool was.

"Mr. Song!" I yelled over the leaf blower. He looked up, saw me and turned off the machine.

"Yes, Mrs. Jennifer," he replied.

"Mr. Song, would you do me a favor?"

"Yes, Mrs. Jennifer."

"Can you come with me for the next little while and sit in my car with Gigi?"

I rambled an explanation that must have made me seem like I was an alien that had dropped suddenly onto Mr. Song's planet.

Moments later Mr. Song, Gigi and I were buckled into the car.

I screeched to a stop in our church parking lot with a minute to spare.

I handed Gigi a bag of Goldfish and a board book, and looked at Mr. Song.

"Mr. Song. Gigi." I spoke to them like soldiers. Like I had some control over what was about to transpire. "I will be back in twenty minutes."

Gigi looked at Mr. Song, then back at me, her face calm but confused. I looked back at Mr. Song, who nodded. I said officially, "Thank you, Mr. Song."

Within two minutes I was sitting quietly and calmly across from Gigi's two preschool teachers who had been co-teaching at this preschool for over twenty-two years. They were similar to an old married couple, speaking for each other, interrupting, and feeding off of each other, but in a wonderful loving way.

Over the next twenty minutes, they told me how well adjusted and happy Gigi was. That Gigi was a lovely girl, she had many friends, and that she was a pleasure to have in the classroom.

All I could think about was how they didn't know that Gigi was outside in our car with Mr. Song. How on earth was it possible that she was well adjusted? It was clear to anyone who really knew that I was not capable of this motherhood gig.

After our allotted time was over, I shook their hands, said, "Thank you. Thank you so much for taking care of my daughter so well."

Then I ran back to the car.

It was like time had stood still. Mr. Song and Gigi were in their same seats, facing the same way, except the goldfish were gone and Mr. Song had a huge grin across his face.

"How'd it go, Mr. Song?" I asked, completely and utterly relieved at the sight.

"Just fine, Mrs. Jennifer."

I looked at Gigi. She was smiling too.

"Mr. Song, thank you so much. Thank you so, so much."

Once back home I unbuckled Gigi and took her out of the car.

Mr. Song got out of the car and strapped back on his leaf-blowing machine again.

"Thanks again, Mr. Song," I said.

I shut the door to the house and wondered just how other moms pull off this Motherhood job.

~Jennifer Quasha

34

The Interview

Raising children is a creative endeavor, an art, rather than a science.
~Bruno Bettelheim

When my son Bailey was seven years old and in the first grade, mornings trying to get him up and out the door for school were a continuous fight. Each day we were faced with tears and tantrums about how boring school was and how he didn't need or want to go.

One morning after weeks of arguing with him my husband announced that he understood and told Bailey he no longer needed to attend school. You can imagine the surprised look on my face. For a brief time Bailey's expression changed and the excitement on his face showed that he thought he had won the battle and was now open to a day of play at home while his friends had to sit in that boring classroom.

I just knew my husband would not give in to this crazy demand, and of course not going to school at seven years old was not an option, so I patiently waited to see what he had in mind to solve the problem.

We went about our normal morning routine—ate breakfast, made the beds and then the announcement came.... My husband instructed Bailey to get dressed in his best pants and collared shirt, as it was time to "hit the pavement" and look for a job. I sat with my cup of coffee wondering how this little boy, who thought he was too smart for school, would react to the instructions. Would he be smart enough to just laugh at the idea?

The next thing we knew Bailey stomped down the hall and a few minutes later emerged dressed to impress. Was he simply calling our bluff?

As we pulled into the McDonald's parking lot and walked in we instructed him to ask for the manager and request a job application. You can imagine the expression on the manager's face as I quickly explained that my son was "too smart for school" and was ready to enter the workforce. The manager must have been a parent because he immediately played along and handed Bailey a pen and application.

As we approached the table to have our child who could barely write his address legibly fill out a job application, the tears came hard and fast. Bailey then announced, "School isn't so bad. It may be boring but I guess I'll go." We asked if he was sure, explaining all the benefits of being able to eat French fries and seeing the new release of the Happy Meal toy before his friends. His reply was a simple, "please take me to school."

We thanked the manager for his time and headed to school. We never had another problem getting him up and ready again. Bailey is now sixteen years old, a straight-A student and has received perfect attendance every year since the day he experienced his first job interview.

~D'ette Corona

35

Men in Training

Boys will be boys, and so will a lot of middle-aged men.
~Frank McKinney "Kin" Hubbard

Three generations of boys were sitting on the floor on Christmas morning—the grandfather, the father and the toddler. The toddler had just opened the last gift under the tree. It was an amazing train set, the kind of train set the grandfather and father had only dreamed about as little boys. The toddler was so excited. The grandfather and the father were even more excited, judging by the gleam in their eyes. The train cars were ready to roll so all that was needed was to put the track together the way you wanted it. Simple you say. Not even close!

The various configurations that you could assemble filled a twenty-page booklet. Did you want a simple oval? Are you kidding me? A figure eight? How boring. How about an up and down and over and around and through? Now that sounded much better to the older boys. The toddler would have been pleased with the simple oval but his playmates wouldn't hear of it.

Out came all of the parts. No one bothered to look at the instructions—oh, no… why would anyone bother to follow directions? The grandfather and the father proceeded to try to put the pieces of the track together. How frustrating. Nothing seemed to fit right. Part A really didn't go with part B. And part C was nowhere to be found. After much grumbling and mumbling and a few pointed "I told you so's" the track was put together and ready to use. The toddler was so excited. Finally he would be able to play with his gift.

Well, not exactly. The grandfather and the father explained to the toddler that, being the loving and concerned people they were, they wanted to test it out to be sure everything worked correctly. How thoughtful of them. And so there they sat, grandfather and father, having a play date on the living room floor. The only things missing were the engineer hats.

The train made its own sounds, and thank goodness for that. At least the grandmother and the mother didn't have to listen to two grown men making choo-choo and chug-a-chug-a-chug-a-chug noises. Unfortunately the only sound the train didn't come equipped with was the whistle, but the two big boys more than made up for that. Each time the train went around a curve or started up a hill, or down a hill, the grandfather and the father made lovely and quite realistic train whistle sounds complete with arm movements. Whoo-whoo. Can't you just hear and picture that? They took turns driving the train and actually got along quite well except for the time the father thought it should be his turn to make the whistle sounds and the grandfather was sure it was his turn. The toddler had to step in and settle the dispute.

What's a toddler to do when his grandfather and his father won't let him play with his very own toy? What are a toddler's grandmother and mother to do while they watch this whole scene? They tried to console the toddler and distract him with his other new toys. They tried to explain to him how nice it was that the grandfather and the father cared so much about him and were taking all of this time to work on the train so it would be perfect for him.

The toddler was smarter than that. He knew exactly what was happening. The grandfather and the father had taken his toy and wouldn't share. But finally, after what seemed like hours, they invited the toddler to come over and sit cross-legged with them on the floor, next to the train. They even let the toddler drive HIS train… up and down and over and around and through. And they let him make the whistle sound… but not all of the time. The grandmother and the mother watched this all happening and decided that for the next Christmas, identical toys needed to be bought for all three boys... the grandfather, the father and the toddler. No sharing necessary. Boys will be boys.

~Barbara LoMonaco

Chapter
5

Parenthood

Stop and Smell the Roses

*The moment one gives close attention to any thing,
even a blade of grass, it becomes a mysterious, awesome,
indescribably magnificent world in itself.*

~Henry Miller

Mud Puddles

The world is mud-luscious and puddle-wonderful.
~E. E. Cummings

I t was a typical spring day—overcast, windy, and cold. And the rain had just stopped so there were puddles everywhere. I was taking my son to the local Walmart. Shane was old enough that I didn't have to hold his hand with a vise-like grip but still young enough that I dared not take my eyes off him even for a split second. We were both in a particularly good mood that day. As a working mom, I was happy to spend some time with my son, and for Shane, it was fun to go out, no matter where we were going.

As we walked towards the store, I tried to steer Shane away from the numerous puddles in the parking lot. We managed to bypass several until we came to the granddaddy of them all, smack dab in middle of our path. Before I could stop him, Shane jumped right in the middle of the muddy pool of water. His brand new Nike sneakers were soaked. His ironed Levi jeans were splattered with mud.

As I looked down to scold him, I saw a little boy with curly red hair, a huge smile and big blue eyes looking up at me in excitement. There was only one thing I could do. I jumped into the puddle with him. My brand new Nike sneakers were soaked. My ironed Levi jeans were splattered with mud. As I looked down at my son, I was rewarded with his laughter. It was at that moment that I learned what I had forgotten so long ago, that jumping in mud puddles was fun.

As we reluctantly left our newfound source of entertainment and continued on our way to the store, I noticed a man in a truck driving by with a big smile on his face. He had been watching us. It was then that I realized that my three-year-old son had just managed to make himself, his mother and a complete stranger smile by giving in to such a natural impulse.

When I first learned that I was going to be a mother, I thought of the many things I would teach my child: love, respect, honor, patience, dignity. The list was endless. What I have discovered as a parent is that it is our children who end up teaching us the really important things in life, like taking time out to jump in mud puddles.

~Denise Seagren-Peterson

Priorities

If you haven't time to respond to a tug at your pants leg,
your schedule is too crowded.
~Robert Brault, www.robertbrault.com

This afternoon I had something of a wake-up call. Actually, it was more of a wake-up scream....

It had been a dismal morning. In one hand was the stack of bills I needed to pay, in the other was my checkbook and, as often is the case, the two did not meet in the middle. There was also a list of e-mails marked urgent in my inbox, a list of honey-dos taped to the fridge, the house was a mess, and the coffeepot had died before breakfast.

Now, I'm a fairly optimistic guy, and any one of these would not typically bring me down, but cumulatively, the load was feeling huge and heavy. What I wanted to do was just forget about it all and go play with my daughter; what I had done instead was spend the morning staring at my computer screen and worrying.

That's when my two-year-old daughter, who was napping in her room, screamed.

It was a scream I'd never heard from her before, not frustration or even fear, but pain.

You know what? I was up and out of that chair in a heartbeat, and all those worries, which had seemed so important, disappeared just as quickly. Suddenly, nothing in the world was imperative except making sure that my girl was okay.

Luckily, it was nothing more than a leg trapped in the slats of her crib, which had twisted when she tried to roll over in her sleep. Ten minutes in the rocking chair and a sippy cup of milk later, she was back asleep, safe and sound.

Still, in the few seconds that it took me to get from my desk to her door, I was treated to a blinding flash of the obvious. Bills would be paid, or they wouldn't... we weren't going to starve. Chores would be done, or not, and there was always next weekend. Nothing on my worry list was more than a B priority at best, and my A priority needed my help.

Nothing on my worry list would have made me sprint away from my screaming daughter.

An hour later, I still hadn't made much of a dent in the lists, but when my daughter woke up for real, I put a pair of sandals on her, turned off the computer, and we went to the park to play in the fountain.

The bills will get paid... they always do, and all of those things that need to get done will eventually get done; and the ones that don't?

It's okay, I'm not going to worry about them, because they're not my priority.

Hopefully, I won't need a scream to wake me up again.

~Perry P. Perkins

Metamorphosis by Mud

A boy is Truth with dirt on its face, Beauty with a cut on its finger,
Wisdom with bubble gum in its hair, and the Hope of the future with
a frog in its pocket.
~Author Unknown

y dinnertime on warm summer days, I am covered in dirt, water, melted Popsicles, sidewalk chalk or goo. My hair is decorated with leaves and crumbs from Goldfish crackers. My clothes are often drenched from water balloon fights or attempts to wash my car. I look a mess, even on days I'd showered and fixed my hair. I am the mother of boys.

The funny thing is, at thirty-seven, the mud has created a kind of madness that has made me, well, calmer. I am chilling out and letting myself and my life get a little messy for the first time — and it's okay. My two- and five-year-old sons have turned my visions of perfect breezy afternoons upside down, like our old striped hammock that lies sideways and dusty in our back yard.

In the woods behind our house, I follow my boys through knee-deep leaf piles and across the muddy creek. Without hesitation, they peer inside fallen tree trunks for proof of life, a squirrel's home, or big bugs. Some moments, I hang back, fearful of what they may find or what might jump out. But their excitement and bravado makes me laugh and then I'm right there with them.

They follow baby frogs from the neighbor's smelly pond and want to touch them, germs and all. Growing up, I was a girly girl who didn't walk in woods or get my hands dirty, and Kermit was the only frog I saw. Now I contemplate getting a little green guy as a pet.

Nothing makes my sons happier than water and me—combined. Their favorite outdoor activity is spraying me with a hose or washing me while they wash my car. I've stopped wearing mascara during the day.

My friends who have older kids often tell me to cherish these moments when the kids are still young enough to want me there to play. Last year, I shook my head and looked forward to when they'd be old enough to stop making me a mess. This year, I try to memorize those moments. Maybe it's because I'm a year older now, or I am noticing my boys growing up so fast. Maybe it's because these two little nature lovers have changed me.

When we moved here when my older son was two, I looked at the woods behind our house and appreciated the beauty. But, now I'm living it. I think my first son made me appreciate life, and my second son made me change the way I live my life. Some early evenings, the last thing I want to do is have to change into fresh jeans or a dry shirt, but in the end, it's more a mission accomplished than a chore.

As a girl, I'd imagined having a daughter or two someday. I pictured a house full of dolls and purple dresses, pink rooms and places for hair bows and ballet slippers. Instead, I am surrounded by bug vacuums, mud puddles and football cleats, and I couldn't be happier. My life is much messier than I ever thought it would be. And better.

~Erin Mantz

Today

A boy is the only thing that God can use to make a man.
~Author Unknown

Some day you will be a grown man with rough skin and whiskers; but for today, I luxuriate in kissing your sweet, smooth cheeks.

Some day you will work hard to make a living and support your family; but for today, I sit on the floor and stack building blocks with you.

Some day you will run up the stairs, two at a time; but for today, I hold your chubby little hand while we navigate the steps together.

Some day you will get up every morning and don a suit and tie for work; but for today, I let you stay in your jammies so we can snuggle until noon.

Some day people will have respect for the authority in your deep, commanding voice; but for today, I savor the sweetness of a tiny boy earnestly calling out, "Mama!"

Some day you will face a world that will treat you unfairly; but for today, my lap is your protection from the world.

Some day you will walk with a determined step and even gait; but for today, I relish the sound of your chunky bare feet pattering across the kitchen tile.

Some day you will have to make decisions that will not be easy; but for today I can guide you and whisper the answers in your ear.

Some day your toys will include cars, sports equipment and electronics; but for today, we play pat-a-cake and read your favorite storybook.

Some day you will dine with business colleagues in fine restaurants; but for today, we sit at the kitchen table and share a peanut butter sandwich with extra jelly.

Some day you will sleep in your very own house far away; but for tonight, I tuck you into your crib and rest my hand upon your head while we pray.

Some day you will help me in and out of the car, and steady my arm; but for today, I lift you high into the air and listen to your squeals of delight.

Some day I will be thrilled to hear you say that you've found "the one;" but for today, I cherish being the most important woman in your life.

Today, I will delight in your snaggle-toothed grin, laugh when you growl at the cat, and kiss your skinned-up knees; for someday, a man will emerge in the place where my precious boy once stood.

~Ginger Truitt

Am I Beautiful?

A daughter may outgrow your lap, but she will never outgrow your heart.
~Author Unknown

y two-year-old and I were home alone while her mother and older sister were out. I was sitting in the living room working on some schoolwork, and I could hear Hannah playing in one of the bedrooms. When it grew quiet for too long in the back of our small apartment in the student-housing complex, I walked down the short hallway to check on her.

As I turned into the bedroom doorway, I found a glittery cloud of pastel colors. I looked around the room and discovered that nearly every surface—the throw rug, the wooden floor, the bed-spreads—was covered in powdery splotches of pink, lavender, mint green, and sky blue. Hannah was sitting in the middle of the pastel explosion, covered from her hair to her shoelaces in powder and glitter. She had found the play make-up set that her older sister had recently received as a Christmas gift and was looking into its tiny mirror, still in the process of painting her face—and everything around her.

"Hannah!" I exclaimed, ready to scold her for the huge mess she had made of herself and her room.

"Am I boo-ful, Daddy?" she asked, so completely absorbed in what she was doing that she was oblivious to the alarm in my voice.

I laughed, picked her up in my arms, and kissed her pastel-powdered cheek. "Yes you are very beautiful," I said.

And she WAS beautiful—not because of the make-up, of course, but because she is my child and I love her. She was and is and always will be beautiful to me.

Now, many years later, when I see parents in stores or other public places losing patience and getting angry with their children for being children while the parents are trying to accomplish some adult task, I am tempted to interrupt them and advise them to calm down, to relax and cherish these moments with their children. I am tempted to tell them that one day, when they're old like me and their children are grown and gone, they will give anything to have just one more day to chase their little ones around a store. I want to say, "Your children are beautiful! Cherish them!"

Sometimes it's easy to see that our children are beautiful—when they're dancing at recitals, or playing soccer with innocent abandon, or sleeping peacefully. Other times we lose sight of their beauty. But even when our children do things that are not very pretty, we need to keep sight of the beauty we see in them. And we need to be especially careful not to let our own stress, anxiety, or exhaustion be the cause of our losing sight of our children's inherent beauty.

"Am I beautiful, Daddy?" Hannah had asked. Now, when she calls to share news of her life, I hear her asking that same question over again. And I try to communicate with her—and with her sister—in such a way that they always know that they are beautiful.

~David Fillingim

Perspective

We do not remember days; we remember moments.
~Cesare Pavese, The Burning Brand

My son played his final high school basketball game last night and for perhaps the first time in I don't know how many hundreds of games over the years, I decided to just sit, watch and enjoy. As I drove to the game I reflected on how many times I'd seen him play over the years and since this was the last time I would see him on the court for his high school team, I was going to focus solely on him.

There was so much that I did not see last night. I did not see the clock running when it shouldn't have been. I had no clue what the score was or that the scorekeeper forgot to put up one of our points. I had no clue the refs missed a foul on the other team nor did I know that they couldn't tell the difference between a block and a charge. I didn't hear the opposing coach berate one of his players for a missed shot. I was oblivious to the parent seated behind me who called to his son every two minutes, encouraging him to "forget the team, do it all on your own!" For the first time I missed all of this. My self-imposed "tunnel vision perspective" allowed me to selfishly focus on my eighteen-year-old son who had been playing basketball since he was old enough to bounce a ball.

What I saw was a confident young man playing a team sport and having the time of his life. His athletic ability was obvious but what was more evident was the decent, respectful, caring person he'd come to be. He was a true leader in every sense of the word. Patient with his teammates, respectful of the officials, attentive to his coaches, and leading by his example of hard work, sportsmanship and positive attitude. His actions off the court were even more exemplary. In the few minutes he spent on the bench, he encouraged his teammates and was fully involved in the game.

At half time, I saw him gather his teammates into a huddle. Every one of them listened intently; there was a huge burst of laughter after which they all took to the court with huge smiles on their faces for the second half. It was all over before I knew it and when I looked at the clock for the first time, the score confirmed that this indeed was his last high school basketball game. I watched him as he shook hands with officials and then went to his coaches and individually thanked them for all their time and hard work over the season.

Perspective is a remarkable thing. I realized there and then that over the years I really should have just watched him play. I shouldn't have cared what level of team he played on. It shouldn't have mattered if he was a starter or not. I should have not paid any attention to the behind-the-scenes ugly politics that can be part of youth sport. For this final game I changed my perspective and finally did what I should have been doing all along—I just watched him play. When I finally did this, I saw in that one game a young man who anyone would be proud to call his or her son and luckily, he was mine.

~Rosemary Smiarowski

42

The Fabric of My Memories

A father is always making his baby into a little woman.
And when she is a woman he turns her back again.
~Enid Bagnold

ith three young girls, laughter, squeals and giggles reverberated off the walls, filling every corner of our home. One of their favorite, and thankfully, less boisterous activities, was playing "hair salon." I would be called for my "appointment" after they'd run out of options on their own flowing braids. Back then I had enough hair to beautify with their plastic barrettes, colorful ribbons and stretchy rubber bands. Sitting patiently, three pairs of small hands worked through my hair, I'd hear a snap, feel a slight tug on my scalp, and then snickering behind me.

"Ohhh, that's looks so beautiful, doesn't it?" More laughter.

"Yes, it is so much prettier than before." Clapping and jumping accompanied the giggles.

When my appointment was finished I was handed a mirror. Of course, I conveyed my approval of their work as they pointed out their own contributions.

Through the years, as their hair grew in length, mine crept in the opposite direction. For the girls, a scrunchie, a cloth-covered hair tie, became the rage. Available in all sizes, colors, and textures, they pushed the rubber band into obscurity. Hair fashion hit the youth market. The girls' ensembles were not complete without a matching scrunchie. It didn't take long for the bathroom drawer to overflow with enough of them to stock the local Claire's boutique.

When my daughters started playing team sports, it became necessary to fashion hair ties in colors to match their uniforms. Under the guise of team bonding, pizza parties served as a means to create coordinated hair decorations. Pinking shears and colored fabric covered the floor. By the end of the evening, shreds of material were everywhere, often accented by pizza sauce or a chocolate milk spill.

By the time my oldest daughter reached nine years of age, she enjoyed watching basketball games on television. As a special treat for her, I acquired two tickets to a Seattle Supersonics basketball game. Our father/daughter outing kicked off with a gourmet meal at McDonald's followed by our arrival at Key Arena shortly before tipoff. During the first half, we enjoyed popcorn (over-salted) and soda (over-sugared and under-carbonated).

My daughter's first NBA game needed a memento, something besides a ticket stub. I suggested we go look for something to take home. She jumped out of her chair and was already skipping up the stairs before I got out of my seat. Out on the concourse we located a souvenir stand and her skipping resumed. Pom-poms, stuffed animals, mini basketballs and T-shirts hung on metal hooks. She was undecided until her gaze focused on a scrunchie emblazoned with the Sonics logo. Her finger shot out as if she'd seen an elephant across the room.

"That. I want that... the scrunchie."

I paid for the ridiculously over-priced hair tie without further consideration. Returning to our seats, we enjoyed our food and drink, cheering a rare Sonics win. My "date" fell asleep on the one-hour drive home, her new Sonics scrunchie taken from her hair and moved to her wrist for safekeeping.

Her collection of scrunchies continued to grow, until the fashion changed. Without warning, slimmer, sleeker athletic style hair bands replaced the scrunchies. Eventually most were sold at garage sales or given away. But not all of them found their way to a new home.

When the time arrived for her to leave for college, I was worried.

Foremost, had I done the right things to prepare her for life away from home? Then next, would she eat enough or get enough sleep? All of the things I could no longer control scared me.

On the morning of her departure, with most of her life and its few belongings loaded into her car, I picked up the final piece to be loaded—her nightstand. Carrying it down the stairs, the top drawer opened a bit. From the back of the drawer slid the Sonics scrunchie purchased nearly a decade ago. I hadn't known she had kept it and I decided to keep the discovery to myself. The day was difficult enough. Any new emotions from me would only dampen her excitement. I maneuvered the nightstand onto the back seat, pulled open the drawer and took one last look at that souvenir scrunchie. Dabbing the tears from my eyes, I closed the car door.

"Looks like you've got everything, at least the important stuff."

"Yeah, I think I've got it," she replied, not knowing how true that was, at least for me.

She pulled out of the driveway, starting the next chapter of her life. Knowing that her Sonics scrunchie was going with her made it a little easier to say goodbye.

~Dean K Miller

43

Off the Beaten Path

The work will wait while you show the child the rainbow but the rainbow
won't wait while you do the work.
~Author Unknown

ere we go again. It's back-to-school time. Two-year-old
Hewson, having played with his sisters all summer, is
broken-hearted to watch them climb the steps of the old
yellow school bus. He insists we watch until the bus is a
speck in the distance. Now what?

I decide a walk through the autumn woods might be just the
medicine for my little broken-hearted boy. We head for the trail at the
back of our property, carrying an empty basket to fill with leaves. We
hold hands and sing Sesame Street songs. Enough leaves have fallen
that we can crunch them under our feet and Hewson forgets his tale
of woe. Toddlers are so easy.

Not far into the woods, he heads off the trail. "No, no, sweetie.
We have to stay on the trail or we'll get lost." He protests for a second,
then allows himself to be led back down the path. I find some pale
yellow leaves and a few orange ones, some yellow-and-brown-spotted
ones and an interesting golden one—but no red.

Hewson grabs any old, brown crunchy foliage. Pine needles,
bark, sticks, moss—it all goes into the basket. Not much farther
down the path, he heads off again. I explain that there may be stick-
ers or poison ivy, neither of which means much to a two-year-old.

I say there might be spiders or snakes, which only makes it more intriguing.

"Come on," I urge. "We'll be at the river soon." He is not swayed.

Now I pride myself in letting my kids color outside the lines—explore and discover, make their own mistakes and test their limits. I've let them get dirty and play in the rain. They've taken baths with their clothes on just 'cause. They've had ice cream for breakfast and breakfast for dinner because rules are made to be broken.

Right now though, I'm enjoying the safety and familiarity of the trail. We could get lost if we leave it. Well, not really. Whichever way we go, we're bound to run into the river on one side or a neighbor's property on the other. What about snakes or spiders? How many times have I told them, "Snakes are more afraid of you than you are of them?" As for spiders, my children have inherited my fascination with arachnids. That excuse won't fly either.

I look at Hewson's gap-toothed grin and ask myself whether I want my children to be happy following the comfortable, familiar path that someone else laid for them rather than forging their own. The answer is obvious. We begin to duck under vines and over fallen trees. I let him lead and he does so without looking back.

Farther into the unknown, I notice trees I've never seen before. A massive red maple stretches up and out of the pine cap. Here are the red leaves we were looking for. A spider's web curtains the trail in front of us still jeweled with the morning's dew. The earth smells so dark and rich you can almost taste it. Birds call little two and three note songs on either side. Squirrels clamber to safety, then stop to watch us pass. The temperature is five degrees cooler and droplets of dew stick to our faces, hair and clothes. Moss decorates the ground and the sides of tree trunks. Here and there a shaft of light slices through. I see flowers I imagine don't even have names yet. It's like we've discovered a hidden world.

Looking ahead, I see Hewson far in front and I thank God for putting this little person in my life to take me off the beaten path, to get me out of the known and into the who-knows. I'm not sure where he will lead me but suddenly I'm excited to be going.

~Mimi Greenwood Knight

Chapter
6

Parenthood

Learning from Each Other

*Always walk through life as if you have
something new to learn and you will.*

~Vernon Howard

De-faced

You're never too old to do goofy stuff.
~From the television show Leave It to Beaver

"We need to talk," I e-mailed.

Two days later my cell phone rang.

"Are you stalking me again?" a perturbed voice questioned.

I paused. "Pardon?" I asked.

"You'd think you'd learn!"

"Because you de-faced me?"

"'De-friended' is the word."

"All I wrote was a simple question: Is it wise to post party pictures on your Facebook page when you are pursuing a professional degree?"

"You wrote more."

"Is it a good idea to tag your brother when he's resembling Charlie Sheen?"

"Since you worry so much about my Facebook albums, I told you, I'd take care of it. You wouldn't be exposed to those sorts of pictures ever again. I'd spare you that."

"So, you de-faced me?"

"De-friended."

"I wasn't passing judgment, just offering a little motherly wisdom."

"Hmm."

"Anyway, I'm glad you re-friended or befriended me again, which brings me to the comments I saw recently on your page. You wrote on your page that you got paid 100 bucks to ride in a sled and eat a pickle?"

"Yes?"

"And I saw a comment from your sorority sis who said she wanted an update 'you know what about' she put. That's kinda cryptic."

"Your point?"

"The sled? A pickle? Is that code?"

"Bahaha!" my daughter chortled.

"What?"

"Mom, I was in a pickle commercial. The man rode me around in a sled through the grocery store for the theme of 'It's in the chilly section... or something.' So random! There was fake snow, a polar bear-man shopping, penguins, and everything. One of the 'stops' was a pickle station where I had to pick from these two jars standing in artificial snow with their labels turned away from me. I had to pick the fresher pickle and then eat the pickle!"

"You hate pickles."

"I know! I thought I might have to do some acting... but I liked it. It was fresh, and it didn't have that nasty pickle smell."

"Like our decades' old jars in the fridge?"

"The two men dressed for the Alaskan sled race drove the sleigh with me in it to the freezer section and gave me a free jar of pickles. Then, one picked up roses for me as he drove by the floral section, although they did end up taking the flowers back, off camera!"

"OH?"

"The cameramen did several videos with different people. It's slated for an Internet commercial. They must have spent hundreds on volunteers. I think they could have gotten us for twenty bucks or maybe free. Ha! I'm not complaining."

"When do you know if yours is chosen?"

"One or two months."

"Neat!"

"And I'll get paid more if mine's the featured one."

"You've been discovered! It's your fifteen minutes of fame!"

"Huh?"

"Andy Warhol said, 'In the future everyone will be famous for fifteen minutes.'"

"Andy who? Huh? What?"

"A generational allusion."

"O-kaaaay! Now you gonna stop stalking me, Sherlock?"

"What's an empty nester to do?" I answered.

"Ah, check up on my brothers? Who knows what they're doing with those animals in Farmville?"

~Erika Hoffman

45

First Flight

The water is your friend... you don't have to fight with water,
just share the same spirit as the water, and it will help you move.
~Alexandr Popov

"D on't!" My panic swelled up within me.

My husband pulled our toddler up from under the water. "She needs to get used to putting her face under water."

Knowing I overreacted, I said in a small voice, "I don't think she likes it."

On the way home after our morning swim my husband sighed. "You know, you need to try to move past it." He gave me a sideways look. "For her."

"I know."

I had fallen into a pool at the age of three. I had floundered under the water, kicking and sputtering. Like a good girl, I had patiently waited underwater for someone to save me. No one had come. There had been many distractions at the pool and no one had noticed a three-year-old struggling under the water.

Miraculously, I had kicked my way to a step and pulled myself out. Hearing my labored gasps and choking coughs, people had come running, patting me on the back and helping me as I vomited in a towel.

To this day, I don't know how I managed to rescue myself. I had never had a swim lesson and my experience in water was minimal.

The event left me with a deep-seated fear. I could barely tolerate even the shower streaming over my face.

After the swim accident, my parents bought me a shallow backyard pool to teach me a few swim skills. There, I learned how to float on my back and do a pathetic doggie paddle. But, I feared deep water intensely. I had stayed clear of pool play dates, water parks and the ocean my whole life. Not an easy task in Southern California.

Then, I had two children. I re-experienced the intense waves of anxiety whenever one of my daughters was in the water. I pictured her as myself, floundering at the bottom of the pool, the water pounding in my ears and seeping into my lungs. I would grip my children in the shallow public pool like a vice, willing myself not to let go.

By the time my daughters reached the ages of three and five, I knew I needed to get them private swim lessons. I knew my fear was rubbing off on them. I found an instructor who specialized in teaching children and who had an indoor salt-water pool.

Her pool wasn't deep. I could stand and hold one daughter while she worked with the other. I mentioned my fear to the teacher and she was sympathetic. "I understand. My brother almost drowned as a child. The trauma can haunt you."

I usually watched from afar, clinging to the steps, as she showed my daughters how to hold their breath and how to move under water. She would calmly explain how to work with water to keep safely afloat. Her words made sense. I began to absorb what she was saying.

"The water is like a blanket that surrounds you and holds you up. You need to lie down in order for that blanket to do its job."

I realized I had always envisioned the water as some sort of monster intent upon doing me harm. I had escaped it once. And it was waiting patiently to get me in the end, like some sort of ominous crocodile.

My heart would swell when I watched my daughters' bravery. After initial protests, they both put their heads underwater to retrieve a toy. Soon, they were swimming underwater across the width of the pool on one breath. I cheered and cheered. Once, I noticed tears in my eyes. I was overwhelmingly relieved to know they would not inherit my fears.

After a few weeks, the teacher asked my older daughter to swim the length of the pool. She had done this before while the teacher stood by, holding the back of her swimsuit. She was awkward as she worked to coordinate her arms and legs. But, like a baby bird taking a flight out of the nest she managed to wiggle her way across. Now, the swim instructor wanted my daughter to try it on her own. My daughter wouldn't budge.

"No, I'm scared." She covered her face with her hands.

We both tried to coax her, but she shook her head back and forth, her wet pigtails slapping her face.

"I'll show you." The teacher dove underwater and swam to us, her muscular legs and arms in perfect unison. She was a dolphin in a swimsuit. How could my daughter mimic her actions?

Suddenly, I had an idea. Maybe another beginner could encourage my daughter.

"Sweetie, watch Mommy try." I shocked even myself as I spoke the words.

I hesitated a moment before I took one full breath and dove in. I vigorously kicked my legs and moved my arms. I was uncoordinated. I was fearful. I didn't know what I was doing. But, I knew the pool wasn't deep and I could always stand up. An overgrown bird, I flapped furiously on this first flight of mine. I almost gave up halfway across as the sound of the water drummed in my ears, sending my heart into palpitations.

But, I remembered the teacher's advice. I had been listening intently, after all. I blew bubbles. I used my head like a compass. I kicked swiftly. I pulled the water away, cupping my hands as I reached out in front of me. And, I lay perfectly flat, allowing the water to hold me.

Just like she said. When I came up for air, sputtering and reaching for the side of the pool in desperation, I received applause.

"Look how brave Mommy is!" The teacher gave me thumbs up and my trembling eased. "Do it again!"

Again?

"I'll do it with my daughter."

At the edge of the pool, my daughter and I were side by side as we pushed off from the step. We kicked hard and moved our arms quickly. Uncoordinated, but brave, we made our way across the pool.

We were a mommy bird and her baby making their first flight together. Maybe it was a bit unconventional. It was certainly awkward. It was absolutely not coordinated.

But, it was brave.

And, I knew it when my daughter kissed my face afterwards.

"We swam like mermaids," she said.

My daughters continued with swim lessons and I became a student as well. We cheered our progress and encouraged each other during fearful moments. I was surprised by how quickly we made progress as we worked together in that pool.

Next summer, my family will be vacationing by the sea where, together, my daughters and I will take our first ocean swim.

~Michele Boom

46

Different Paths

While we try to teach our children all about life,
our children teach us what life is all about.
~Angela Schwindt

"And where is your daughter going to college?" the woman asks my friend Ellen. We are at a fundraising luncheon, networking with the best and the brightest. My friend's face tightens. Her daughter has been struggling through her alcohol addictions in a treatment center and won't be going to college next year.

"She's going to work for a year," Ellen tells the woman.

Ellen and I move deeper into the crowd. "I hate it when that happens," she says. "I feel so embarrassed. I never know what to say."

We find our table. Kate is there, a woman I haven't seen for several years. Her son Mark and my daughter went to high school together. While our kids were easy friends, I always felt inadequate in conversations with Kate.

We greet each other and she instantly tells me what a success her older daughter is. "... Harvard Law School and now works for a big New York firm and has a darling little girl and a husband who's in environmental architecture. What about Jessica?"

My mouth feels dry. How can I tell Kate that my daughter dropped out of college, that she's bounced from job to unemployment to job? How can I explain to someone so put together and achievement-oriented that my daughter struggles with depression and cannot move ahead on a straight path? I have spent hours looking for the words to convey the brilliance and individuality of my daughter, brilliance not proven by any advanced degree or outstanding job success.

"She's still searching," I say.

My mouth is stretched into someone else's smile as I prepare for Kate to assault me with the litany of Mark's successes. But surprisingly, her face loses its starch.

"I am so relieved to hear you say that. Mark, well you know he started out at MIT, but he dropped out after a year and moved to Florida. He works as a janitor and he shows no signs of going back to school. At first, I couldn't believe it. We didn't raise him to be a janitor and well… but anyway, he seems happy so I guess that's all that really matters."

I take a breath and relax. A happy child is all we really want.

"Tell me more about Mark," I say, and Kate's smile returns.

Later that evening, I drop by my daughter's apartment for a quick visit. I am exhausted from the luncheon and from a long meeting. I spent the last hour of the meeting trying not to stare at the glossy photos of my client's children in various poses of glory — graduations, award acceptances, medal winning, weddings. While I was listening to him discuss the project, I was battling envy — these children were easy to talk about in a crowd. These photos proved he was a good and able parent.

Jessica answers the door, dressed in sweats and carrying a book. Her hair is uncombed, which means she probably didn't go to work today. "What are you reading?" I ask.

"Culture and advertising," she says beckoning me into her book-strewn living room. "It's really interesting the impact that both gender and advertising have on us."

She gestures to a stack of books, telling me the salient points of each and the status and professional qualifications of each author. She has read more in the last month than I have in the last year. She has learned as much about the subject as she might have at graduate school. She has done this on days when she was too depressed to face the outside world.

I pick up a couple of books and settle in the blue armchair that was in my living room when Jessica was growing up. She opens one of the books and dissects an ad. She tells me about the subtle but strong messages that impact us every day.

As I listen, I realize I am imprinted with some of those messages. I am wishing my daughter were easy to codify, easy to explain to people, easy for me to understand.

I think of all the stories I've heard, quietly, from parents who felt their children didn't turn out "right." Some of these children suffered with mental or physical health issues, struggled with learning disabilities, were trapped in addictions to drugs, alcohol, or food. Other children weren't able to excel in high school, to go college, get a good job, find a wonderful spouse, and live happily ever after. Still other progeny were rebels, adventurers, preferring to follow their own paths.

Yet as my daughter's face shines with her intellectual discoveries, I realize the gift she is giving me. She is pushing me out of my stereotypical thinking and into brave territory where I celebrate her for who she is. She is stretching me beyond my own narrow pre-conceived notions and inviting me into her world — a world of struggle, a world of hope, a world of creative excitement and possibility.

I put the books back on the chair when I leave. I hug my daughter goodbye. My daughter is making a difference in the world by talking about what she has learned with me. She is making a difference by showing me it's fine to struggle, to not conform, to explore who you are.

My mother has two children. One finished college in four years; the other ran off and got married after her sophomore year, and didn't get a degree until years afterwards. During those unschooled years, I learned enormous amounts about life and myself. During those years, I learned tolerance for those who don't follow the prescribed path. And what I didn't learn then, my daughter is thoughtfully teaching me right now.

~Deborah Shouse

47

The Soldier and His Daughter

The guys who fear becoming fathers don't understand that fathering is not something perfect men do, but something that perfects the man. The end product of child raising is not the child but the parent.

~Frank Pittman, Man Enough

y daughter and I were alone in the hotel pool when I heard the door open. I didn't want company. Clara was learning to swim and I pictured her fledgling courage being washed away by some child's cannonballs.

As the soldier walked through the door, I never saw a body so built for trouble. He was a solid six feet, but his rippling physique and obvious military bearing made him look taller. His limbs hung loose and powerful like a panther's, calm but ready to spring. There was a large, angry scar on his stomach. His right shoulder was adorned with a tattoo of the Marine Corps insignia, while his other arm displayed less-friendly artwork.

Despite his frame, I felt at ease. Why? His eyes were gentle and he held the tiny hand of a jabbering little girl.

The soldier eased into the cold water without a flinch, and then helped his daughter down the steps. She needed help; her legs were tiny and she was encumbered with a pink inner tube. My daughter stopped splashing and looked with obvious envy at the tube.

As soon as the girl's spindly legs were submerged, she began to kick furiously and babble in a language I didn't understand. Her father gently encouraged her to swim to him, which she did with the maximum amount of syllables. When she met his goal, he wrapped her thin frame in his large arms. His skin was healthy but pale, while hers was the color of stained wood.

My daughter, acclimatized to the soldier and his daughter, began once again to launch herself off the steps in a fearless and, to this point, futile attempt at swimming. It was my job to keep her from drowning.

But I was torn. I had been travelling with Clara for a week and a half and had rarely seen a father solo with his daughter. Used to being the chromosomal abnormality in Mom groups, I tended to want to embrace other hands-on fathers.

Eventually, an opportunity presented itself. My daughter, finally tired of swallowing water, headed to the hot tub. She sat on the top step with her feet dangling in the water and waited patiently while I went to talk to the soldier. She was smart enough to know that parents need socialization to stay happy.

"On vacation?" I asked him lamely, thinking of no other opening.

"Kind of," he said as he dutifully threw his daughter across the pool. While she paddled back, he explained that he was on leave from Iraq. He took the time to take a trip to the States with his daughter, who usually lived in Thailand. He was no longer with her mother, so it was just the two of them. "She doesn't speak English, and I don't really speak any Thai, but we do the best we can."

She tapped his leg and he threw her again. I mumbled something inconsequential and shook his hand, then went to join Clara. I wanted to spend the whole day bonding with the soldier about fatherhood, but I knew that it would be too selfish to continue the conversation. His time with his daughter was too short to ask him to share it.

My daughter and I outlasted them. I was still busy catching Clara as the soldier wrapped up his chattering daughter in a towel emed to engulf her. Despite the towel's bulk, she ran to the ... He waved to me as he followed her.

Long after my daughter went to sleep that night, I thought about the soldier and the courage it took for him to be there with his daughter. The early years of childrearing are fraught with rejection for fathers, as Mom is equated with comfort in a baby's mind. During those lean times, many a father turns in his keys to his child's heart, accepting a reduced role as a provider.

I am not so blind in my adoration of fathers to assume that this soldier is a perfect parent, or even is a supportive co-parent. But to persevere in a long-distance relationship with a child who speaks a different language, that's nothing short of heroic. The soldier's story reminds me that it is not whether we always are there for our children, but that we keep trying to be there for our children. Parenting is about stealing moments of grace to love our children in a sometimes broken world.

~Craig Idlebrook

48

My Son Made Me Tweet

What would life be if we had no courage to attempt anything?
~Vincent van Gogh

t's my son's fault I'm on Twitter. Or rather, blame it on @ jamestweeting—his Twitter handle.

My son James is thirty now. He's got a beard and a job. He's independent. Very independent. He has been since he left for college over a decade ago.

His self-sufficiency brings me both joy and worries. I am proud of him for forging his own path and making what he wants out of his life. But I'd like to know what he's doing. And, of course, I sometimes have motherly advice I'd like to share.

I have few opportunities to grill him about his activities or plans, or to provide the guidance I sometimes think he needs. James rarely calls, except on Mother's Day. He doesn't write, beyond an infrequent e-mail. He seldom even posts on Facebook.

But a few years ago he began to tweet.

James explained to me how I could see what he wrote on Twitter, even if I didn't have my own account. For many months, I followed him by lurking. I read his tweets and kept tabs on what he was doing—at least when he published his activities to the world. I learned when he had a business trip, and found out about some of his weekend fun with friends.

Occasionally, I responded to what he tweeted by e-mail, but

not on Twitter. I didn't want to open my own Twitter account. Why would I want everyone to know what I was telling my son?

Apparently, my reluctance to join Twitter became a subject of discussion in my son's workplace and made me an object of amusement among his friends. He told me his colleagues all wanted me to tweet. I have no idea what they thought I would say.

Finally, in June 2011, I relented. I signed up for my own Twitter account. I started with a semi-anonymous handle and I only followed James. I sent out a tweet telling him he had shamed me into it. But after my first tweet, I reverted to lurking.

Not long after I opened my Twitter account, James tweeted that he was ill with a cold and trying to get work done from home. I could hear his misery through the wireless network. Like every mother, I received antennae at childbirth that interpret what my child doesn't say.

As James's mother, I had to reply. I tweeted him: "So sorry you're sick, but glad you are productive. Chicken soup."

I kept my response well under the tweet limit of 140 characters. Turns out a mother can say quite a bit in a tweet. Maybe this Twitter thing was useful after all.

James re-tweeted (forwarded) my chicken soup advice, with the comment: "This is why you want your mom on Twitter."

Guess he thought I was a successful tweeter, too.

Some of my son's friends started following me. I think it was the oddity of a fifty-something woman tweeting to her son. They suggested new handles for me. One of his friends even started a fake James's mother online—@jamesmomtweetin—to provide motherly advice to my son when I was not active enough.

I responded to the fake mom tweets with my own. The real @jamestweeting's mom—me—does a much better job of giving snarky advice than the fake @jamesmomtweetin ever could. After all, I have thirty years of experience to pull from.

I haven't been quite sure of the protocol on Twitter. Should I follow my son's friends? His work colleagues? His girlfriend? Somehow, it feels like stalking to get too involved in his life. It's one thing to follow my son, whom I love and cherish, and who invited me to correspond with him on Twitter even though he left my nest long ago. It's another thing to interject myself into the world he has built for himself, filled with people I have never met. So I'm careful, and only follow his friends who follow me first, and even then with hesitation.

Over time I became a little braver and started to use Twitter for my own purposes. I now have a transparent handle—@MTHupp—labeled with my name. I follow others besides my son—my own friends (yes, some of them are on Twitter), as well as other writers, publishers, news sites, and people knowledgeable about my profession.

In my writing group, I've become the expert on Twitter. I provide most of the Twitter feed for Write Brain Trust, a group of writers working together on digital publishing and marketing. Little did I know that my attempts to stay in contact with my adult son would turn me into a social media guru.

Yet the real benefit of Twitter has not been humorous exchanges with people I don't know, nor the knowledge I've gained in using a new social media tool. It has been the window into my son's world. When he tweets, I get an inkling of what he is doing and feeling. I have an opportunity to communicate in real time with my son, if only in 140-character increments.

His friends may chuckle at my responses, but I will put up with a lot of ridicule to know how my adult child is doing. As a mother, I do whatever I can to communicate with my son. Somehow, I have to be sure my voice is heard in the turmoil of his life.

Right, @jamestweeting?

~Theresa Hupp

"You kidding? I have *tons* of friends — Max10AT, Badgirl4D9, Metalhed66, 007 Cowboy ..."

Baggage Control

Love is what's in the room with you at Christmas
if you stop opening presents and listen.
~Author Unknown, attributed to a 7-year-old named Bobby

I t had been a long Christmas day at the in-laws and I knew my nine-year-old son's patience was wearing thin. We had done everything except the one thing Joshua had wanted to do—open presents. I was preparing for a tantrum intervention when my mother-in-law said the magic words: "Let's open presents!"

Thank goodness, I thought. And then she said, "We got you all the same thing!"

Now I had to pause and wonder—why would she get us all Power Rangers? No way was my daughter going to like a Power Ranger. I mean, what other present could she possibly get that my nine-year-old son would want?

"Here they are!" She excitedly wheeled into the living room four carry-on sized suitcases in four different colors. Just as she said, there was one for each of us. Panic rose in my gut and now I really prepared to do an intervention, expecting my son to have a meltdown at the sight of his long awaited present—which turned out to be a suitcase. He spoke before I could get my hand over his mouth.

"Wow! That is so cool!" he shouted. He quickly picked the navy blue suitcase for himself and began opening up the different compartments—the removable net bag for your delicates, the luggage lock and key, the retractable handle—it all fascinated him. I let out a sigh of relief. Disaster averted. Clearly I had a quirky young son who liked a nice piece of luggage, but if he was happy, I was happy.

All was well until he went back to school after Christmas vacation. The teacher told all the kids that they could bring in their favorite present from Christmas for show and tell.

"What are you going to take, Josh, your White Tigerzord?" I asked.

"Nope," he said, with confidence and determination.

"Are you going to take one of your video games?" I checked his expression in the rear view mirror as he sat in the back seat—it was nothing less than smug.

"Nope. I am going to take my suitcase. And, Mom, can we put it in a big bag so no one can see until I take it out of the bag?" Again, I checked his expression to see if he was serious. He was. I could feel the blood drain from my face. Visions of my son standing in front of the class, building the suspense with his suitcase hidden away in the darkness of a trash bag, preparing the big reveal while kids sat on the edge of their seats expecting… a puppy, a remote control car, a snake… anything more exciting than a suitcase! I began to imagine the years of therapy it would take to correct the emotional damage caused by the trauma he was sure to experience if he took his suitcase in for show and tell.

"Really, Josh? Your suitcase? Are you sure you don't want to take your super cool, totally awesome Tigerzord? I bet the kids would think that was really rad!" I tried to throw in every kid adjective I could think of, but to no avail.

"Nope. I am going to take my suitcase. It is so cool! They are going to be so surprised!" Oh, my sweet child, you don't know how much they are going to be surprised, I thought.

The big day came and I had given up hope of changing Joshua's mind, so I found a big trash bag, put in the suitcase, and closed it carefully with a twist tie. I dropped my precious son with his surprise cargo on the school curb and I could hear the kids as I pulled away, "What's inside, Josh?" "Wow! That's a big bag—what did you get for Christmas?" My son beamed with his secret safely nestled inside the bag. I reluctantly drove away and spent the day doing what any mother would do—I prayed!

The day passed without a call from the school, which I took to be a good sign. I pulled up to the curb to pick him up and he stood looking no worse than when I left him. In fact, he seemed to be in good spirits with no visible signs of emotional damage. But still, I decided it was best to proceed with caution.

"How did your day go?" I asked, spying in the rearview mirror again.

"Great!"

"The whole day?" Of course I wanted to come out and ask him about show and tell, but if it had gone badly, as I suspected it had, I didn't want to open a tender wound.

"Yup! Great!" Well now I had no choice but to ask point blank.

"Even show and tell?"

"It was awesome, Mom! My friends were so surprised!"

"Really...?"

"Yup! They thought my suitcase was so cool!"

"What did they like?"

"Everything! They thought the handle was really neat and Eric really liked the lock and key."

I was dumbfounded. Who knew? And I was also relieved. I really didn't have a lot of extra money for therapy.

"Hey, Mom, I have a question," my son continued.

"Yes, Josh?"

"Do you know where Nana got that suitcase? Eric really wants his mom to get him one."

I learned something that year about parenting and control, about letting go and realizing that you can't put bumper guards around every area of your kids' lives. My fearful thinking had convinced me that my son was heading for some emotional pain—but I didn't know that for certain. I did everything I could to control the situation and prevent him from being hurt. It's what we are supposed to do as parents; but sometimes our overprotective tendencies might actually keep our children from experiencing some pretty cool stuff—like being the big man on campus with the rad suitcase. I'm glad my son was determined to take his favorite Christmas present to school that year for show and tell. I'm also glad that second graders think luggage is cool.

~Lynne Leite

Frozen Moment

*You've developed the strength of a draft horse while holding onto the delicacy
of a daffodil... you are the mother, advocate and protector of a child
with a disability.*

~Lori Borgman

I watched the woman's retreating back as she grabbed her young
daughter's hand and practically ran down the frozen food aisle
of my local Wegmans supermarket. I looked down at my son
Joe. "Geez, was it something we said?" He glanced in my general direction and gave me that smile. The smile that somehow con-
veys sweetness, wisdom, and the smart aleck side to his personality
all at once. It breaks and melts my heart every time I see it.

Joe was born sixteen years ago, a surviving identical twin,
severely brain damaged and challenged from the start. Through the
years he failed to accomplish any of the milestones most children do.
That day in the grocery store, he was shopping with me as he has on
many occasions, loving the activity and challenge of maneuvering
through a crowded grocery aisle.

I was pushing Joe's wheelchair through the aisles with one hand
and pulling the cart behind me with the other. It sounds a lot harder
than it really is. Other shoppers were giving me the usual looks, ranging from the averting of eyes to smiles of pity and/or compassion. I
smiled at those whose eye I happened to catch, and politely turned
down an occasional offer of help from a Wegmans employee.

As I continued to chat with Joe, asking him questions about what to buy, not expecting him to answer with words, but secretly hoping I would get a response, even a "Gosh, can you just shut up, Mom?" Parents of nonverbal children will take what they can get. I was happy with his crooked smile and a brief glance from those beautiful brown eyes. The occasional giggle at something I said was always a plus.

I've learned to live in the present with Joe, and not focus 24/7 on his future or what he can or cannot do. Joe has always been gifted with a pretty easygoing personality, and his laugh is positively infectious. People laugh a lot around Joe.

There we were, laughing our way through the pasta aisle, which we always seem to spend extra time in since Joe is half Italian and pasta is his favorite food. I am not Italian but I'm pretty sure that returning from the grocery store without at least one product of Italian descent is somehow a sin. As I explained this to my shopping companion, he seemed to agree since he giggled, and so did the dark-haired gentleman with a box of rigatoni in his hand.

From the pasta aisle we made our way to the frozen food aisle. As I stood in front of the Eggo section, a little girl wandered up and stood next to Joe's wheelchair.

"Why is he sitting in that?" She pointed to his wheelchair. I looked down at the little girl, and then looked up to see if there was an adult nearby. The only other customer in the aisle was a frazzled-looking woman pushing a full cart and talking to her imaginary friend. She was gesticulating wildly as she insisted her imaginary friend do something about the mold on her back deck. As she turned to drop something into her cart, I saw the Bluetooth earpiece. So I was wrong about the imaginary friend. She caught sight of the little girl standing next to Joe and me, and pushed the heavy cart towards us.

"You have to stay near Mommy. You can't wander off, Taylor."

"Mommy, why is that little boy in that?" She again pointed at the wheelchair.

"He's... sick." She gave me a strained smile, averted her eyes and went to grab Taylor's hand.

The little girl avoided her mom's hand, and looked up at me. "Does he have a boo boo?"

I smiled down at the little girl. "Joe is not sick, but he does have a boo boo in his brain."

The little girl looked thoughtfully at Joe and coughed. Joe jumped, as he sometimes does at loud noises. Sometimes they don't even have to be loud, he will startle anyway. Being naturally curious, the girl asked why he did that.

As parents, we have to seize certain situations and use them as "teaching moments." I have tried to use them over the years with my children, and many times I have experienced my own teaching moments at the hands of my children. My hope is that other parents who have met Joe have used that opportunity to explain his challenges in a positive light. Even just encouraging your child to smile and acknowledge a challenged child or to realize that they are more like any child, regardless of their abilities, than not. Sometimes that simple bit of information is all that is needed, depending on the age of the child asking. What Taylor would have learned that day is that having a disability doesn't mean you are ill, natural curiosity is not a bad thing, and children in wheelchairs are not to be feared.

That day the little girl seemed to learn the complete opposite as her mother took her daughter's hand and pulled her through the aisle with one hand and pushed the heavy cart with her other hand. It is none of my business what parents teach their children but I am an optimist, and would like to believe that the mother later sat down and gave her daughter a better explanation for a child's disability other than that they are "sick." I also hope she resolved her mold problem.

What the mom did not see, as she was dragging her daughter past the frozen pizzas, was the little girl turning around to give Joe and me a little wave and a sweet smile as she disappeared around the corner. Had she taken a moment out of her busy day, that mother could have found herself smack dab in the middle of her own teaching moment, courtesy of her daughter.

~Laura Guman Fabiani

Reel Joy

Honesty is the first chapter of the book of wisdom.
~Thomas Jefferson

ur children Emma and Tucker learned early in life about the joy of fishing, whether from their grandpa's boat, casting from the shore, or snapper fishing off the jetty at the beach near our summer home. It focused them on the moment, with no video games, no TV, no distractions.

Whether we caught something or not, it was the quest that counted and the fun we had together enjoying nature. They learned how to bait the hook, cast, and "present the bait." They learned how to snag the fish and bring it in. They also learned how to clean and filet their catch and prepare it for dinner. They learned the patience and persistence that it takes to be successful.

And of course there was always a little bit of competition and sibling rivalry that added to the fun as long as it was by the rules.

Each year, toward the end of July, our beach association held its annual "Snapper Fishing Contest" (small bluefish that have not yet come of age for the deeper water) at the marina inlet. It always drew quite a crowd. All of the kids were full of energy and anticipation. The parents were a bit anxious and wondered where the hook would actually end up when the cast was made.

To start the competition all the kids would line up along the inlet and when the "First Mate" would sound the horn, everyone would cast their lines into the water in hopes of coming away with the biggest fish of the day. It was like something out of a Norman Rockwell painting.

It was a mixture of talent, from the "experienced" anglers just crushing the cast, to some of the more inexperienced kids who spent most of the time tangled in yards of monofilament. There was an occasional scream of pain, as the hook would get caught on a finger or other body part, or even a parent. You could also tell which parents grew up with a rod and reel and which ones had just purchased the starter set.

Help and guidance was always within easy reach. Although it was considered a "contest," most parents understood that it was a fun way to introduce everyone to the sport of fishing. The more experienced parents would help anyone who needed it. Overall it was a great day of fun, with no distractions from the outside world.

Determination was written all over those little faces. As one of the kids would catch a fish you would hear a screech of excitement: "I GOT ONE!" There were squirming, slippery, smelly fish flying everywhere, wiggling, trying to get back into the water. The kids giggled and wrestled their prizes into the bucket.

When they caught what they thought was their biggest fish, they would take their prized catch to the judging table under the pavilion on the beach. There, the "First Mate" would carefully place the catch on the scale. Then the kids would release their fish back into the Sound from the jetty.

One year, however, when our daughter presented her fish to be weighed, the judge reached over and sliced open the fish, removed its entrails, and then weighed it.

My wife Jeanne and I were shocked. "Joe," I asked. "What happened to catch and release? Why do you have to clean each of the fish?"

Joe looked up with a rather apologetic look on his face, and whispered, "We found that last year some of the fathers were dropping fishing weights down the throats of the fish before the kids brought them over for the weigh-in. So their fish would be heavier."

We were dumbfounded. A simple, fun competition between

five- and six-year-olds became a crass example of how adults had lost touch with right and wrong. Their lust for winning had tarnished something that was a pure, fundamental joy.

It was Emma and Tucker's excitement that snapped us out of the harsh moment. We all gave Emma a big hug and congratulated her as Joe announced, "We have a new record to beat." Emma was at the top of the leader board and she was excited.

As we walked away from the weigh-in table we took notice of the father and son behind us. The father was anxiously pushing his boy up to the table. When his fish was weighed it came in four ounces lighter than Emma's.

The father became irate and insisted that it be weighed again. When it came up the same, he grabbed his son and pulled him back to the inlet. The father handed him his pole and said, "Are you going to let a girl beat you? Get your line in the water. Catch a bigger one."

Jeanne and I gave both kids a big hug. Together we had a good laugh and figured he was probably one of the fathers who had stuffed weights into the fish the prior year.

Emma just shrugged. Exhibiting understanding beyond her years she grabbed her little brother and together they headed off to fish some more. For them it was just fun.

The kids are grown now but fishing continues to teach us all valuable lessons. Watching my kids experience its joys has become the prize catch for me.

Some folks take a little longer to really understand what fishing is all about. All we can do is hope that they will soon realize the joy that's found in its simplicity.

Cast the line. Have faith. And enjoy the reward of what you reel in. It continues to be a thrill in our lives.

~Jack Blandford

Putting Down Roots

It takes hands to build a house, but only hearts can build a home.
~Author Unknown

It's not easy to be a stay-at-home mom. It's even more difficult to be a stay-at-home military mom. I know, because I've been both. From military bases to apartments to mobile home communities, the one thing we could always count on was moving. Goodbye to old friends, hello to new ones. So long to the old school and on to the new. From climate to climate and town to town, I found myself wondering if my children would ever be able to put down roots.

It's true that I would be there for them, but money was always short, and sometimes my husband's pay record would be lost for months. Pinching pennies became an art form. Have you ever gone grocery shopping with a bag full of small change? Well, I have. From dusk to dawn, I made my children's clothing, often redesigning hand-me-downs. I became their nutritionist and gourmet chef. I was once asked what made me so creative. My answer was both brief and honest: desperation. It was hard, but it was also a joyful experience that was both rich and rewarding.

My children adjusted with courage and humor. Their strength amazed me. But with no extended family, I often wondered if they would ever feel that they had roots. Oh, how I had wanted those roots when I was a child. Would my children be harmed in the long run by moving from place to place? What could I do? Then one day, when they were very small, I had a revelation.

Jenny was about five years old and Helen was little more than a baby. That was when I began the gardens. Tiny things, at first. Just a child's garden, filled with baby carrots, herbs, and annual flowers. To hear Jenny and Helen tell about it nearly thirty years later, one would think we had owned a farm. Adults now, they often talk about what it felt like to fill little baskets with their own growing things.

From tiny vegetables and flowers we moved on to flowering shrubs and garden design. I made it up as I went along. To tell you the truth, I hadn't a clue. Finally, in Charleston, South Carolina, we planted the apple tree. I think that we harvested one apple and split it four ways. South Carolina is not exactly the perfect apple state. But that was never the point.

We lived in Charleston for nearly eight years and our garden grew larger each year. With each new plant, I learned more, and my girls and I would discuss just what those fibrous roots signified. What about the roots that we planted, only to leave them behind for someone else? Not long ago, we did a search on Google Earth, and we found the duplex that had contained the laughter and dreams that we shared for eight years in Charleston Navy housing. We scanned closer and closer—down, down, and down—and there it was, our little apple tree, alive and well.

Bittersweet tears spilled down my cheeks as I remembered the day we planted that tree. It had survived hurricanes, drought, and much sorrow, and so had we. At that moment, I finally understood. The apple tree's roots, growing deep in South Carolina soil, were much like our family. Deep in the soil of shared joys and sorrows, our roots are strong in one another, in faith and in love.

~Jaye Lewis

53

Getting the Sad Out

A single conversation with a wise man is better than ten years of study.
~Chinese Proverb

rowing up in the seventies and eighties—during the era of everyone "finding themselves" and "looking out for #1," there was no shortage of children living in homes shaken by divorce. I was no different, my parents having split when I was seven, my mom remarrying shortly after to a wonderful man who raised me as his own, and as I grew older also having a loving relationship with my real dad. What I had little to no experience with was friends who had lost a parent at a young age, families that were struggling to overcome the loss of a partner, hero, caregiver who had been taken far too soon from a family that loved them. I certainly never expected to be one of them.

My whole world changed when I became a widow at thirty-four years old, with a two-and-a-half-year-old son, living a fairytale life in Southern California with a man I was truly, madly, deeply in love with. Jackson was so young when it happened, too young to realize what he had lost—a realization which I was to discover later would hit him over and over again as he grew up and entered new phases of "manhood."

Initially, I could distract him with toys, treats, pets and generally anything that a little boy would find engaging. I think I did it more for myself than for him, wanting to shield my son and myself from the pain I knew he would inevitably feel. I would do anything to keep him from being sad, and cried my own tears in hiding never wanting him to see how much I missed his father and how sad I was for him not to know him.

This worked really well until he was about seven, when all his friends' dads were playing football with them, coaching baseball and soccer, and teaching them to do what Jackson called "boy stuff." I still tried my hardest to distract him and change his focus when he was sad and breathed a sigh of relief every time I succeeded.

One day, my extremely wise seven-year-old caught me off guard with a question I never expected. He asked me why I never let him cry over his dad and why I never let him see me be sad. I answered that it was because I didn't want him to be hurt or sad. He then put his arms around me and told me that he loved me more than anything in the world, but he still was sad that he didn't have his dad, and even when I made him think about something else "he was still sad on the inside." I thought about this long and hard. I wondered who I was really protecting, my son from feeling pain, or me having to witness my child dealing with a pain and loss I could never fix. As a parent we all know that there is nothing worse than seeing our child suffer and not being able to make it right.

That Christmas, Jackson and I went to Fiji with one of my three best friends and her family. We had the most extraordinary vacation ever, Jackson played full out, experiencing all that the island had to offer. One night, half way through our trip, we went back to our beachfront bure to go to sleep and Jackson started crying, saying that he wanted his daddy. For the first time ever, I didn't say "it's okay, everything will be okay," or "don't worry honey, you have me" or try to distract him with promises of fun-filled days. I just let him cry. He cried his little heart out, sobbing, wailing, calling for his dad over and over again. This went on for two hours, two of the longest hours of my life. I cried with him. Instead of telling him it would get better, I just said, "I know honey, I miss him too, so much." We held each other and cried until we were cried out. Finally, he fell asleep in my arms.

The next morning, he woke up so calm, so at peace, so happy.

He gave me a huge hug and told me that it felt really good to get all that "sad" out of him. I had to admit it felt good to me too.

I learned that as much as we try to shield our children from pain, sometimes life has another plan. Parenting is not only protecting our children from sadness and loss, but it's also showing them how to handle it, letting it be alright to go through your own process, to grieve, to cry—to experience all the emotions that comprise the human experience. I wanted Jackson to learn to be resilient, but I learned that resiliency isn't born from denial, it is born from honesty and love and the ability to go through the pain and come out the other side.

Jackson is one of the happiest, most resourceful, resilient and soulful people I have ever met—I would love to take credit for that, but I can't. Instead, I need to give him credit for making me a better parent by showing me that we could endure anything by handling it together. That day brought us even closer, it made him trust me even more, because he saw the real me, and my authenticity gave him the freedom to be real and honest with me. Now, at thirteen, he truly feels he can talk to me about anything, and knows that I will accept and love him no matter what. My most important parenting lesson came from my child—learning from our children is perhaps the greatest lesson of all.

~Joelle Jarvis

Chapter
7

Parenthood

Treasured Moments

The best thing to hold onto in life is each other.

~Audrey Hepburn

54

First Date

Love is foolish... but I still might try it sometime.
~Floyd, age 9

ecently I went on a first date, something I hadn't done in over twenty years. My husband Mike knew all about it. In fact, he went along, and so did our fourteen-year-old son Taylor. It was actually Taylor's very first date. Several months earlier Mike and I found out from one of Taylor's more talkative friends, Matthew, that a girl was pursuing Taylor. When I questioned him about having a girlfriend, Taylor looked first alarmed, then embarrassed, and finally said, "Oh, no, we're just friends."

Despite Mike's warnings to let the topic drop, I persisted. "Are you sure?"

"Oh, yes," Taylor continued, "Megan says we're just friends."

"Sucker!" Mike grinned before I could stare him out of the room.

Some time later I was serving freshly baked chocolate chip cookies to Taylor and Matthew, thinking that the subject of the upcoming eighth grade dance might just happen to come up. Now I had been asking Taylor for weeks if he was planning to ask Megan. Each time he told me no. He was planning to go with a bunch of his buddies. I had a feeling, however, that Matthew just might have different information.

I knew if I poured enough lemonade, eventually Taylor would

have to go to the bathroom. Four and a half glasses later, he reluctantly left the kitchen.

"So, Matthew, are you going to the dance?" I asked ever so casually.

"Yep."

"Are you taking a girl?"

"No, just gonna hang with Chris and the guys."

"And Taylor?"

"Naw. Taylor's taking Megan. His girlfriend. You know that, Mrs. Stephenson."

Okay, so I had my information. What was I going to do with it? Confess to Taylor that I had been bribing his friend with chocolate chip cookies?

Mike insisted we keep this new information to ourselves and wait for Taylor to tell us himself. The dance was in two weeks. I would wait a week for Taylor to come to us. I waited two hours before going to him.

"Taylor, I hear you asked Megan to the dance."

"Did Matthew tell you?"

"Why didn't you tell me?"

"Because you would want to talk about it."

"Of course I want to talk about it! This is a big deal."

"No it isn't. Unless you make it a big deal. Please don't make it a big deal, Mom."

"Okay, I promise. Here's money to buy the tickets tomorrow," I said handing Taylor two five-dollar bills.

"Thanks," he said, returning one of the bills. "Tickets are only five dollars."

"Sweetie, you have to pay for Megan's."

"She bought her ticket the other day."

"What? You're supposed to buy her ticket."

"It doesn't matter, Mom. Relax."

I attempted to take a deep breath. This wasn't going very well. And yet, I, of course, continued. "What time did you tell Megan we'd pick her up?"

"We're not. I told her I'd meet her there."

"YOU CAN'T MEET HER THERE! YOU ASKED HER TO THE DANCE!" Yes, I was practically yelling by this point.

"Mom, are you starting to see why I didn't mention it?" Taylor asked, much calmer than his near-hysterical mother.

"You tell her we will pick her up at 6:45, or I WILL CALL HER MOTHER."

"DO NOT CALL HER MOTHER!" Apparently I had Mister Calm's attention. "I will talk to Megan. Tomorrow. At school."

Let me tell you, I did not want to call that mother and tell her I had birthed and raised the boy who had invited her daughter to a dance, made her buy her own ticket, and told her he'd meet her there. But I didn't promise not to get her mother's e-mail from the school directory and e-mail my profoundest apologies.

The evening of the eighth grade dance arrived. In his new suit Taylor looked somehow both adorably cute and astonishingly grown up all at the same time. To my surprise, Taylor said he wanted both Mike and me to journey to Megan's house and then the school. Apparently it would be "too weird" for one of them to sit in the front with a parent and the other to sit alone in the back seat. Whatever the reason, it did come with a caveat: I was NOT under any circumstances to take my camera. Apparently, no one's mother takes pictures.

Naturally Taylor had neglected to ask Megan for directions to her house. I, however, had referred again to the school directory, so we were covered.

At exactly 6:44 we pulled into the drive. I peeked over my shoulder at Taylor. His face was as white as his shirt, and he made no move to open the car door.

"Son, aren't you going to get out of the car?" Mike asked gently.

"I'm not getting out unless both of you come too," was Taylor's surprising reply.

So, the three of us climbed the eleven steps to Megan's house and waited for someone to answer our ring.

When the door opened, there stood another threesome: Megan

and both of her parents. Peeking around the corner was a little sister.

"Come on in," Megan's mother invited. After introductions and small talk—neither Megan nor Taylor uttered a word—Megan's mom whipped out her camera and took several pictures of the silent couple. "Didn't you bring a camera?" she asked me.

In the days and weeks following the dance, I would frequently ask Taylor about Megan and was always told she was "fine." Once I wondered aloud if Megan and Taylor might run into each other during the summer. "Who cares?" was the response. "We broke up a long time ago."

"Taylor, promise me something. The next time you have a girlfriend tell me yourself so I won't have to find out from your friends."

"You won't have to find out from anyone. I'm never having another girlfriend."

"Smart man," was Mike's helpful reply.

Stay tuned. We're headed to high school.

~Julie Stephenson

55

Ten Precious Minutes

Kids spell love T-I-M-E.
~John Crudele

As a courtesy I grab my daughter Marissa's backpack and load it into the car before our ten-minute ride to school. The last time I checked she only had books and folders in the backpack. As I lift the backpack it feels as if it has been loaded with bricks. I feel for my daughter.

Then I do a double take as I notice that my little girl has grown into a young lady. She has much more style than I ever had or ever will have. Her hairstyles have become more sophisticated. She walks gracefully but with a purpose and asks if we have everything we need for the day. I tell her that her glasses, backpack and water bottle are all loaded in the car.

I open the garage door, fire up the engine of my Toyota Camry and back out of the driveway. Another day is beginning for both of us. It is about a ten-minute drive to school if there is not too much traffic. My daughter takes only a second to reach for the knob of the car radio. She changes channels quickly trying to find a song to her liking.

Soon Katy Perry and Snoop Dogg are telling me why California Girls are so wonderful. She loves the song and I secretly do too. I talk about the Beach Boys and how they sang about those California Girls too. I always tell her about the "old school" days when the music was the best. She doesn't care and someday down the road her kids won't care about her music either. Actually, they might care but they won't admit it openly.

The good thing is that we are talking. Music is a common bond between us. I love the fact that my daughter has inherited my love of music. Sometimes, she will fall in love with a song I like or a group I think is great and vice versa. This broadens each of our musical horizons and I must admit it also keeps me young, or at least young at heart.

The music also becomes a perfect conversation opener that often leads us into other discussions. How my daughter's friends are doing, what's going on during the day, how her classes are this week, etc. Because she is a teenager the answers are usually quick. Still we are conversing and I have gotten a brief summary of the upcoming day in her life. Out of the blue the DJ tells a funny story and we both relate to it and laugh. We hear some shocking celebrity gossip and we each gasp and look at each other.

When your child becomes a junior in high school the moments when you can bond become fewer and farther between. You learn to truly appreciate each moment you get. You also feel guilt for the times you have missed. Earlier in my daughter's life it was vital for me to get to work earlier and put in a long day. Thankfully, my wife, who has always been the ultimate mother, drove my daughter to school day after day without complaint. I am deeply appreciative.

From preschool until high school I missed out on a gift, the gift of time with my daughter. Knowing that I missed that gift has led to guilt and in some cases sadness as I understand that even ten minutes a day can have a positive impact on both her life and mine.

It is actually pretty easy to find those extra ten minutes a day to spend with your child. When I first began the task of taking my daughter to school, I grumbled and looked at it as something that I didn't want to do. It was similar to starting a new exercise program. I had to motivate myself to do it. I didn't think I could give up ten minutes a day. In the end, those ten minutes a day have become precious. Like ten minutes of exercise, they have helped my physical and mental well-being.

My daughter grabs her backpack as we arrive at the drop-off area of her school.

She lugs the pack onto her back and taps me lovingly on the knee and I tap her arm. It's a simple ritual we have. We tell each other to have a good day as Lady Gaga sings "Poker Face" in the background. I watch the young lady that I am so proud of walk into school. I pull away and quickly switch the music to a U2 song. Bono is reminding me that it's a "Beautiful Day." Thanks to those ten minutes I get to share with my daughter each morning, every day is a little more beautiful to me.

~David R. Warren

56

Midnight Madness

Mothers are all slightly insane.
~J.D. Salinger

This year I did something I once swore I'd never do—shopping at midnight on Black Friday. I know, I'm crazy. That's what I said to the gazillions of other people who were clogging up the roads when they should have been sleeping off their turkey dinner. "Why aren't these people home in bed!" I shouted, as we sat in the left-turn lane through yet another red light. After all, this is the twenty-first century. You can get great deals online from the comfort of your own bed while sipping a hot cup of coffee. So why would I endure three things I despise—traffic, cold weather, and crowds—for a few bargains?

Teenagers.

Before you shudder and mentally add teenagers to the list of things you despise, let me say that I have two of them, and despite all that entails, I still love them with my whole heart. Even though, for them, spending time with Mom is usually down on their list next to homework and picking up the dog poop. I am no longer the one with whom they want to share a secret, play a game, or just hang out. It's a fact of life, and I get it. The natural progression of things. But that doesn't make it any easier on parents who are not ready for this sudden shifting of their universe. I miss my kids.

So, when they asked me to take them shopping at the outlet mall at midnight on Black Friday, my first reaction was definitely no! First of all, I am rarely awake past 11:00 p.m. anymore. Add the fact that we're talking about midnight after Thanksgiving, when the tryptophan of the turkey meal usually kicks in at around 5 p.m. Not to mention that the outlet mall consists of designer stores where a T-shirt costs $50. I mean, it's a T-shirt! How much designing really goes into that? A T-shirt should be $10 or less, period. But my son, who usually runs the other way if I mention shopping, wanted me to take him shopping.

I felt needed. Okay, I'm not so naïve that I didn't know it was my wallet and a ride, not quality time with Mom that they wanted. But still...

There was the hour car ride. We belted out songs on the radio, laughing at who got the words wrong and who was off key. We talked about the deals we hoped to score and what my son wanted to get for his girlfriend. I still can't believe my baby boy has a girlfriend! Now that I think about it, the timing of this union coincides precisely with his desire for $50 T-shirts.

We took turns yelling at the idiots who cut us off or pulled some stupid traffic tricks. I had ample opportunities to give them lessons on what not to do when driving. The kids bickered back and forth as usual, and I had to keep the peace. That's what moms do.

And we all bonded as we sat in bumper-to-bumper traffic with crazed smiles at midnight.

The kids scanned for a spot once we finally made it into the overflowing parking lot, and we rejoiced at our luck when I randomly turned down one lane just as someone was pulling out. High-fives all around. And there's something about standing in a line that snakes around the building in the freezing cold that brings people together.

Once inside, we had to work as a team, one going this way, one the other, hoping to come together with just the right size and color. Searching for a particular shirt for my husband was proving to be a losing battle as I dug through mound after mound of disheveled clothing. Giving up in defeat, I turned to see my daughter coming toward me, shirt in hand and victory on her face. "I got the last one!"

So we emerged at 3 a.m. with some bargains. Nothing earth

shattering, nothing we couldn't have found online or in stores at a reasonable hour. But for me, I got so much more. Quality time with my kids. The definition has changed since they were little, but I'll take it where I can get it.

Driving home bleary eyed and running on nothing but adrenaline, I said, "Next year, no shopping before 7 a.m." But then I looked in the rearview mirror at my children's sweet faces, both dozing in the car like they did when they were little.

The truth is… if they ask me to go again next year, I'm in.

~Lori Slaton

Got the T-shirt

The first river you paddle runs through the rest of your life.
It bubbles up in pools and eddies to remind you who you are.
~Lynn Noel

ith different definitions of the word "safe," my husband and I often disagree on extracurricular activities for our children. I believe parents should protect their offspring, so my idea of adventure is trying a new restaurant. He believes parents should let children experience death-defying feats, building their self-esteem. Unfortunately, Michael's ability to persuade the children into partaking in thrill-seeking escapades leaves me outnumbered when the family takes a vote.

"Whitewater rafting? Awesome. Count me in," our fifteen-year-old son Holden says, responding to Michael's suggestion for our afternoon entertainment while vacationing in the Smoky Mountains.

"Me, too," our daughter Piper says, avoiding being overshadowed by her older brother.

I attempt to appeal to her preteen femininity in order to stop the hazardous outing from materializing. "Piper, your hair will get wet."

"So."

"I mean… like… soaked." She shrugs. "With nasty river water," I add.

"No big deal. I'll just shower when we get back to the cabin."

My husband unfolds the brochure with pictures of smiling families paddling through perilous rapids. The kids clamor for a peek. He asks, "Do we want the excitement of level three and four rapids, or the wimpy level two?"

"What about a level five?" Holden asks.

Michael chuckles. "If you fall out of the raft on class five waters, you die."

Concern flashes across Piper's face. "So what happens on level-four rapids?"

"You can suffer serious injury, but most likely you'd survive," Michael assures her.

"Well, that's certainly a bonus." I point to the brochure. "Look, Piper, you wear a helmet, so you don't smash your head open on the boulders like an overripe cantaloupe. And you have to use a stinky, everyone-has-worn-it-but-it's-never-been-washed, life vest so you don't drown."

"Nice, Mom. Scare the children, why don't you?" Holden says.

My eyes narrow. "That's my plan."

Then Michael pulls the ultimate move. "Just think of the bragging rights."

"You have to stay alive in order to brag," I remind them as we pack for a day on the Pigeon River.

Standing in the gift shop, Michael pays for our impending demise while I thumb through the T-shirts. The thought of advertising my sense of adventure via such a shirt has me excited, until Michael walks up behind me, holding a shirt that announces that the red vest doesn't save one's life, but merely makes the body easier to locate.

The kids laugh and Holden says, "I want one of those."

A video of the churning, level-four rapids playing on a nearby monitor increases my anxiety. I spy a bench in the corner of the shop. "Why don't I just stay here and wait for you guys to come back." I grab a T-shirt and turn toward the sales counter. "I'll pay for this and wait over there."

Michael grabs the shirt and returns it to the rack. "No rafting, no T-shirt."

Before we board the bus, I double and triple check the straps and latches on the kids' helmets and life vests, tightening them as much as I can.

"Mom," Piper says, "I can't breathe."

"Good," I say.

A guide hands us paddles as we climb aboard. I fight the urge to sideswipe Michael's head for spearheading the dangerous trip. We veer down the serpentine road toward the riverbank, and the guide instructs us to bang our paddles on the roof of the bus to show our excitement.

Piper nudges the motionless paddle within my white-knuckled grip. "C'mon, Mom. This will be fun."

"Yeah," Holden says in between strikes to the roof, "it'll be great."

After the banging stops, the guide warns us of the dangers ahead: capsizing in rough waters, flying out of the craft when hitting unforeseen rocks, slamming our heads on said rocks, becoming entangled in river debris and drowning, striking ourselves, or those in close proximity, in the face with our wayward paddles and breaking noses or losing multiple teeth.

"You'll end up with summer teeth," the guide says, pointing to his mouth. "Some are here and some are there."

"Wow, this does sound like fun," I say loud enough for my family to hear.

They look at me and then at one another before banging their paddles on the roof of the bus.

Luckily, our guide looks experienced and rugged, able to save our lives if need be. He reassures us that he never takes unnecessary risks, which alleviates a smidgeon of fear until he announces a series of approaching rapids. "We're coming up on Razor Blade and Aftershave, followed by Veg-O-Matic."

"Veg-O-Matic?" I ask.

He laughs. "Yeah. It used to be called Meat Grinder, but that scared people."

We navigate the treacherous waters with the help of his verbal cues on when we should paddle and when we should pray. After successfully steering through Duck and Run, and Thread the Needle, I become a little cocky. "Woo-hoo," I shout, picturing the T-shirt that will inform the world of my newfound bravery.

"We're coming to the Rock Garden," our leader announces.

Suddenly, we lurch forward when a boulder catches the front of the raft, and Piper bounces off her seat. She clings to the side of the raft as the whitewater rapids prepare to swallow us at the bottom of the waterfall. Instinctively, Michael and I grab her by the red vest and heave her back into the raft as we remain tilted on the rock's edge.

"Everyone lean back!" the guide yells, and we tumble over the fall. Once stabilized at the bottom, he says, "Nice save."

"Thank you," Michael and I say in unison. We glare at one another, but neither of us forfeits the glory.

For the rest of the trip, I watch the kids use teamwork and problem solving to navigate tight spaces, overcome trepidation when approaching frothy waters and, instead, embrace the challenges placed before them. They respect the guide's directions, yet aren't afraid to improvise when necessary. Doling out high-fives when reaching the safety of still waters, they exude confidence and self-assuredness, qualities we hope to impart to our children before they leave the safety of their childhood home. I realize that the day's daredevil parenting compressed years of character education into a six-mile journey in turbulent waters.

Heaving the raft onto shore, I turn to Michael. "Now do I get my T-shirt?"

He nods. "Well, I guess you earned it."

"You know, we should make this a yearly event," I say as we walk to the gift shop.

Michael and the kids look at me in dismay. "What?" Michael asks. "I thought it was too dangerous. That we were all going to die with our heads smashed open like overripe cantaloupes."

"Oh, that." I wave off his comment. "Sure. It could've happened. But it didn't." I unlatch my helmet and take off my red vest. "Besides, parents should teach their children to be risk-takers."

"Mom," Holden says, "are you sure you didn't hit your head on a rock?"

~Cathi LaMarche

58

The Special Plate

The more you praise and celebrate your life,
the more there is in life to celebrate.
~Oprah Winfrey

ne day when I was browsing a garage sale, with my three children in tow, I found a big red plate that caught my eye. It was right before Valentine's Day and the words on the plate read… "You Are Special Today!"

"Should I buy this and use it to serve Daddy a nice Valentine's Day dinner?" I asked the children.

"Yes, Daddy… dinner." They agreed. Or at least the toddler did. The other two were busy digging through the box of toys selling for ten cents.

I bought the plate for a steal… just one dollar. On Valentine's Day I prepared my husband's favorite meal, decorated the table with a tablecloth and candles and placed the pretty red plate with its special message for the special man in my life. "So, I'm special today?" he asked. "Why today?" He was teasing… he never forgot our anniversary, my birthday or Valentine's Day.

This started the tradition of "the special plate." As my family grew the red plate was used often. The birthday boy or girl always got it. If anyone had a special accomplishment at school or work… they got it. When baseball or football games were won… and sometimes when they were lost as well… the plate was brought out. It was used for celebrations but also to perk up spirits when an arm got broken or someone was ill. Visitors and special guests of honor were given use of the plate. As the children grew and invited friends over for sleepovers they would ask, "Can my friend use the special plate tonight?"

So many times... and for so many occasions the special plate was brought out over the years. Through celebrations and tragedies alike the plate made each of us feel special when it was our turn to use it.

The special plate has made it through our three children, thirteen grandchildren, and many foster children. Adults and children alike recognized it and even came to expect it. On occasion feelings have been hurt because the special plate was not offered when it should have been... an oversight for certain... never intentionally.

My husband and I are alone now. Everyone comes and visits from time to time. Still, in all the hustle and bustle of our busy lives the plate is not being used as often. On special occasions no one thinks of the plate until the meal has begun and it's too late to bring it out. I found it a little sad that this was the case at our last family gathering. It was my birthday and I missed being honored with the special plate. It had been forgotten, no longer an important part of our lives. How had this happened to something that had been so much a part of us for so long a time? After family had gone home I took out the plate and looked at it. One chip and a few scratches marred the surface but the plate was still bright red and the words still legible. I bought a plate hanger and hung the plate in a place of honor over our dining room table.

Since giving the plate a place of honor I have enjoyed watching the reactions of family members as they notice it on the wall. Not one person has seen it without sharing one or two special memories about the plate. "I remember when I broke my arm...." my son recalled.

My older daughter shared, "You brought me home from school on my birthday and we had a special mother/daughter luncheon together. I felt so pampered and special. Because my birthday is on Valentine's Day you had the table set in red and white and I ate on the special plate."

My husband shared, "I got laid off and dreaded telling you...

I felt like a loser. That night you served me on the special plate, reminding me that it was me and you against the world. Suddenly I felt ten feet tall!"

Even my best friend had a memory to share. "I said hurtful things to you. I feared our friendship was over. You invited me to lunch and served my favorite sandwich on the special plate."

My younger daughter recalled, "When I was fourteen and my best friend, Erica, died in my arms... I was having a difficult time dealing with her death. I ate on this plate for over a week."

I also enjoy telling my own stories when acquaintances and friends comment on the plate.

As I write this I cannot help but compare this plate to the cycles of life... especially my own. As a young wife and mother I was in much demand. Everyone wanted or needed me. Like the plate I shined brightly because I served a purpose. As time passed I wore many hats... wife, mother, grandmother, sister, aunt, teacher and friend. Like the plate, I may have a few chips and scratches but I am still useful and well loved after all!

~Christine M. Smith

59

Mommy, Can You Come Up?

Always kiss your children goodnight—even if they're already asleep.
~H. Jackson Brown, Jr.

From the time my son could talk, he had something to say. Every night after we put him to bed he'd call down the stairs, "Mommy, can you come up?" And every night I would answer the call and go back upstairs to hear what was on his mind. Sometimes he had something serious to discuss and other times, not so much.

We discussed everything from his belief, at five years old, that he'd have to move to Florida when he grew up, to his curiosity about what was here before dinosaurs. When he was in elementary school he'd tell me about things his friends were going through and ask me what advice I'd give them. At about eight years of age he wanted to know if he'd have to move away from home to go to college. When I told him he didn't have to but I was pretty sure he'd want to, he assured me that he wasn't going to leave home—ever!

At one point he changed his request from, "Mommy, can you come up?" to "Daddy, can you send Mommy up?" I'm not sure why this happened but the result was still the same; I went up. One night my husband turned to me and said, "You know why he doesn't ask me to come up? He knows I won't go." My response was simple. "When Aaron becomes a teenager he's going to have serious things to discuss. I want him to know he can always talk to me. No matter what time of day or what the subject may be, I want Aaron to know that he can trust me to take it seriously and take the time to talk to him. It's going to matter."

I'll admit there were nights when I really didn't want to go back up and talk about anything. On one of those nights I asked Aaron why we couldn't talk about these things earlier in the day. His answer? "Because I don't think about them then." Enough said! It was at night, when the day was done and he was relaxing, that the mysteries of life invaded his thoughts.

Aaron is now a teenager and there are many more things to think, and talk about. Teenagers these days deal with a lot of issues. From drugs to grades, from teen pregnancies to friends' parents divorcing, the list of possible real-life topics is endless. And then there are the not-so-serious issues teens deal with like acne. On any given day my son is dealing with these issues. On any given day he knows he can talk with me about any of these issues. He knows I'll take them seriously and take the time to listen because when he was little I always answered the call. And as I knew then, it really matters now.

~Diane Helbig

"I've been yelling for 34 seconds.
What took you so long?"

The Meet

Your children need your presence more than your presents.
~Jesse Jackson

I sat on the hard bleachers at the gymnastics meet, inhaling the smell of sweat and chalk, I clasped my hands together to keep from biting my nails. My daughter Lucy was suffering from a bad cold that day and was not at her best. As I watched her miss skills in her routines that she normally performed with ease, my heart sank. This would be her last chance to score high enough to move on to the next level of competition, Sectionals. If she didn't attain a certain score, her season would be over until next year—after only two meets. If she were feeling well, she wouldn't be struggling. In addition, the judges at that meet were scoring the athletes particularly hard. It was just bad luck—at the worst possible time.

Even though eight-year-old Lucy had been taking gymnastics classes since she was a toddler, the sport doesn't allow competition until Level Four, which she had just reached that season. She had waited a long time for this, and her excitement for finally competing knew no bounds. She showed her competition leotard to anyone who would stand still long enough to admire the shiny red, white and blue costume. We practiced fixing her long hair in the regulation bun, winding it tightly to withstand cartwheels and back handsprings without coming loose as it had in the past. At the last meet, she had missed the required score to be entered into Sectionals by a mere three tenths of a point. Her coach told her it was unlikely she would fall short of the score this time. My daughter had also told all her schoolmates that she would be competing on that weekend—meaning that on Monday, they would ask if she'd "made her score."

It was a big set-up for what now might be—at least in Lucy's eyes—a long fall.

When the meet concluded and the scores were announced, her coach informed her that she wouldn't be competing at Sectionals. She broke down in tears, and my stomach clenched. At that moment I knew just how upset she was. Tears are seldom seen during competition, because gymnasts are repeatedly told that crying in public at meets is not allowed.

Her teammates and coach tried to comfort her, but she was inconsolable. I ran down to the competition floor and hugged her. Then I shuffled her to the car while trying to figure out how to best handle her grief.

To buy myself some time, I took her out to lunch. As we awaited our food in the restaurant, I tried to make her feel better. I delivered a long-winded speech while she sat across from me, looking small and miserable. I talked about winning and losing, luck, and the subjective nature of scoring in gymnastics.

"You've chosen a tough sport," I told her. "In soccer, when the ball goes into the net, that's a goal. In gymnastics, some of the scoring will be based on the judges' personal preferences. Sometimes you will have bad days. All you can do is go out and do your best."

Her response to this speech was to start crying again and say that she wanted to quit the gymnastics team. I couldn't blame her. All those years of hard work, and her season was over after one mediocre performance. Even as an adult, I thought it was unfair! How could I possibly explain this to an eight-year-old? I took deep breaths, trying to suppress my anger at the unforgiving gymnastics system. But no matter how angry I was, I needed to make my child feel better. As I pondered how to do that, she cried. Soon, our food arrived, breaking our tense silence.

When we finished our lunch, I asked her what she wanted to do next. She looked at me in surprise. "You mean we don't have to go home?" she asked.

"No," I answered, making a snap decision. "It's your day with Mommy." When she heard my answer, her face lit up.

My little gymnast is my middle child, and between the demands of the other kids and, well, everything else, she and I seldom get uninterrupted time together.

She furrowed her brow, thinking long and hard about this important decision. I suggested ice cream, a movie, or the mall. She finally decided she wanted to go for a bike ride. "But," she said in stern tones, "just you and me."

We left the restaurant and went home to change clothes and get our bikes. Then we rode around the neighborhood and she showed me some of her favorite places. The weather was warm and sunny. We chatted about everything—that is, everything except gymnastics. We didn't do anything extraordinary, but it was a nice afternoon. We returned home at dinnertime, both feeling much better.

Later that night, Lucy told me she'd decided not to quit gymnastics.

A few days after that fateful meet, I was looking through her school papers and came across her "Weekend Update." It's the report that her second-grade class writes on Monday, telling of their weekend activities. I cringed inwardly, wondering what she wrote about the gymnastics meet. I opened the folded sheet and began to read. My vision blurred as tears filled my eyes. In the box at the top of the page she'd drawn two stick people riding bicycles. The bikes had impossibly large wheels, and the people long spindly legs, but they were obviously meant to represent the two of us. A bright crayon sun shone in a blue sky. The smaller figure was drawn with a half-circle smile, which filled her face.

Lucy's report said absolutely nothing about the gymnastics meet. She had written instead about how much fun she'd had having lunch and riding bikes with me.

I've heard parenting experts say that children want time with

Mom and Dad above all else. That no amount of gifts or other material things can take the place of time spent together.

I keep that paper as a reminder. A reminder that I won't always find the right words to say when my children have disappointments, but that sometimes, just being there is enough.

~Tiffany Doerr Guerzon

A Reminder of Love

The love of a family is life's greatest blessing.
~Author Unknown

As I prepared to slide a pumpkin pie into the oven, I discovered that the oven was still cold after preheating for thirty minutes. "Something is wrong with the oven," I called to my husband Clay. He checked the breaker box in the garage, wiggled the knobs on the stove, and confirmed that it definitely was not working. With fingers crossed, I reached for the phone to call the repairman, and luckily he was available. What a relief, we would be able to cook Thanksgiving dinner after all!

While waiting for the repairman to arrive, my husband pulled the stove away from the wall. We had lived in our home for almost twenty years, having moved into it the year after we married. Since that time, as newlyweds, we had become the parents of our son and daughter and had watched them grow from babies into teenagers. The stove was the original one that came with the house when it was built. I will confess, pulling out the stove and cleaning behind it is not high on my list of necessary routine cleaning tasks! Therefore, I knew that there would probably be many surprises behind and beneath the stove.

With the broom and dustpan in hand, I began sweeping up the debris of nearly twenty years. Amidst the petrified raisins, breadcrumbs, dust bunnies and various other mystery objects, something colorful caught my eye. As I bent to pick it up, I was puzzled at first as to what it could be. It was a small object, purple, and plastic... a purple magnetic letter "L" from a set of multicolored magnetic alphabet letters. Why, I had not seen one of these letters in years!

As I stood examining the letter in my hand, I was mentally transported back in time. I remembered a time when our refrigerator was covered with these magnetic alphabet letters. I could clearly remember two precious little sets of hands playing with these letters. My children learned the alphabet, how to read and spell using these letters. In my mind, I could hear the echoes of little voices asking, "Mommy, how you spell my name?" "C... A... T... spells cat!" "Mommy, how do you spell love?" The letters grew into words and the words into sentences. "Look what I can spell, Mommy—'I love you!'" The little letter brought back many special memories of the love and laughter of a little boy and girl in the heart of our home—the kitchen.

As my children grew from toddlers to attending elementary school and middle school, the bright, colorful letters that once covered our refrigerator were taken down and packed away. Stored for several years in a box in the garage, they were most likely sold at a yard sale to make room for more grownup things. However, this one little letter remained, a precious reminder, a visible symbol of the love in our family. As I grasped the little letter firmly in my hand, I thankfully remembered the love that will always bind our family together even as my children grow to adulthood and eventually start their own families.

Walking to the kitchen sink, I carefully washed my new treasure. After gently drying it, I crossed the room to the refrigerator. There, I restored it to its rightful place where it will always be a sweet reminder of the love that will forever connect our family. Children grow up, families grow, and change, but love will always bind us together. This little letter will always be a precious reminder of that love.

~Tanya Shearer

Chapter 8

Parenthood

From the Mouths of Babes

Children make your life important.

~Erma Bombeck

Solo Flight

*Being a single parent is twice the work, twice the stress and twice the tears
but also twice the hugs, twice the love and twice the pride.*
~Author Unknown

"Y ou're pregnant." I stared at my doctor, trying to grasp his words. Pregnant? True, I hadn't been feeling myself lately, and I seemed to have gained a few pounds. But for the last several months I'd been dealing with a difficult divorce, fighting depression, and trying to find my identity. In my late twenties, nothing about my life seemed normal anymore, so I passed off a few physical oddities as part of the fallout. I never dreamed I was pregnant.

Numb, I walked to my car and attempted to collect my thoughts. Then a mixture of delight and excitement raced within me, along with a determination to raise this child alone. Because of some warning signs he had shown, I didn't think the father of my child would make a good parent.

For my safety and that of my child, I would fly solo on this trip. All I needed was love, prayer, and a commitment to being the best mom I could be.

Family and friends welcomed my news with a flurry of hugs and excited chatter. In no time, morning sickness and cravings for Mexican food became part of my routine. So did fatigue and a bulging belly.

But with the growth of new life within me came the growth of a new uneasiness. Though I was at peace with my decision not to marry, what would my child think about it one day? Would he or she resent me because a father was never around?

"You have enough to think of right now," my mother advised me when she heard my concerns. "God will take care of things when the time comes. Just pray."

I did pray, and with the busyness of baby showers, shopping for maternity clothes, and working full-time, the matter slipped my mind. Then, nine months of waiting and thirty-four hours of labor ended when I held my son, James. I stared into his dark eyes and stroked his head. Love burst within me and with it, a fierce determination to give him the best home I could give. But guilt also needled me: Would he hate me one day because I never allowed him to know his father?

Nevertheless, I took off into the skies of parenting and discovered just how wild the wide blue yonder is. Late-night feedings, diapering, laundry, cooking, and holding down a job kept concerns about the future far down on the ground below. On weekdays I deposited James at daycare, logged in eight hours at the office, picked him up, and returned home, exhausted. But on weekends and in the evenings I set dirty dishes and housekeeping aside and spent time with James.

As James grew, we snuggled on the couch and watched *Cinderella*, *Lady and the Tramp*, and dozens of other movies and TV shows. I smiled down at my son and whispered, "I'm glad there's just us." His freckles spread into a grin. "Me too."

When Father's Day came around each year, James scrawled his name on a card and gave it to my dad. He spent a lot of time with my parents and played for hours with his aunt. Overall, James seemed content and secure. He didn't indicate that he missed having a father.

When my son started school, however, I met my first threat of turbulence. At the end of one school day in early September, James told me, "The teacher wants us to bring a picture of our family to class."

I froze, and that old familiar fear tugged at me. What would he think when he saw other kids' fathers in those pictures?

James didn't seem bothered by the project. He selected a photo of himself posed with his grandparents and me, and proudly mounted it on construction paper. The next day he skipped off to school, photo in hand.

At work I could hardly concentrate. I fussed the whole eight hours, wondering what emotional damage was being done to my son through a few family photographs. When I picked him up after work, James seemed fine. "How was school?" I cautiously asked. His "good" answer and broad smile put me at ease.

But once at home, his smile vanished. When I walked into my bedroom to change clothes, James followed me, crying.

"What's wrong, honey?" I asked.

"My picture wasn't like everybody else's," James blubbered.

My heart beat faster, and I forced my voice to sound lighter than I felt. "Why wasn't your picture like the other kids' pictures?"

"Because our family isn't like the other kids' families."

As I held my son, guilt and dread suddenly gushed into the open. "James," I squeaked, "are you upset because you don't have a daddy?"

He stared at me. "No. I'm upset because I don't have a dog."

A dog...? I could hardly process his words. What about a father? I explained to my son that we lived in an apartment and couldn't have pets. But maybe one day we could have a dog. Content with that answer, he trotted off to play.

For the first time in seven years, I relaxed at the controls. My solo parenting had paid off in ways I'd never realized, building security and happiness in a little boy who loved our twosome as much as I did.

Years later, in his teens, James did ask about his father—more out of curiosity than a desire to complete our family. I told him as much as he wanted to know and invited him to talk about his dad whenever he wanted. Now in his twenties, James wants to marry and have children one day.

I've thought a lot about my commitment to single parenting. There were times I could have used an extra pair of hands with day-to-day tasks. Another salary would have helped, too. But I don't regret my decision. This flight will never land; I will always be James's mom. And I will continue to enjoy wherever it takes me—on a wing and a prayer.

~Rachel Allison

Parenting on Four Wheels

A child seldom needs a good talking to as a good listening to.
~Robert Brault, www.robertbrault.com

t was late and I was tired, but my infant son's cries from the back seat had finally died down. Late night car rides were as relaxing for me as they were for Connor. Both of us were lulled by the hum of the engine, the ticking of the turn signal, and the occasional rhythmic whooshing of the wipers.

As my son grew, so did his seat in the car....

At two, Connor sang along to the toddler songs I played on the car stereo, grinning at me in the rear view mirror as he clapped to the beat. He practiced his words on me, pointing to objects so that I would name them.

At five, he was promoted to a booster seat from which he watched over his baby brother in the infant carrier next to him. He'd happily retrieve dropped bottles and binkies and sound out street signs on the way to school, giving me a high-five from the back seat every time he read a word correctly.

By second grade he'd outgrown car seats, and having learned to read silently, had long since stopped shouting out words to me. He was a quiet kid, but in the car, when he wasn't reading, he would talk—about his school day, his friends, his favorite song on the radio.

Before long, he was sitting next to me in the front passenger seat, his younger brother and baby sister taking up the back. It was at this point that Connor took over as car DJ and we began talking about our shared love of music, specifically the lyrics. He'd play his favorite songs for me and tell me about his favorite bands. And I, in turn, would give him a taste of the 70s and 80s, instilling a strong appreciation for "good music" like Pink Floyd, Journey and Michael Jackson. Conversations about music led to other topics: school, friends, even girls. Serious subjects were saved for car rides, too: relationships, divorce, sibling rivalry.

I've learned more about Connor, and his brother and sister, driving in the car, than I have anywhere else. I can tell how well they're getting along by the seat they choose. When there is tension between them, Jack will lift the third row seat and sit alone. When the oldest and youngest are getting along, six-year-old Ella will request that he sit next to her rather than in front by me. Their body language speaks too: when the boys are getting along, Connor will turn his head to talk over the seatback and Jack will lean forward against his safety belt to listen.

As a single parent, car rides have given me a glimpse into my kids' lives when I'm not with them. They point out the places they've been, the restaurants they want to try, where their dad takes them for pizza.

Car rides are also where I've learned about my kids' friends, and the real reason I always offer to serve as taxi on the weekends. I learn about the type of music they're listening to, who is doing well in school, which boy likes which girl. It's all there, right inside those four doors. Fifteen years of talks, music, laughter, peaceful quiet and even sometimes, tears.

It is late and I am tired. Connor has just sent me a text asking me to pick him up from his friend's house, up the street and around the corner. It is 11 p.m. Curfew. As I pull out of the garage, I am reminded of all the car ride memories that I hold dear....

The six-month-old infant snuggled in his car seat on the way to the babysitter.

The five-year-old kindergartner dressed in his crisp white uniform shirt and blue shorts, ready to begin his school career.

The ten-year-old soccer player, he and his teammates crammed like sardines into my minivan after the big game, dirt on their knees, sweat soaking their shirts, huge grins on their faces.

The fourteen-year-old high school freshman, in black blazer and pink tie, the color of his date's homecoming dress.

I pull into the driveway and walk around to the passenger side. Connor comes out and, seeing the driver's seat empty, climbs behind the wheel to drive his mom home. I watch as my oldest child carefully navigates our subdivision streets and wonder silently where the years have gone.

~Beth M. Wood

Reprinted by permission of Mark Parisi and
Off the Mark ©1995.

64

A Little Hand Up

Never worry about numbers. Help one person at a time,
and always start with the person nearest you.
~Mother Teresa

I bundled up my six-year-old daughter, Renee, against the Minnesota cold and a forecasted snowstorm for her short walk to school. Snow pants, coat, scarf, gloves, and her new wait-until-payday boots, all princess pink and a half size too big to allow for growing. Renee was so excited about her new boots that she had worn them in the house all weekend, only giving them up for bath and bed.

It pleased me to slip her feet into them, knowing each precious toe would be warmly nestled into the deep soft lining. It pleased me almost as much as throwing out her old ones with the sticky zippers. They definitely hadn't made it into the box of freshly laundered and packed clothes that Renee and I had spent Saturday morning sorting out of her closet for her younger cousin.

Kissing Renee on her eyelids, the only uncovered part of her body, I opened the front door. Her two big brothers tossed me a kiss and a "Love you, Mom," as they each grabbed one of their sister's hands and run-skipped the block to the crossing guard.

I poured myself another cup of coffee, turned on the radio and began mentally checking my things to do. I wasn't too far into dance-cleaning the kitchen before "Get up and Boogie" was interrupted by the happy news that school was closing early due to the snowstorm.

Within a few minutes, my boys exploded into the house and out of their winter wear. They gave me a "Yippee!" high-five and headed for their game system.

Renee wasn't able to wiggle-dance out of her winter bundling.

"Mommy, I'm stuck all over," Renee said, doing an off balance, toe to heel, boot push move until she plopped to the floor, thankfully cushioned by the seat of her snow pants.

I bent over to help her. "Renee?" I asked, surprised at the grimy boot in my hand. "Where are your new boots?"

"These are my new, new boots," she smiled at me.

"No, honey, these aren't your new boots. Look, they're dirty. The clasps are broken and the snow got in through the hole in the side."

"Yup," she agreed, not realizing the implied question in my statement. "My friend's clothes are all like that and these boots were too small for her."

"But what happened to your pretty-princess boots?"

"Mommy," she smiled at me. "My friend needed boots. She outgrew hers and her feet were cold. My boots were warm and they fit her, and she looked pretty in them. She was happy and that made me happy too. She gave me her boots as a hand-me-down and I gave her mine as a hand-me-up."

Suddenly, the ugly boot in my hand became as beautiful as the fabled glass slipper. The simple clarity of truth filled my heart. I had felt generous setting an example for Renee by giving away outgrown and no longer needed clothes because it was the right thing to do.

But, not only had Renee done the right thing by giving her new boots to someone who needed them, she had done it the right way. She was a cheerful giver. She reminded me that God hands us down His blessing so that we may cheerfully hand-me-up His abundance to others.

~Cynthia Hamond, S.F.O.

65

Listen to the Children

And a little Child shall lead them.
~Isaiah 11:6

There was a time in my life that I felt no hope. I had become lost and consumed by depression. Every day was a struggle. I had lost all faith, and the desire to live. I was dying inside, and had given up.

One day, after the usual crying spell, my nine-year-old son looked at me, and with so much concern in his face asked, "Mom, Why are you crying all of the time? What is wrong with you?"

I looked back at my son, crying, and replied, "I am tired, and at the end of my rope." He stared at me in confusion, then so innocently and sweetly questioned me, "Do you know what I do when I am at the end of my rope?"

I said, "No, what do you do?" He then giggled, and grinning ear to ear told me, "It's so easy Mom, I climb!" That day became the first day of a new life. It was, just that simple, and from the mouth of a child, came truth and resolution. God speaks to us in many ways, but none more precious or moving, than when spoken through a child.

~Christina J. Hunt

Big Sister

Having a sister is like having a best friend you can't get rid of.
You know whatever you do, they'll still be there.
~Amy Li

hile my twenty-two-month-old son Keegan napped and my four-year-old daughter Priya was busy coloring pictures beside me on the couch, I seized the rare quiet moment in my house to phone my mom for a chat. With my parents living out of town, it is rare for us to have an in-depth phone conversation without getting interrupted by a request to brush a doll's hair or wipe a runny nose. As we caught up on the latest family gossip and upcoming weekend plans, I mentioned that I was finally ready to give all of my baby toys and infant items to charity.

My mom asked, "Are you sure you are done having kids?" As I watched Priya drawing pictures and listened to Keegan's soft breathing on the monitor I sighed with happiness. "Yes Mom, we are definitely happy with what we've got. I think Keegan is it — I don't want another baby."

To this, Priya's ears perked up and she gave me a funny look. Pressing me further as only a grandma would, my mom suggested again, "Come on, how about one more baby."

With a serious tone I replied, "No, Mom. No other babies. We are happy with what we have and Keegan is the last one." Then I turned to Priya, who had put down her crayons and was now intently listening to my end of the conversation. "Priya, would you like another baby brother or sister?"

All of a sudden, her lip started to quiver and Priya began to cry. I asked her what was the matter, to which she replied, "I don't want another baby—I want to keep Keegan!"

As a parent of two young children, it's so easy to get caught up in the craziness between the siblings. Fights over toys, hair pulling, and who got the bigger piece of dessert—but the sweet innocence of the love between a big sister and her little brother makes it all worth it... and almost makes me want to have another baby. Just almost.

~Ritu Shannon

Body Language

Speak the truth, but leave immediately after.
~Slovenian Proverb

"Is that when I get my peanut?" asked my two-year-old daughter. We were talking about what her life would be like when she was four like her big brother and how she would be able to do all the big-kid things that he did.

"What are you talking about?" I asked.

"My peanut. Do I get my peanut when I'm four?"

Oh.

Maybe Freud was right.

My disappointed daughter listened to my explanation about the difference between boys and girls, and how she would not grow a peanut like her brother's by the time she was four. Then, presaging the day she would become a doctor, she proceeded to interview random men on the street in our town, asking them, "Do you have a peanut?" Luckily, none of them knew what a peanut was either!

Her patient assessments resumed when she was about four. I had, of course, worked hard to indoctrinate my children on the danger of smoking, and in fact one of their grandfathers had already contracted cancer from smoking. So I shouldn't have been surprised when my budding doctor approached a man on the street one day, and loudly announced, "That man is stupid and he's going to die." I can only hope that was the last straw for him and he decided right then and there to quit.

My son's medical education was limited to one, most important lesson. We all know that the best way to have a conversation with your son is to have him sitting in the back seat of the car right behind you where you can't see him except with the eyes in the back of your head. So that was when my seven-year-old felt comfortable asking me, "How do you make a baby?"

It was a little earlier than I had expected to have the conversation but I forged ahead and told him: "When a man and a woman love each other and get married, the man puts a seed inside the woman to grow a baby." You could practically hear the violins playing.

But that wasn't enough and he pressed on, so I had to expand a bit on the methodology. When he demanded a full explanation because he couldn't understand how this could possibly happen, unless the woman swallowed the seed like a pill, I was forced to divulge all the gory details. There was a long incredulous pause, and then I heard a tremulous little voice in the back seat saying, "So how do you adopt?"

~Amy Newmark

Taking His Vitals

They have the unique ability to listen to one story and understand another.
~Pandora Poikilos

We were there for a simple wellness checkup, nothing more. And, as any forward-thinking mother would, I spent time prepping my preschooler. Reminding him that he'd been there before. Assuring him there would be no shots this time. Explaining that the doctor simply wanted to make certain he was healthy and getting bigger. I knew that my well-prepared child would sail through the exam.

But the pediatrician's office was chock full of sick children. Hacking coughs, runny noses, flushed cheeks. Crying babies, rowdy siblings. Kids fighting over toys. Kids chewing on large Lego blocks and their fingers. The oppressive heat and noise in the stuffy waiting room unsettled me and I could see its effect on my quiet son, as well.

Almost-three-year-old Koy scooted nearer on the Crayola-red bench and tucked his legs up under him. "Wouldn't you like to go over there and work a puzzle?" I riffled his mop of red hair. He shook his head and pressed close against me.

"There's nothing to worry about," I said. "This will be fun! Now, why don't you pick out a book and bring it..."

"Koy," called the nurse from the doorway. "Koy, you're next."

Gathering my purse and our jackets, I started towards her. Koy hung back.

"Come on," I urged and took his hand. "She's waiting."

His uncertainty was obvious to the observant nurse. "There's nothing to be scared of," she reassured him as she led us into the small examination room. "The doctor just wants to look you over and see how big you've grown. Okay?"

His slight nod was jerky, nervous.

"Remember?" I murmured. "Mommy told you all this."

He gave me a doubtful smile.

"Now, first," the nurse carefully explained, "we'll go down the hall where I'll take some important things."

"Important things?" His eyes widened.

"Yes," she nodded. "I'll take your height and your weight. Then, we'll come back here to this room and I'll take your temperature and your blood pressure."

Startling both the nurse and me, Koy locked his arms around my knees and buried his face against my thighs.

"Mommy," he raised his voice in alarm, "she's going to take my things. All my important things!"

"It's okay, Sweetie." I tried to pry him loose.

He clasped me closer and wailed even louder, "But what if she never gives them back?"

~Carol McAdoo Rehme

Teething Pains

If you have a lot of tension and you get a headache, do what it says on the aspirin bottle: "Take two aspirin" and "Keep away from children."
~Author Unknown

I am certain of two things. First, your three-year-old will misinterpret what you tell your six-year-old. Second, your kids were put on this earth to embarrass you.

"Why are my teeth falling out?" Zach asked, as he gripped the tiny tooth that had come loose from his mouth.

I tried to reassure him that this happened to all kids. I brushed the tears off his face and told him, "Your baby teeth have to fall out to make room for your adult teeth to grow in."

"But I like my baby teeth."

"If you put your tooth under your pillow, then the tooth fairy will take it and give you money."

I was hoping that all of my pleading, and let's face it, bribing, would calm his nerves. He seemed to forget the trauma caused by parts of his body coming loose. However, it brought up a new concern—a small fairy.

"Is she going to fly around my room?" Zach asked.

"I guess so. That way she can get under your pillow."

"She is going to crawl under my pillow?"

"That is probably what she will have to do to reach your tooth."

The whole time I was explaining the workings of the tooth fairy to Zach, my daughter Caitlin sat and listened attentively. She never made a peep. I was wondering if I should explain this process a bit more to her. I wasn't sure if a three-year-old could grasp the concept of a tooth fairy.

"What is the tooth fairy doing with all of the teeth?" Caitlin asked.

"She needs the teeth to give them to the new babies, so that they can have teeth until their adult ones come in."

This seemed to be exactly what she wanted to hear. Days went by and I didn't hear any more questions from her. Zach got his money, just like he had been told, and Caitlin seemed content. That is, until we went to a local department store.

I walked up and down the aisles pushing Caitlin in the shopping cart. Several times we passed an elderly lady with worn-out clothes that had seen better days. Her hair was gray and stringy. It had been a while since a comb had tamed it. Caitlin stared, turning all the way around in the cart just to get a peek.

"Caitlin, it's not polite to stare," I said.

"But Mom...."

"Caitlin, you heard me. Stop staring."

As we turned down the next aisle, we crossed paths with the elderly woman one last time. I saw Caitlin's eyes drift in her direction. However, before I could reprimand her, she opened her mouth and in a volume I was sure the whole store heard, she said...

"Look, Mom. The Tooth Fairy took too many of her teeth!"

~Helen R. Zanone

Phone Messages

A child can ask questions that a wise man cannot answer.
~Author Unknown

I was baffled! Why wouldn't this man return my phone calls? I just couldn't understand it. I had recently remodeled my kitchen. It was everything I had dreamed of except for several cabinet doors that were loose. Although the cabinet man, Bill, had been working in the kitchen just six short days before, I was still having major problems. I was not happy. I called him over and over. I was convinced Bill was avoiding me. Each time, I reached what I assumed to be his grandchild.

"May I speak with Bill, please?" I would ask.

"He's not here," a small voice would respond.

"When do you expect him?" I would inquire.

"Don't know," the same little person would tell me.

"Can you please tell him to call me?" I begged. The child assured me that he would. By then, I wanted to cry.

Irritated, I began the task of preparing dinner. Although I knew better, I impatiently opened the defective cabinet door to the pantry. When I did, the entire door fell off in my hands. My dream kitchen was turning into a nightmare! I began to vent out loud, not caring whether my five children heard me.

"I can't understand it!" I complained. "I keep calling and I just can't get Bill on the phone. I need him to come over and fix these cabinets."

My six-year-old son then reached into his pocket and pulled out a cell phone.

"I need him too," he said impatiently. "I keep answering the phone that he left here last week and I have lots of messages for him."

~Tracy Minor

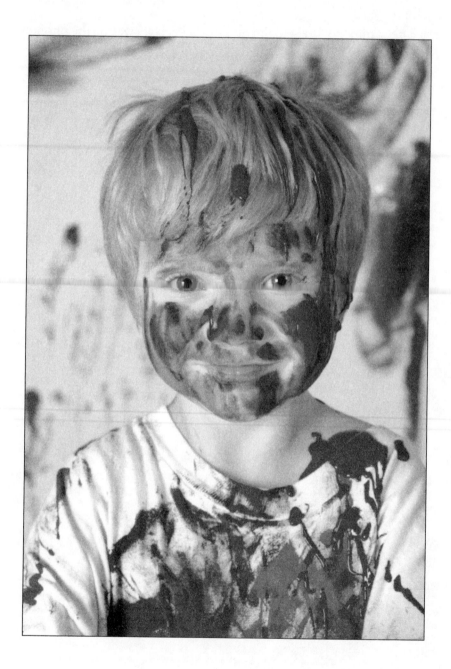

Chapter
9

Parenthood

What Goes Around
Comes Around

*Whatever we do lays a seed in our deepest consciousness,
and one day that seed will grow.*

~Sakyong Mipham

71

The Hot Seat

No matter how calmly you try to referee, parenting will eventually produce
bizarre behavior, and I'm not talking about the kids.
~Bill Cosby

"I am so sorry about the blue cup."

There was a pause on the other end of the phone line, and then I heard my mother's confused voice.

"The blue cup? What blue cup?"

"The one from your Tupperware set." In a rainbow of cups, there had only been one blue, and when my older brother Mark and I were kids, we had battled for it like it was the Holy Grail.

"I can't believe you don't remember it. We used to fight over that cup all the time!" (Along with who got to ride in the front passenger seat of her car, whether we watched *The Brady Bunch* or *Star Trek*, and whose turn it was to wash the dishes.)

How on earth had Mom forgotten the blue cup? She laughed when I apologized, and acted like our quarrels had been nothing.

"Those were the best days of my life," she said. Mark and I had obviously driven her sanity over the brink and she had never fully recovered.

The comeuppance I was getting from my own two children, five-year-old Andrew and two-year-old Gracie prompted my phone call. One morning at the breakfast table, they argued over the only brown chair in a kitchen full of white chairs.

"It's my chair!" Andrew yelled and pried his sister's fingers loose from the chair's spindles. "No, it's mine!" she retorted, her eyes flaming and curls bobbing furiously.

I froze, spatula in hand. They had never fought before, and I didn't know what to do.

Before the chair incident, I had adapted to parenting with an ease that pleasantly surprised me. Pregnancy? I loved it. Over twenty hours of labor for each child? I considered it a worthy cause. Breastfeeding, sleepless nights, and full-time motherhood? I acclimated and then flourished. But sibling rivalry? I was clueless.

I hoped the feud over the brown chair would dissipate, but each morning I was greeted with shrieks as they brawled over the chair like it was the last seat on a Titanic lifeboat. I tried the calm "let's take turns" approach. "Today Gracie can have the chair, and tomorrow it will be your turn, Andrew."

"That's not fair! I had it first!" Andrew wailed. He wasn't buying the judgment I was doling out. He was right to be dubious. As the days went by, I lost track of whose turn it was, and we were back to crying and hurt feelings.

I tried a spiritual approach, explaining the Golden Rule and reminding them to love one another. I told them everything was a gift from above and they should share. The next day, Andrew, who already shows promise for a career in litigation, was ready with his arguments.

"It's not your chair, Gracie!" he exclaimed with a pious air. "It's God's chair." And Andrew was certain that God wanted him to have the chair.

Gracie, who is not quite as eloquent with comebacks yet, let out a blood-curdling scream. That's when my husband Jesse laid down the law — if he heard any more fighting over the chair, he would pack it up and haul it back to Grandma's house and reunite it with my old high school desk.

That brought peace for a few days, but then my little Hatfield and miniature McCoy discovered there were plenty of other things they could fight about. They bickered over who got to sit on the middle couch cushion, who got to hug Daddy first when he got home from work, whether we watched *Dora* or *The Avengers*, and whose turn it was to go down the swing set slide. Andrew complained when Gracie looked out his car window. She screamed if he touched her tricycle. He banned her from his room when she set one toenail over the threshold. She swooped in and snatched her doll from his clutches if he got too close. After one particularly trying day, I escaped to Starbucks when Jesse got home from work.

Between sips of raspberry mocha and sounds of soothing jazz, I thought about why my children's arguing bothered me. I knew my children loved each other. When they weren't fighting, they enjoyed one another's company. Most siblings argue. So why did it feel like I was in the hot seat whenever they disagreed? It wasn't a coveted seat, like the one on a popular game show, or even the hotly contested brown chair. In this seat I felt pressure because my resolutions affected my children's health and happiness. When my attempts to restore peace fell short, I felt helpless, and I panicked inside. All parents have areas of weakness where they feel the burden of producing the right solutions. I buckled with each sharp word and every angry glare that came from my children. Their arguing felt like a personal affront to my parenting abilities.

When I left Starbucks that night, I felt less stressed, but I still didn't have all the answers. Parents never can. It was my children who gave me a new perspective a few days later.

Gracie was running down our hallway when she suddenly fell and began to cry. Andrew reached her first, running furiously to her side. I wanted to scoop her up and rock her, but when I saw his concern, I stopped. "Gracie, are you okay?" he said, looking directly into her eyes.

"Oh, my toe," she told her big brother. Andrew began gently rubbing each of the toes on her feet. "Is it this one, Gracie? Does this one hurt?" Gracie stopped crying as Andrew massaged her toes. I wanted to sit down beside them, but I didn't want to interrupt the moment. I'm glad I didn't because of what happened next.

"I love you, Gracie," Andrew said.

"I wuv you, too, Andoo," Gracie replied.

With their words, my anxieties drained away. When it mattered most, my children would be there for one another. And maybe what I had been teaching them was getting through, despite my own uncertainties.

These days I'm learning to be more resilient when my children bicker. I'm an optimist; I know if I don't lose my mind, one day I can rejoin the workforce as a professional referee or hostage negotiator—my children are training me for endless possibilities. And I understand better about my mom and the blue cup. Maybe it's not so much that she forgot our fights, it's that she remembers more vividly the times Mark and I loved each other. I believe that one day I will remember my children saying "I love you" to one another more than I will remember their spats over an old brown chair.

Years from now, one of my children may call and apologize about the brown chair. When that day comes, I already know what I will say.

~Janeen Lewis

72

Hopelessly Hip Mom

*When we weren't scratching each other's eyes out, we were making
each other laugh harder than anyone else could.*
~Lucie Arnaz, daughter of Lucille Ball

"**Y**ou can't buy that!"

My thirteen-year-old daughter was aghast.

I spun to the left, then the right, in the dressing room mirror, as the double-ruffled skirt flipped playfully above my knees. Squinting my left eye just right, I looked almost five years younger.

"Why not?" I asked, squinting my right for confirmation.

"Because," Kelsey stammered, "it's... not a mom outfit."

In that instant, I knew another battle line had been drawn in the mother-daughter drama of life. The arena: the junior fashion department. The honor: hippest woman of the house.

There wasn't room for us both.

How did this happen? From mother-toddler sundress sets to matching holiday sweaters, we'd always been an amiable dressing duo. When initial purses were in vogue, I bought Kelsey her "K"; she bought me my "J."

If anything, I'd expected our fashion issues to involve debates about appropriate teen attire. I'd even imagined offending my off-spring with my conservative parental "uncool."

But nothing had prepared me for my daughter's derision over my desire to dress with style, or, more specifically, her style.

I love clothes, but Kelsey has better taste. After all, she tracks the trends, collects countless catalogs and surfs online stores. I'd be a fool to waste such valuable research.

Thus, my daughter became my unwitting fashion consultant due to her savvy sense of style and keen eye for color. Flippy skirts? Great idea! Shell ankle bracelet? Me, too! And how was I to know my hair looked great straight before Kelsey bought the flat iron?

It's not that I was a total style slouch before Kelsey's teenage wardrobe revelation; she had simply been too young to notice. Now, nothing I don escapes her critical eye: a hem too short, a color too bright, a hairstyle too close to her own carefully coiffed do.

It all came to a head one late summer day over a pair of pale blush, corduroy shorts—make that two pairs. When Kelsey grabbed one off the junior rack I snuck one for myself. Then we each popped out of our respective dressing rooms for a look in the three-way mirror.

I was caught pink-shorted.

"Oh, no you don't!" she commanded.

"What?" I pleaded innocently.

"You can't buy the same shorts!" she shot back.

"Kelsey," I explained calmly, "you're young. You look great in everything. I don't, so I need them more than you do."

My middle-aged logic fell on deaf, red-hot ears.

"Then I'm not wearing them," she countered.

This called for drastic action.

I invited her into the changing room for a mother-daughter chat. Negotiations worthy of a world-power summit ensued.

Her proposal: We would both buy the shorts. However, we'd never wear them together, and under no circumstances would I wear them to her school.

Mentally, I traveled back to my own teenage years, with memories of midriff top tussles and platform shoe blues. The conflict hadn't been about the clothes, I realized, but about carving out my own identity: one that had nothing to do with my mother. I looked at my daughter with new respect. This was quite a teenage compromise.

"Deal," I said.

Later that day, we found the first fall catalog stuffed in our mailbox. I nestled next to Kelsey on the couch as she flipped open the cover.

"Dibs on the peach-flowered miniskirt," she announced.

I pondered thoughtfully the feminine floral skirt to which her finger was possessively pointing.

I chose my words carefully.

"That is so cute… but it might be a little young for me, don't you think?"

"You'd look good in it, Mom," offered my fledgling diplomat, "but maybe you're right."

I gave Kelsey my most gracious smile.

Peach isn't my color, anyway.

~Judy O'Kelley

"You've been hanging around
with us too long, Dad."

73

Polka Dots and Stripes

It's always the badly dressed people who are the most interesting.
~Jean Paul Gaultier

"I'm at my wit's end," my daughter complained. "Maddie insists on wearing that old pink tutu over her clothes everywhere we go. It's embarrassing! And why are you smiling?"

Yes, I was smiling as I thought back to a time twenty-eight years before when it was this very daughter of mine who was "embarrassing."

Life with two daughters had been happy and normal for several years... until my younger started kindergarten and wanted to choose what to wear to school each day.

Oh the struggles we had! Like clockwork... every morning. She wanted to wear polka dot shirts with striped pants, or plaids with teddy bears. The colors didn't even come close to matching. Of course, I insisted she choose from the clothes I picked, which resulted in tears and drama. She would leave for school wearing perfectly matched clothes and unfortunately, a frown on her face. I'm sure I wore a frown too.

Although I hated to send her to school feeling unhappy I did anyway. Why? I was concerned about what others would think, or say, about her appearance. Would her teachers think I was colorblind? Or even worse, that I did not get up and get her ready for school? Or that I just didn't care?

Unhappy school mornings were becoming the new "normal"

around our house and I didn't like it. Fortunately, a change did come about, thanks to the wisdom of a kindergarten teacher.

During a conference with my daughter's teacher I learned that her morning disposition was interfering with her learning. She would seem sad and unable to focus at times. Tearfully I told the teacher of our daily power struggles over what she should wear to school.

Her teacher told me that as long as my daughter was dressed appropriately for the weather I should let her decide what to wear and stop worrying about what others would think. "Let her go to school happy and ready to learn. Parents have to choose their battles."

I took this teacher's words to heart and began letting my daughter wear whatever she wanted. (Although I often cringed when she came out of her room with her polka dots, stripes and smiley face on.) Her teacher saw immediate improvements in her grades and interest in learning. My husband and I were enjoying our stress-free mornings. Such a simple change, yet it made all the difference.

Why was I smiling? As I watched my little granddaughter spin around the room dressed in a T-shirt, jeans, and pink tutu I noticed that she too had her smiley face on.

"Let me tell you what a wise teacher once told me, " I said.

~Carol Emmons Hartsoe

74

The Good Parts

*A mother is a person who seeing there are only four pieces of pie for five
people, promptly announces she never did care for pie.*
~Tenneva Jordan

When I was growing up my mother ate the most disgusting things. Dry crusts from my sandwiches, burnt toast, the soggy last few inches of pizza slices that I always left behind. She ate the dark meat, gizzards even, broccoli stems and the dust of crushed chips left in the bottom of the bag. Hers were the broken crackers, the baked potatoes with the black spots in the middle. She'd peel an apple for me and eat the skins, which was horrifying, and then when I was done, she'd eat the fruit I'd left around the core. I thought something was wrong with her.

My mother dressed ugly too. She never got herself a decent looking pair of sneakers and her sweatpants were all faded. I never understood why she dressed so badly because she always bought me really cute, trendy outfits. She still had some awful velour sweatshirts from the 70s and I'd pray she'd never show up at my school wearing one. If she did, God forbid, she'd probably be eating a burnt pizza crust and a peach pit.

My mother was so embarrassing.

Then one morning, recently, I finally got it. After eating my daughter's unwanted toast crusts and a plum skin for breakfast, we went shopping. I needed new shoes for a wedding we were attending that weekend. Except, once we got to the mall I realized that my feet weren't growing. It was just a party. No one was going to be looking at my feet. But the baby? She'd nearly outgrown all of her shoes and would be in a new size soon. She needed new shoes more than I did.

I considered a new sundress, but did I really need one? No. My little one was going to be in a size 2T soon and I wouldn't have a thing that would fit her. I decided to wait and spend the money on her.

When we got home, we had lunch. She ate the fluffy tops of the broccoli and I realized I'd learned to love the tough stems. I peeled her a peach and sucked all the flesh from the pit while she ate the good parts. I wanted a graham cracker but there were only two left, so I decided that I didn't really like graham crackers as much as I did when I was little anyway. Neither did my mom and that's why she always let me have the last ones in the package too.

When you're a parent, you don't mind giving up the good parts. I don't need a bunch of new stuff because I have all I need. I have my daughter and her happiness and I have a mother that I finally appreciate—a mother who once gave me all the good parts in hope that one day I'd grow up to be that kind of parent too.

~Victoria Fedden

75

Outnumbered

No one will ever win the battles of the sexes;
there's too much fraternizing with the enemy.
~Henry Kissinger

What is it like being the only female in a house full of males, the only female parenting three boys... four if you include my husband? It does have its very positive aspects. I always had someone around the house who was stronger than I was, who could open those stubborn jar lids or stuck windows or change a light bulb. I didn't have to share my clothes, shoes, make-up or jewelry with anyone. Well, I did have to share my clothes once, at Halloween, but that's another story. I always had someone who watched out for me and protected me.

There were negative aspects too. I hate crawling, creeping creatures... snakes, lizards, bugs, frogs... you get the picture. The boys would bring something home to share with me. I should have been a good role model and calmly asked my boys to take their treasures outside. But instead I would run screaming from the room. We finally compromised; they could bring those icky things home but they—the creatures, not the boys—had to stay outside behind the garage. And they couldn't tell me what creatures were living in the yard. Not even a hint.

As parents, my husband and I felt strongly that we should eat dinner together as a family most nights; no television allowed. It was time for conversation and sharing. When the boys were really young our conversations were about the things that were important to them at the time — what they saw on *Sesame Street* or what they did at the park that day. But as they got older their interests turned to anything automotive. This fit in perfectly with my husband's interests but left me out in the cold. Oh, I cared about cars. I wanted one in my driveway that could take me where I wanted to go. And I knew how to put gas in the tank and where the key went in the ignition. But other than that, I really didn't understand the mechanics of how the darn things worked.

Our dinner table conversations became technical symposiums: engines, spark plugs, exhaust manifolds, catalytic converters, engine blocks, horsepower, tires. Each night, just as we started the salad, one of them would bring up an article he had read in a car magazine, or a cool car he had spotted that day, and off they'd go. Without me.

Occasionally I would try to steer the conversation to a different topic… something that I could participate in. And that did work… for about two minutes. Somehow, when I wasn't looking, the conversation would come back to cars: differential clutches, spider gears, torque converters, transaxle housing, or some other fascinating topic. Occasionally one of my guys would ask me what I thought about a clutch shoe or a camshaft. I knew about shoes but what did they have to do with a clutch? Wasn't a clutch a purse that matched the shoes? Didn't I really prefer coil springs to the air springs or the leaf springs? Really? I didn't have a clue.

So I did the only thing a parent could do when the odds were against her. I zoned out. I stopped listening. My eyes glazed over and my mind took me to different places. Lovely places. Places I wanted to go; places I could understand. And the car conversation continued to swirl around me, non-stop.

Then one by one, my sons became adults and moved out. I was no longer outnumbered. But there was a problem. For so many years I had zoned out at the dinner table, I had to be retrained to listen, focus and participate. Too many times over those first few months, my husband would say, "Barbara, are you listening?" And I would answer, "Are you talking to me? Wow, what a concept." So I listened and I discovered all over again that my husband was an interesting person. And he could talk about things other than cars. I knew there was a reason I married him!

Now, each of my sons has added a wonderful girl to our family and so I have three women on my side. When the eight of us are all together for dinner, we don't talk about cars. Well, most of the time. Every once in a while, those cars do intervene and the "boys" start up again. When that happens the girls and I give each other "the look" and start our own conversation. And believe me it's not about cars.

We added our first grandchild a couple of years ago… a grandson. And, believe it or not, he is interested… in cars. One of the first words he said was "Jeep." My other two sons are starting their families too. What do you suppose the odds are that they will have sons too? Check back with me in a few years to see. If I seem zoned out and don't hear you, you'll know that the boys once again outnumber the girls, car talk has taken over family gatherings, and I'm just not listening.

~Barbara LoMonaco

Who's Teaching Whom?

It is amazing how quickly the kids learn the operation of the DVD, yet are unable to understand the vacuum cleaner.
~Etienne Marchal

I have many special memories of my older son's graduation from college. I remember sitting with my parents in the arena and trying to spot Scott's face among a sea of mortarboards. I remember cheering when his name was announced. I even remember my joy when I realized I'd written my last tuition check to his school—forever.

One of my favorite memories, however, came after the graduation and celebration dinner were over. Because Scott's apartment was small, we gathered in the lobby of my parents' hotel to see Scott open his graduation gifts. He plowed through them quickly, building a pile of gift bags and tissue paper under the coffee table. Then we settled back to enjoy the free coffee and some rare family time.

During a lull in the conversation, my mom told Scott about a problem with her cell phone. "I can't hear my ringer," she said. "Do you know how to fix that?" Within seconds, Scott was kneeling by his grandmother's chair with her phone in hand.

I turned to talk with my dad, but he had followed my mom's lead and asked my younger son about a cell phone problem. My son was leaning over my dad's chair, holding the phone and guiding my dad through the resolution process. My husband and I looked from son to son and then at each other. Then we stopped talking. Our special family night had morphed into a tech support session.

I wondered when this had happened. When did my children learn things that my parents and I don't know?

As our children grow, we move from potty training and time-outs to lessons about doing chores and turning homework in on time. We teach our children about friends and romance and character. We assume information flows from parent to child. The parents are supposed to be the teachers, right?

But parents and children change roles over time, and the process starts long before we parents qualify for senior citizen discounts. Our sons and daughters develop passions and interests that we don't share. When they do, we face some choices. Are we willing to learn about new things like rock climbing or motorcycles or a vegan diet? Can we talk openly about our values and beliefs with someone who may challenge them? Will we embrace something we've never cared about simply because it matters to our children?

When my sister and I talked years ago about the craziness of parenting teens, we developed a motto: "It's their journey." The motto reminded us that our children would probably travel different paths to maturity than the paths we followed. No matter how much we hoped they could duplicate our experiences, we knew it probably wouldn't happen.

Now that my sons are adults, I rely on the same motto, but for a different reason. My children's unique life experiences have helped them develop knowledge and insights they can share with others, including their mom. Why should I be surprised by this development? I don't question the travel expertise of friends who lived overseas for several years. Why shouldn't I offer the same respect to my kids when they've acquired knowledge unfamiliar to me?

In some ways, I will always be my children's teacher. By word and example, I will continue to share important truths about endurance and commitment and integrity. I also hope to teach my sons about living with passion and purpose no matter how old you are.

But I hope my children will teach me a few things as well. I bought a new phone today, and I need some help.

~Donna Finlay Savage

A Painful Journey

Little children, headache; big children, heartache.
~Italian Proverb

I was sitting on the studio floor carefully piecing together tiny photos for my son's final elementary school yearbook when Jenny arrived home from school. This was the day the eighth graders studying French had waited for throughout their middle school years. A rite of passage, if you will. The day their trip was finalized, roommates confirmed and trip agendas distributed. The kids would be traveling from Connecticut to Quebec to experience a little bit of French culture. And along the way, who knows what adventures they would encounter?

I was waiting to hear the door slam and her feet run up the two flights of stairs to my studio, breathlessly relaying the news and presenting every detail of the much anticipated trip: when they were leaving, what they would bring, what they would see. But all I heard was her quiet footsteps from the living room to her bedroom.

"Hi Jenny, how was the big day?" I shouted down the hall. "You girls must be so excited that the trip is almost here!"

After a few minutes Jenny appeared in the doorway with a sweet-sad expression on her face. "I'm rooming with a girl named Latoya."

"What?"

"Latoya."

"Who is that?"

"I don't know."

"Wait a minute. I thought you were allowed to pick your room-mates. What about Alex? Maria?"

A few seconds passed.

"They picked someone else to be in their room."

For some reason I wasn't processing what she was saying. "I don't understand, pumpkin. I thought you girls have been planning this for years."

No response.

"They picked someone from their new group of friends."

"What new friends? I thought this was already decided? Did they say why?"

No response.

"Should I call their moms and see what's up?"

"No," she said. "It's okay."

"No it's not. You guys have been talking about this trip since elementary school. What's up? I know you haven't been seeing the girls as much lately, but…"

"It's okay really," Jenny interjected.

And then she said something that stopped me in my tracks.

"Maybe if I go with someone who doesn't know me she will like me for who I am."

Those words cut through me. What I knew in my heart finally reached my brain. "But honey, these girls are supposed to be your friends."

"It's okay Mama, really." And off she went to her room.

For the next few days I thought and thought over the last year. The girls who had befriended her throughout her childhood, who had slept over, who had been in her Girl Scout troop and vacationed with us, had denied Jenny their company lately. Not inviting her to parties, not returning calls, embarrassing her in public. My heart cried for her as she always made excuses for them. I couldn't get my head around it.

A truly sweet, giving girl, Jenny had always looked out for the underdog—for the girl who was sad because she had lost her dog, for the boy whose parents denied him attention, for the girl whose mom passed away. She constantly was helping others. The whole thing didn't make sense.

That weekend I was at a baseball game when I saw Maria's mom, Barb, who was also a friend of mine. I went over to her. "Barb, can I ask you something?" She looked at me with huge Bambi eyes that surprisingly were filling with tears.

"I wanted to ask if everything was okay between Maria and Jenny."

Before I could get another word in, she started to cry.

"I am so sorry, Anna. I am so embarrassed. I just didn't know what to do."

"What are you talking about, Barb?"

"The girls. The party in seventh grade."

"What party?"

"At Alex's house. "

I was totally lost. And then she explained.

A popular girl named Trish invited a mixture of old elementary school friends and new middle school girls to a party at Alex's house. Anyone invited felt honored. And even though Jenny was best friends with Maria and Alex, she was not invited. The girls held a vote and decided not to talk to Jenny. Trish had dictated that no one was to return Jenny's calls or invite her to the movies or parties. Jenny was like the plague and as such, if any girl were to be seen with her, she would catch the same disease.

Unbelievable. I would never have believed it if this mom, a friend, hadn't heard it from the mother who hosted the party.

"I am so sorry. Even though Maria hasn't been outright mean, she has stood by and has done nothing to defend Jenny lately. She just let the girls act that way. I know that is just as bad. I just didn't know what to do."

Thinking back, Maria had been nice to Jenny, but kept her distance in public. Working on projects at our house they giggled like close friends, but out in the world there was a distinct line. Evidently study alliances were permitted because school demanded it.

Even more unbelievable to me was that a grown woman, a friend no less, could stand by and do nothing. Maybe by being a friend to me and advising me of the situation, we might have learned something that would have helped the girls adapt.

"I am so embarrassed for how Maria acted, Anna."

"Please don't be embarrassed for your daughter," I replied. "Maria is a good girl. You should be embarrassed for yourself."

The years have passed. In many ways it was harder for me to get past the hurt so Jenny could move on. And move on she did. Jenny has grown up to be the most caring, understanding adult. As painful as those years were for her, she came out of them a strong, confident woman who has chosen a career in which she can help young people grow self-esteem and confidence.

~Anna Koopman

The Buffy Tree

Change always comes bearing gifts.
~Price Pritchett

When I was a contrary, hardheaded teenager, my mother often said, "I hope one day you have a daughter just like you!"

"One day" came twice. I was assigned not one, but two daughters just like me. Their teen years were hard, for them and for me. Every decision was a potential minefield.

I decided to avoid any decisions at Christmastime. There were too many battles. Instead, we would have "traditions."

My traditional menu for Christmas brunch was set in stone: grits and eggs, homemade biscuits, country ham and onion sausage. The Christmas mantel had to be decorated with pineapples and white candles, cedar boughs and Nandina berries. Every Christmas Eve and Christmas morning, we had Christmas punch: equal parts apple and cranberry juice, perked through spiced apple and pineapple rings with cinnamon sticks.

The traditional tree? Cedar, of course. My grandmother always had a cedar, and the sharp smell of cedar was as much a part of my childhood holidays as hanging a stocking on the mantel, swirling sparklers on the porch, or watching *Miracle on 34th Street* on TV. Christmas wouldn't be Christmas without a cedar.

Would it?

The year we moved our family of teenagers to a new home, Buffy rode with me to Buck Cockrell's tree farm to pick out a tree. At the time she was fourteen—every bit as contrary and hardheaded as her grandmother wished her to be.

I asked to see a tall cedar that would scrape the ceiling of our "new" living room. Buffy asked to see anything but a cedar.

"Cedar stinks, the needles stick, and the ooze is icky," she said, folding her arms across her chest.

"My grandmother always had a cedar tree, and cedar smells like Christmas to me. It's a tradition!" I said, folding my arms across my chest. The wind blew cold through the firs and the cedars. I stood my ground; she stood hers.

If ever World War III erupts, my vote for mediator goes to "Mr. Buck." He ever so gently arranged a mother-daughter truce. If we wanted, he said, we could decide to have both a cedar and a fir.

It was an uneasy ceasefire, but the U.N. peacekeeping forces were otherwise engaged.

The trees arrived later in the day, and I insisted that my cedar be set in the living room. I relegated Buffy's fir to the den by the back door, where the cold winds blow.

I further insisted (according to tradition) that the cedar be decorated with ornaments from previous years: the silver drum from a high school band party... the carolers I decoupaged when Henry was in law school and we had no money... the yarn-haired, toilet-paper-roll angel that Walter Munson made in kindergarten....

As for Buffy's fir? She'd have to make do.

At first, it irritated me that she did so well. She salvaged some lights from the magnolia tree in the front yard of our old house. She bought boxes of candy canes, hung them on the tree, and voila!

Okay, the tree was sweet and sort of pretty. I could get used to it, but as for liking it? No way. I wondered: how could a child of mine not want a cedar? It's tradition.

Just because I'm contrary and hardheaded doesn't mean I can't learn. One afternoon before Christmas I was baking in the kitchen when several of Buffy's friends dropped by for a visit. When they left an hour or so later, I overheard Buffy speak to them at the back door: "Hey, take a candy cane for everybody at your house."

They were hesitant about un-decorating her tree, "Oh, no..."

"Oh, yeah," she insisted. "Take a little Christmas home with you."

They demurred but at last she grabbed a fistful of candy canes and pressed them into the hands of her friends. "Here, and tell everybody we said Merry Christmas!"

Take a little Christmas home with you.

Tell everybody we said Merry Christmas.

As I heard those words, shame flushed my face. Maybe Buffy isn't like me, after all. For sure, her tree was not like mine. My cedar was about the past; her fir was about the present. Buffy's vision of Christmas was not limited by tradition, but was focused on the present and on the spirit of the season—on the spirit of giving.

And what a joy it is.

Every year since, we've had a Buffy tree by the back door, decorated with candy canes. Some years we have a star on top, some years not. It may be decorated with Life Savers, candy canes, or old-fashioned peppermint. Whatever I can find, it doesn't matter.

What does matter is that our guests and family—over the holidays—take a little Christmas home with them,

With her generosity of spirit, my daughter taught her hardheaded mother to see Christmas in a new and lovely light.

~Sue Summer

Chapter
10

Parenthood

Love Conquers All

You don't really understand human nature unless you know why a child on a merry-go-round will wave at his parents every time around — and why his parents will always wave back.

~William D. Tammeus

Worth the Wait

When you look at your life, the greatest happinesses are family happinesses.
~Dr. Joyce Brothers

I accepted Bruce's invitation to dinner at his house with a tiny bit of discomfort. This time, his children were going to be there, too. I'd met Megan, Brent and Kevin once before at a picnic. But my sister and her family were also there so I wasn't alone with them. This time it would be obvious Bruce and I were a couple. I was uncertain how the children might react to that idea.

The weather was unusually hot, even for July. Bruce wanted to keep it casual but thought we needed something to do so we wouldn't be sitting around staring at one another. He decided we could wash our cars. Playfully spraying one another with the hose kept us all cool and provided the diversion we needed. Everything seemed to be running smoothly and I was beginning to relax.

Bruce had planned bacon, lettuce and tomato sandwiches for dinner and Megan insisted on cooking the bacon. I was a little skeptical about letting a nine-year-old work with hot bacon grease, but Bruce said she'd be fine. Even so, I went inside to supervise.

The aroma of maple bacon already filled the room. Seizing the opportunity to avoid her father's censorship, Megan wasted no time commencing her own agenda. The questions came quickly. Did I have a husband? Kids? What kind of jobs had I had? Which one did I like best? Why? Where did I live? Did I like dogs? Had I ever owned any? I'd been in job interviews that were less comprehensive. I was amused and suggested I'd set the table while I answered her questions. Forgetting the kids had no idea I was familiar with the kitchen, I automatically went to the cabinet containing the plates. Four-year-old Kevin eyed me with suspicion.

"You don't have to steal those," he said.

Megan didn't notice my faux pas and began yelling at him for being rude. I was about to ask him for some clarification when she let out a yowl. Distracted by her annoyance with her brother she'd brushed the hot tongs against the bare skin of her thigh.

By the time Bruce and Brent came inside, I was finishing up the bacon and Megan was perched on a stool on the other side of the room cooling her burned leg.

"Nice job, Megan," cracked seven-year-old Brent, surveying the damage and shaking his head.

She'd barely paused my interview, so I knew the damage wasn't bad. Bruce took a cursory look and pronounced it "no big deal." Still, I wished it hadn't happened.

After dinner, the kids begged Bruce to pull out the projector so they could show me photos of "when they were little." I was curious, so I went along with the idea—until I understood which pictures they wanted me to see. They were combing through slide carousels in search of the photos that showed each of them being born! I had some friends who'd taken some pretty graphic photographs of their kids entering this world. I was definitely not prepared for that much information and began to squirm. Bruce and I exchanged stressed looks as he tried unsuccessfully to dissuade them. But they were so excited for me to see these particular photographs that I couldn't say no. I searched out a good spot to focus my eyes so I could look away without being obvious, but I didn't need to. Bruce quickly pulled most of the shots that included his ex-wife so he could focus on the individual photos of each child swaddled in pink or blue blankets. All three were convinced I'd taken in every detail and they were thrilled.

By the time we were married I had read every book our library had on stepfamilies. Most were about stepparents with full custody.

Our situation was much different. Bruce's ex and her husband lived nearby so the kids popped in and out unpredictably. One moment we were newlyweds and the next we were a family of five. By our first anniversary I was struggling. I'd had no problem moving to the house Bruce had shared with his first wife. In fact, I rather liked the cozy little Dutch Colonial. And it was the best possible situation for the kids as they still had loads of friends in the neighborhood. What I wasn't prepared for was the growing feeling that I didn't belong.

Bruce put everything he had into helping me feel comfortable. He let me redecorate the kitchen with beautiful hickory cabinets and new counter tops. He even gutted and tiled the upstairs bathroom for me, installing a wonderful jetted tub. He never questioned my ability to handle the kids. In fact, he had more faith in me than I did. Still, I couldn't shake off the feeling of not being part of the family. Every time they visited, the kids brought their memories of family life the way it used to be. I began to feel like I was the stand-in for the real mother as I listened to a running dialog of "remember when" stories. Initially, I'd found them interesting, encouraging their talk. But eventually, I felt myself closing down as soon as they started. I tried to control my increasing sadness and jealousy. I didn't want to be that person and I felt angry with myself for letting it get to me, for being so immature. I knew they had a life before I arrived. The fact that they wanted to talk about it shouldn't have been any surprise.

I wondered whether this feeling was normal, whether it would go away. I knew of no one else with this kind of experience. So I kept searching for answers in books. I don't remember where I read it, but I finally found the one line that hit home: "You need time to develop your own history."

I can't say that everything was immediately fine. I'm not especially patient so I still went into a funk for a while when the kids had one of their "remember when" visits. But instead of giving in to my feelings, I began planning things for us to do together. We started traditions like make-your-own pizza nights and New Year's Eve hors d'oeuvres parties. We had winter floor picnics—roasting hot dogs in the fireplace and gorging on devilled eggs and potato salad as we lounged on my old quilt spread on the living room floor. I searched out tree farms with horse drawn wagons where we could cut our Christmas trees. And I initiated story times, reading aloud to the kids, often as we snuggled together during raging thunderstorms.

All of a sudden, I began to hear stories about the time we went to the apple orchard where we'd seen beautiful dappled gray ponies pulling a wooden cart or the exciting day we got to meet my sister's new parrot, and I realized it had happened. We finally had our own history. It took time and patience. I don't remember exactly when it began. But I can tell you it was worth the wait.

~Barbara Ann Burris

Our Summer of Discontent

A father is a man who expects his son to be as good a man as he meant to be.
~Frank A. Clark

t was the summer of 1991 when we stopped having fun. My thirteen-year-old son was spending vacation with me. We were heading out on a backpacking trip, driving along a bumpy section of dirt road in the Trinity Alps Wilderness Area, searching for the trailhead. Micah was playing one of his rap tapes. The music was loud, a rhythmic rattle of pounded metal slammed to the background by industrial-strength guitar chords. The song was about shooting cops and holding up 7-Eleven stores. I distinctly heard the singer scream the f-word. I hit the eject button.

"Let's see if we can find a different song," I said.

Micah did not enjoy having his music evaluated by me, and he let it be known. I let it be known right back that I did not intend to listen to that kind of trash in my car. It was the first day of vacation and we were already at odds with one another.

As the week wore on the situation grew worse. Micah complained about the food, griped about camp chores and argued when I tried to have a simple conversation with him. When he wasn't arguing with me, he simply wasn't speaking.

I would like to blame our ruined camping trip on my son's poor taste in music, but that was only a small part of the problem. He had arrived for the summer looking as committed to bad times as a death-row convict. He was skinnier than when I saw him last and his hair had been cut in some new, dopey-looking, punk style. Micah wore a permanent scowl and walked with his shoulders slumped. When I spoke to him, he rolled his eyes and gave me a why-don't-you-get-off-my-back look, which would become habitual.

To say that my son withdrew from me that year would have been the greatest of understatements. He disappeared in all ways but physically, his personality vanishing so completely it was as if his life suddenly went on remote control.

Was this the same boy who had visited me last year? The vulnerable and sincere child who respected his parents, worked hard in school, and loved sports? The caring kid who enjoyed nature and brought home stray animals on a regular basis? Was this my child? And if so, how did he change so fast?

That summer turned out to be only the beginning of my son's troubles. Over the next several years his behavior would travel way beyond the pall of wise-guyism or healthy adolescent rebellion. Micah would run away from home, overdose on drugs, and spend countless hours in counseling. His mother would change their phone number, then their address, then her place of employment and the city in which they lived. She would do that so many times in a fruitless search for a safe, drug-free neighborhood. And I would dump my son's entire college savings on a private school that specialized in dealing with troubled kids, only to watch him be expelled after only one week for unruly behavior.

During those adolescent years Micah would flunk out of a dozen schools and be kicked out of a dozen more. He would run counter to all authority, roaming at will in and out of his mother's house, moving through life as if it were little more than an extended trip to the mall, picking through it for drugs and parties.

And I would be stranded almost a thousand miles away, wondering what was happening to my son. Was he still alive? And if he was alive, was he already out of reach? Would he ever turn his life around, or would he simply turn into another street bum and kill himself with an overdose of drugs? God only knows, right?

Who was to blame for Micah's problems? I had no idea. I wanted to help my son. I wanted to tell him to get off drugs, go back to school and start showing his mother respect. I wanted to instruct him to stop acting like a spoiled child and start acting like a man. I wanted to say all those things and more, but during our short time together I tried not to quiz or anger Micah.

I remembered before the divorce, when we were a family and Micah was playing in the yard and stumbled over a yellow-jacket nest. I was in the garage when I heard him cry. I ran out to find yellow jackets swarming around him like an angry halo. I ran to him, swatting at the wasps with my hands, picking them off his skin and hair. He'd been stung a dozen times and I was stung numerous times myself. We ran into the house and slammed the door shut.

"Everything's going to be okay," I had told him that day, nine years earlier. I spoke those same words, willing Micah and myself to believe them as we drove home from our camping trip. Back to civilization and whatever would await us.

It's a natural instinct for a father to want to save his son. Which is to say when a boy begins to tumble at a headlong rate, a father feels it is his duty to catch him before he reaches bottom. But I was unable to provide that help. My parenting was limited to a few weeks of summer vacation. I would suffer Micah's problems with him once a year and then watch him depart.

It took a long time, but my son did turn his life around. At age nineteen he became involved in a church group. Not long after that he gave up drugs, went back to school and got his GED. He began taking better care of himself and eating right.

Today, Micah is a far healthier, happier version of his old self. He cares about life and about those around him. He graduated from college and works for a non-profit organization, feeding homeless people.

It may not seem like much to parents with children who have led more conventional lives, but to me Micah's transformation was a true miracle. My son went to the edge and didn't like what he saw. I'm so thankful he decided to come back.

~Timothy Martin

Bliss Happens

It doesn't hurt to be optimistic. You can always cry later.
~Lucimar Santos de Lima

n 1997, when Valerie was seven years old, I decided to take her to New York to see my sister Nancy. We made our plans months in advance. Valerie was young, but extremely bright, and I knew she would take in a lot—Manhattan would be a notable experience for her. I was greatly looking forward to spending this time with her and my sister.

The big day in early December finally came. Our flight was uneventful and Valerie had considerable fun on board with her crayons, puzzles, and the in-flight headset. Then we landed at La Guardia. As we walked through the airport, Valerie held her favorite stuffed animal, "Bunny," and I carried the luggage. We stopped by the restrooms, and I waited outside while she went to the ladies' room. When she was finished, we left the terminal building, hailed a taxi, and began our trip into the city in the cold drizzle that is typical for New York in December.

Traffic was moderately heavy. About a half-hour into our trip, when we were almost to Manhattan, Valerie exclaimed, "I forgot Bunny!"

I said, "What do you mean?"

"I left Bunny in the airport."

"Where in the airport?"

"In the ladies' room, I think."

"Oh, Val," I said. "It's already been a half-hour. Hundreds of people have gone in and out of that bathroom. Bunny's gone."

"No," she said, on the verge of a great cry, "we've got to go back and get Bunny."

I carefully explained that even if we returned to the airport immediately, there was little chance that her stuffed rabbit would still be there. If we asked the driver to turn around and go back, our ride would cost three times as much and we would miss meeting my sister. If someone had turned in Bunny to a lost and found, whenever we returned to search for him would make no difference.

Logic was earning me no points, and more miles had passed. I made a parental decision. We were going to continue riding to Manhattan. Misconnecting with my sister (these being pre-cell phone days for us) would be one too many disasters in the same morning. Valerie broke into audible sobs. I felt I could console her as I had done successfully so many times before, but this, it dawned on me, was an unprecedented situation. To my dismay, she continued to weep, uncontrollably, for the rest of the ride.

We arrived in Manhattan, met my sister—Valerie's only aunt—and Valerie was noticeably happier. We made our way to the top of the Empire State Building. Then, looking at the rain-covered, bird's-eye view of the nation's biggest city, Valerie couldn't overcome losing Bunny. She resumed her sobbing.

One long elevator ride later, we found a bank of phone booths on the ground floor of the building. On the phone, Valerie explained to her mother what had happened. I called La Guardia Airport and discovered there was no all-in-one phone number. I was seeking to find someone, anyone, who could hunt for the bunny. I shoved in an endless round of quarters. My stress was building as one call after another yielded no results, and the room in which we stood seemed to become busier and noisier. Valerie was still distraught.

I left as many messages as I could to airport and airline officials far and wide. Then I explained to Valerie that people were searching for Bunny all over the airport. I attempted every legitimate maneuver I could conjure up to take her mind off the search. We walked through the first-floor shops. We watched a band play in the lobby.

I came to realize that the grief Valerie felt for Bunny was the same emotion adults feel when they lose a loved one. Still, when we took a picture in front of a lobby replica of the building itself, Valerie composed herself and broke out a toothy grin. I could tell she was trying to be brave and to enjoy the trip despite her loss. It was important, however, to honor Valerie's feelings: that losing Bunny was unthinkable. I didn't want her to suppress her feelings for the sake of approval by grown-ups.

We were to depart the city on Sunday morning, and I promised Valerie we would look for Bunny first thing at the airport. I could picture her mother who, unbeknownst to Valerie, was frantically searching for a Bunny replacement. Sue found and called the manufacturer about the stuffed animal, but the company simply didn't make them anymore. It was a valiant effort, although I already knew that no other toy could replace Bunny. Like a hopeful child, I too wanted to believe we would find him.

Saturday passed rather well. Valerie broke into sobs once in the late morning and once in the evening, deeply lamenting the loss of Bunny. Our day was filled with the sights and sounds, and smells, of the city. We took the full city tour, climbed to the top of "Miss Liberty," and picnicked in Central Park just south of the reservoir.

Sunday morning finally came. We bade my sister farewell and rode to the airport hours before our flight, so early that the long corridors were nearly empty. It was a huge airport with construction in progress and not so easy for retracing steps.

We finally found and checked the bathroom where Bunny had last been seen. No Bunny. Then we examined countertops, ledges, luggage carts, and seemingly every place that a toy rabbit could hide.

We asked the first airport employee we saw where to find lost objects. He pointed us down a long hall in the next building. We walked for quite a stretch — it had to be nearly a ten-minute hike — but for Valerie it was no labor. We were on the Bunny trail, and nothing else mattered. Secretly, I was dreading the possibility that Bunny was gone forever. I knew we were running out of options.

When we reached what seemed to be our destination, it appeared less than promising. Through a crack in the door, we could see a light on in a small, dingy room where apparently dust mops feared to tread. We walked in to find no one there. Then, a woman emerged from a door in the back of the room.

Valerie described the situation at length, and the lady said she'd do what she could. She went back through the same door from which she had come. Valerie followed her to where she could see down a small hallway-like closet. The woman walked a few paces to some metal shelves. She picked up the object most resembling Valerie's description but grimaced slightly, unsure if this was the valued prize. Then Valerie shouted, "THERE'S BUNNY!" Sure enough, Bunny had been "resting" on one of the shelves.

The woman handed over the toy rabbit to an ecstatic young girl. I was stupefied. I am a positive thinker by nature and had been hoping for the best but preparing for the worst. If that shelf had been bereft of Bunny, undoubtedly some of the real work of fatherhood would surely have followed.

In my newfound glee, I thought to myself, "This is like a storybook ending. We lost; we found. Whew!" Would she have otherwise dreaded New York or plane trips or airports forevermore? Would our bond have been weakened?

We strode sprightly from the dingy room to an airport now buzzing with life. Passengers had started arriving. Vendors had opened up shop. Porters were handling luggage. Vending machines and pushcarts and luggage carousels made their merry mechanical noises.

We phoned in the spectacular news to Val's mom, who seemed equally elated. We had nearly two hours to kill, but on such a special morning it didn't matter. My apple spice muffin and Valerie's plain bagel yielded abnormally high levels of edible contentment.

On the return flight, Valerie clung to Bunny with an intensity I hadn't previously witnessed. The one time she went to the restroom, she told me to hold Bunny "with both hands" until she got back.

When we landed, her mother greeted us at the airport as if we had made our way back from across the Atlantic. Sue had heroically located a substitute rabbit from a local vendor that looked somewhat like the first one. Valerie named the second stuffed rabbit "Sunny," as in "Sunny Bunny," and to this day, six years later, she has both of them, though Bunny is still, by far, her favorite.

Probably every other parent has a "Bunny" story. Nine times out of ten, you aren't going to find that rabbit again. Nine times out of ten, it's going to be a sad story. This one turned out sublime. Days following our New York trip, I talked with friends about the episode, and one said, "Look, she's seven years old. Let her believe in Santa Claus and the Easter Bunny and that stuffed animals stay faithful to their owners. She'll have different experiences soon enough." So I offered no resistance to Valerie's belief in all that's good about life.

In the weeks and even months that followed, Valerie basked in the happiness of having her Bunny—her nighttime companion, the daily guardian of her bedroom, her unerringly faithful friend. Who was I to throw a damper on the wonders of life? Grace happens. Bliss happens. Bunnies return.

~Jeff Davidson

Do-Over

The beauty of "spacing" children many years apart lies in the fact that parents have time to learn the mistakes that were made with the older ones—which permits them to make exactly the opposite mistakes with the younger ones.

~Sydney J. Harris

One warm afternoon in late spring, I stood and watched a dark head bobbing down the school bus steps through the driver's window. As my little girl reached the last step and disappeared from view, my heart filled with gratitude, not only in anticipation of the hug that was soon to come, but for the great blessing I'd been given. After surviving the rough years of raising my children, after nearly a decade of enjoying my grandchildren, after I was certain I'd finished with the daily business of motherhood, I was given a do-over.

I had been a young mother. My own mother died when I was only nine and I longed for a complete family. I had my first son when I was nineteen, a second son at twenty-four, and a daughter three years later. However, my mother's absence had left me with a knowledge gap. It was like the time we moved a month into second grade and they'd already introduced multiplication at the new school. I was always a step behind, always uncertain about whether I was doing things right. I read a lot of parenting books and the advice conflicted sometimes, and at other times there was no advice for the problem I was trying to solve. I made a lot of mistakes, but somehow I survived... we all did.

I survived my firstborn's early years. Joey was big for his age, and very independent. Before the age of two, he could climb out of his crib. One morning I woke up to an acrid smell wafting up the stairs from the kitchen. I hurried down when I noticed Joey wasn't sleeping in his bed. A burner was on and there was a frying pan on the stove. The floor was littered with grains of raw rice. Turning off the burner, I saw what was making the awful smell—in the pan there were burning grains of rice and an egg still in its shell. I went to the living room in search of the hungry culprit.

My heart sank to the pit of my stomach when I saw the front door standing wide open. "Joey!" I screamed his name and ran outside barefoot in my pajamas. I found him a few doors down, wearing only a diaper and playing in a puddle of dirty water. I scooped him up and carried him home, relief mixed with mortification at the stares from my neighbors. From then on, I learned to sleep with one eye open. There were other heart-stopping adventures, but we survived.

I wasn't sure I'd survive John's teenage years. My second son was much easier than his brother had been as a young child. But he made up for it as a teenager. By thirteen he'd already begun to experiment with alcohol and drugs. I was a teacher, and the middle school truant officer who came to my house looking for my son was also my principal's husband. He got in trouble with the law. I'd never had a traffic ticket and now I was sitting in courtrooms and talking with probation officers and lawyers. They knew us at the emergency room because of all the times I brought him in with wounds or alcohol poisoning. For five years, my son's bipolar disorder held us hostage. But with persistence and faith, we survived that, too.

My third child, Lynne, was easy compared to the boys. But I was always waiting for the other shoe to drop. I was so involved with the demands of her brothers, that I fear I neglected her. Lynne cried about having to grow up. She wanted to stay little, and, to be honest, I wished she would, too. She was right about adulthood being a challenge. She followed her heart when a more practical choice would have led to an easier life, but I raised her to believe that love trumps comfort. Happiness is being grateful for what you have—you can always choose to be happy. Love, on the other hand, is a gift from heaven that should not be overlooked.

By the time I was forty-eight, my kids were grown. The boys were married to girls I loved and had families of their own. Lynne was in college and seriously in love for the first time. I had close, loving relationships with my children and I delighted in being a grandma. It was my turn now, so I resigned my job at the big, urban school district where I'd taught for twenty-five years, moved to a cozy apartment in one of the "ten best places to live," and accepted a dream teaching assignment in a small school district. Joey and his family moved nearby. Within a year Lynne came too. I had no unfinished business, no regrets, and no empty nest. My life was perfect. I looked forward to travel and the independent life of a single woman.

A few months into my new life, I met a widower with a three-year-old. Remembering my motherless childhood, my heart went out to Jim and Maya, and ignoring the warning signs, I dove headlong into friendship. I admired Jim's strength and optimism. He had loved his wife dearly throughout the twenty-five years of their life together. Her sudden death had left him bereft, but I never heard the slightest hint of self-pity in his voice. I remember the day we looked at each other in disbelief as we realized we were falling in love. Neither of us had expected to ever feel these feelings again, but there it was.

Still, I hesitated when Jim asked me to marry him and be Maya's mommy. I'd been ready to devote myself completely to my teaching. I was looking forward to summers traveling the world. I thought of the tears, uncertainties, and anguish of raising my children. But I also recalled the joy I'd known holding my babies, playing with them, and watching them grow. I remembered little hands in mine, reading stories at bedtime, and love notes with "I love you Mommy" scrawled in shaky crayon letters. Nothing I had done with my life had been more meaningful, important, or gratifying than the work of being a mother. Nothing had brought me more joy. And this time I knew what I was doing; there would be no knowledge gap. This time motherhood would be easy. I married Jim, and Maya became mine.

I smiled to myself. My eyes landed on my young daughter as she rounded the corner of the bus. Then my smile faded and my heart sank. Somewhere between this morning's goodbye and now, Maya had changed into the too short, spaghetti-strapped dress she knew was forbidden for school. "Lord help me," I thought to myself, "she's only six!" None of the other three ever tried that! I took a deep breath, pasted the smile back on my face and went to hug my daughter, knowing that whatever came up, we would survive.

~M. Cristina Ruiz

A Shelter in the Storm

Son, you outgrew my lap, but never my heart.
~Author Unknown

"Where is Tyler?" I asked my son's friend, Haven, trying not to sound upset. My fifteen-year-old son, Tyler, was disappointing me again. And, as usual, I was trying to not think the worst of him.

"Um, he's back at the campsite," she answered, uneasily.

We stood for a while on the slope of the hill, listening to the band playing on the stage, before Haven excused herself to join Tyler. As the sun went down, changing the rolling outline of the distant mountains from green to dark olive, I wrestled with my hurt feelings.

I reminded myself that I was blessed to be camping with my two sons at a resort in New Hampshire, during the peak of summer, attending an awesome four-day Christian music festival. So what if the family bonding moments I had envisioned weren't happening? Even before the car left our driveway to begin the trip, the iPods and earplugs came out, so then "out" went the nice chats I imagined we'd be having. And no sooner had we set up our tents then the kids took off on their own. I would text them over and over again until I finally got a text back saying "We're at the other stage" or "We're getting something to eat." Okay, they did join me on my blanket, once in a while. And I didn't expect them to be by my side the whole time.

But I was getting exasperated with Tyler.

When we set up his tent close to the rest of us he decided to sleep in the car across the street.

When the music groups that I wanted him to experience were performing he was not around to hear.

And when he was with me, I cringed at his rudeness.

Bringing up three other children before this, I knew about the seasons when your child turns into a hostile stranger and you, the parent, feel like an alien. It seems that you can't do or say anything right, attempts at communication are met with stony silence from the teenager, or answered by grunts, possibly combined with looks of disgust.

I had lived through this teenage angst with his older siblings—Naomi, Sarah and Joshua—and learned not to take it personally. But the trouble Tyler had been getting into at school and at home caused me to fear at times that something was serious wrong. I would defend him against any criticism and insist on believing the best of him, yet at the same time wondered if I had lost him. Had I somehow, as his mother, failed him?

As Haven disappeared into the crowd, I put on a brave smile and sat down on my blanket. I tried not to admit the humbling truth that she had probably made an appearance out of respect or sympathy for me. She and Tyler both knew that on this, the final night of the festival, I had really wanted them to join me. The more I brooded over this the sadder I became. Had my son shut me off completely? He obviously had no compassion for others, not even for me. What was he doing? Something illegal?

Dark clouds moved in over the hills, and a light drizzle began. My favorite band, Switchfoot, began playing. The music was inspiring, the light show mesmerizing. I clapped and sang along, but my heart was heavy. Then there was a loud thunderclap and it started pouring. Some of the crowd folded up their chairs, picked up their blankets and scurried under the huge canvas tents lined up at the base of the mountain. Other people opened their umbrellas or stood under large plastic tarps. One family invited me to join them under their tarp, but I declined, choosing to stand stoically under my own umbrella.

Then a figure ran up the hill and stopped beside me. I was surprised to see it was Tyler. I shifted the umbrella to include him.

"I came back for you," he said. "It's really pouring. Do you want to go to the tents?"

"No, I think I'll stay here. It's slowing down a little already," I said. "But you should go if you want."

Instead he took the umbrella from my hands, and held it over us. As we stood together watching the show I felt the presence of my son with a kind of awe. I felt his love. As the rain stopped and the stars appeared in the sky, I realized that I had been given a gift—I had glimpsed the true nature of my teenage son's heart. And I knew that I didn't have to worry—my son was going to be just fine.

~Donna R. Paulson

DNA Stands for "Does Not Apply"

If the family were a fruit, it would be an orange, a circle of sections,
held together but separable — each segment distinct.
~Letty Cottin Pogrebin

"**H**ow would you guys feel if we got married?" Eric and I asked our children in early 2007. Our his-and-hers kids, who ages ranged from twelve to four, were thrilled. They actually happy danced.

So that summer, Eric and I took the plunge. We had a small wedding, with our children as our only attendants. We went on a Caribbean cruise—sans children—but the day we returned, our ready-made family began.

While talking with the kids one evening, I was struggling with how to refer to my new husband. "Eric, I mean, Dad," I stumbled. Finally, I looked at my children and said, "From now on, I'm just going to call Eric 'Dad' when I'm talking to all of you. You don't have to call him that, but it'll be easier if I do."

To my surprise, four-year-old Julia said, "But can we? If we want to?" And seven-year-old Lea piped up, "Can I call you 'Mom?'"

So it was settled. Eric and I became Dad and Mom, and we tossed biology out the window.

We were determined to become a blended family where biology simply didn't matter. We decided that we would love all four of the kids the same, no matter whose blood ran in their veins. We even joked that DNA was no longer the acronym for deoxyribonucleic acid. In our family, DNA now stood for "Does Not Apply." Loving the children equally, regardless of their genes, was the key to making our situation a success.

For a while, our just-ignore-biology philosophy actually worked. And Eric and I could hardly believe how easy it was. "This blended family thing is a piece of cake," we decided.

Since I had my stuff so completely together, I decided to use my infinite wisdom as a brand-new stepmom to help other women in my shoes. I put my writing skills to work on a magazine article. I interviewed two "experts," both of whom had written a book on blended families. The first one I talked to was a really well known author, and I asked him how to successfully blend two families. His response was, "Blended families don't blend. They collide." Yikes.

The female author I interviewed gave just as bleak a picture. "Being a stepmother is the most difficult and thankless job on the planet," she told me. "Stepmoms do a lot of the work in raising the children, but the biological mother gets all the love. No matter what you do or how much you give, you'll always be second to her." Ouch. That one hurt. A lot.

Their advice wasn't what I wanted to hear, so I ignored it. I wrote the article using only the quotes I liked—the Pollyanna ones that said, "If you love each other enough, everything will work out just fine." The article sold and was even reprinted several times, but I'm not sure it really helped anyone. Including—or maybe, especially—me.

Shortly after school started, it was my stepdaughter Lea's turn to be the Star Student in her classroom. She was supposed to take in pictures of her family, and a family member was invited to school for the afternoon. Eric had to work, as did her biological mom, so I became the available family member.

When I arrived at school, Lea introduced me as her mom. Things were going really well until the pictures Lea had brought started circulating the room. "Who is in this picture?" A kid would ask, holding up a picture of Lea's biological mother. I could tell Lea felt uncomfortable with the question. After all, she'd already introduced me as her mom.

And things got worse after the kids began to ask me questions. "What was Lea's first word?" one girl asked me. Another said, "What was Lea's favorite food when she was a baby?"

"How should I know?" I felt like saying. "I've only known her for eight months!" Instead, I stumbled along, finally admitting that I was Lea's "other mom," and I hadn't known her when she was a baby.

When I finally owned up to my "other mom" status, the kids lost interest in asking me questions. "But I know lots of things about Lea," I wanted to say. "I might not know whether she preferred strained peas or pureed sweet potatoes as a baby, but I know she likes sour cream and onion potato chips and that her favorite color is green."

But the kids didn't care. Their message was loud and clear: You're not her real mom and therefore, you aren't important. In other words, biology matters.

In the car on the way home, I apologized to Lea and said, "I hope you weren't too embarrassed."

She shrugged and said, "It doesn't matter. I was just glad one of my parents could make it today."

One of her parents. That's how Lea thought of me. I smiled to myself and decided that despite everything, I'd count the day as a win.

By that Christmas, I was pregnant. When Baby Nathan was born, the kids were as proud of him as Eric and I were.

Nathan's biology was an often-visited topic in our family. One day, Lea said, "Nathan is the only person in our family who is related to everyone else in our family."

"Yes, that's true," I said. "He has a little part of each one of us."

"Nathan is like a little string that ties our family together," she said.

"That's an awful lot to expect of a baby," I said with a smile.

She grinned back and said, "Yeah, you're right. It's a good thing we've already got something to tie us together."

"Oh, yeah? What's that?"

She gave me a funny look and then said, "Well, duh. We love each other, Mom."

I've learned that biology does matter and pretending that it doesn't only complicates things.

Yes, biology matters, but not nearly as much as love.

~Diane Stark

"Finally! We have enough players
for a team!"

You Gotta Be Cool in Middle School

You can tell a child is growing up when he stops asking where he came from and starts refusing to tell where he is going.

~Author Unknown

When you're in middle school, the need to look "cool" outweighs any desire to get good grades or please your parents. Social status is everything! So when my son, Dylan, asked to ride his bike to school, rather than be dropped off by his apparently "uncool" mom, I tried to consider his new status as a middle-schooler.

On the one hand, I was terrified of sending him off to school alone. I'd always been there to drop him off and watch him safely enter the school building. If he rode his bike, I wouldn't have that reassurance that he'd arrived safe and sound. What if he got hit by a car or accosted by a stranger? There was also bad weather to consider. Fortunately, middle school started at 9:00 a.m., so at least he wouldn't be riding in the dark.

On the other hand, I knew that I couldn't baby my son forever. He was a typical boy for his age, seeking independence and separation from his mother. At some point, I had to learn to "let go" and give him his wings, despite my fears for his safety. Besides, neither of us wanted him to be "that kid" whose mother was constantly hovering over him. Definitely not cool.

So, with fingers crossed and prayers said, I reluctantly told my son he could ride his bicycle to school. That gave me the title of "cool mom"—at least for a day or so. Everything went well until the day that Dylan temporarily lost his coolness....

As he described the scene to me later, he was just leaving the school on his bike at day's end when he was apparently distracted by the crowd around him. Other kids were streaming out of the school; cars were everywhere; people were shouting and laughing. Naturally, Dylan was checking out the sights around him instead of the path ahead. Suddenly—BAM!—he rode his bicycle straight into the side of a big metal newspaper box, knocking him to the ground!

Sheepishly, Dylan looked around to see if anyone had seen his misfortune. Due to the chaos, it appeared that his tumble hadn't been noticed by too many people. But it wasn't over yet. As he began to rise to his feet, Dylan spotted a police car parked on the other side of the street. The police officer in the car was looking right at Dylan. And then he raised his megaphone to his mouth:

"Are you all right, young man?" he bellowed across the street.

Hundreds of heads suddenly turned to see Dylan rising from his fallen bike, which had clearly had a collision with the newspaper box. Dylan's face turned red. He gave the officer a terse nod and the "okay" sign with his fingers, and then quickly hopped on his battered bike and rode as fast as the wind, never looking back.

"I was so embarrassed, Mom," my son told me that evening. "I'll definitely be watching where I go from now on!" Lesson learned.

And I learned a lesson, too. My son would most assuredly get into some scrapes as he traveled the road to independence, but he would get through it on his own. And, as often happens in middle school, Dylan's uncool incident was soon old talk as other kids managed to embarrass themselves in various ways. Thankfully, Dylan and I both survived middle school!

~Susan M. Heim

86

Just a Word

When the world says, "Give up," Hope whispers, "Try it one more time."
~Author Unknown

Our son Brendan was born in 2003, and he was the perfect manifestation of our love for each other. His deep dimple and sparkling brown eyes made me melt. Then I began to notice a change in him at about eighteen months. The handful of words he was speaking stopped. His eyes no longer sparkled. He was diagnosed with autism.

I felt as if we lived on a lonely island. His behaviors were so drastic that we were no longer welcome at restaurants—and play dates with neurotypical peers and their moms had become impossible. I began focusing on the "why me?" question constantly.

One day, as I tearfully reviewed every possible cause of our son's loss of language and connectedness, my loving husband finally said, "It doesn't matter how it happened; we love him exactly as he is. Autism is just a word—the important thing is that it is now our life's work to do everything we can to ensure that he reaches his potential. That is our job. Spending our time wondering why this happened or being sad is not helpful to him. We need to be together on this; we need to fight for him every day. Put your energy into the fight; we have to do this for him."

Wow. It wasn't about me. It was an epiphany of sorts, that moment with Tom.

Thus, the fight began. It was time to get off the lonely island

and reach out to my sweet little Brendan. I was going to make it my mission to do everything possible to give him what he needed to be as happy and comfortable as possible, and I made a pledge to myself that I would never lose sight of the possibility that he would one day speak again. Tom was my inspiration in that—he always believed—and we worked tirelessly from that point on.

We spent our days with strangers who quickly became family—speech therapists, special education teachers, occupational therapists, social workers—you name it. Most of them could barely pay their bills because they were so underpaid, and yet they were the highest class of people we had ever met. They were extraordinary and gave us all the love and support we needed, along with our families and our dearest friends.

And, despite the fact that he was unresponsive, I told Brendan each and every day, many times a day, "I love you deeper than the sea." I knew I might never get a response, but I said it anyway. Our team encouraged us to keep talking to him, despite the fact that he didn't respond. We narrated everything as we went about our day. It was emotionally brutal to do this with no response, day after day, but we did, because we love him. One day, they said, he just might respond, and it would all be worth it.

We learned sign language too. One day, he wanted more cereal, and so he popped his fingertips together repeatedly to tell us. A few months later, he did the same thing, signing "more" and even vocalizing it with a word, "mo." That moment was transformational. He wanted to communicate!

Every night during those years I kept saying it: "Brendan, I love you deeper than the sea." Then, one night, to my total surprise, he said it back. I cried tears of sheer delight, bliss, profound joy—and I realized that we were all going to be just fine. My heart swelled with gratitude, and yet, I also discovered that I had come to feel grateful for who he was, with or without the words. He was the center of our universe and, autism or not, he lit up our life and gave us meaning.

That was five years ago. Today, he is thriving in fourth grade with his peer group. We still experience meltdowns, and socialization has its challenges—but that seems to be the case for most children on some level. And, every night, before bed, he says, "Mommy, I love you deeper than the sea." And he sleeps, and my husband and I enjoy the celebratory glass of wine—another day of success. Success now not necessarily because of his development, but success because we have embraced him for who he is—he feels our love—and we feel his. And today, I ask, "why me?" but in a very different context; "Why me? How did I get so lucky to be the mom of a child with autism, who would teach me everything I need to know about hope, optimism, perseverance, and unconditional love?" What a gift to be the parent of a special needs child.

~Elisabeth Bailey

87

Two Makes a Family

It's hard growing up without a father,
but it's easy when you have a fantastic mother who plays both roles.
~Author Unknown

anny had been in kindergarten about two months when he brought home a note announcing that the next Friday would be Bring Your Father to Lunch day. Why a school feels it necessary to open that particular can of worms is beyond me, but there it was in black and white with a reminder at the bottom that adult lunches were $2.50 and to please notify the teacher in advance so she could plan for seating.

I called to let his teacher know that Danny would indeed have a guest for the lunch. I arrived at his class on the designated day. There were a few curious looks from other children in the class when I turned up, but Danny was perfectly at ease. We all went through the cafeteria line and then Danny and I sat down at a table with three little girls, two of whom had their fathers joining them for lunch as well. The little girl across from me chattered on and on about how her daddy would be there soon but that he was at work far away.

Without hesitating for an instant, the three little girls at our table (including the two whose daddies were sitting with them) handed Danny their milk cartons to be opened. It must have already been a well-worn ritual for him—several other children brought Danny their milk cartons to be opened during the course of our meal. I had to smile as I handed him my own milk carton. Trust Danny to come up with a way to be known. I could see him going off to college simply known as: "Danny, the Kid Who Opens the Milk Cartons!"

We all sat eating and chatting about school and bus riding versus car riding and who could tie their shoes all by themselves. Curiosity finally overcame the little girl across the table from me and she blurted out what had apparently been on her mind from the moment I had sat down at the table with them: "How come you're here and not Danny's daddy?"

The two fathers sitting at the table shuffled their feet and hands in turn and for some reason, it seemed as if the lunchroom chatter volume turned down a notch or two while this curious child awaited my answer. Danny didn't look up at me, but I knew from the angle of his head he was acutely tuned in and suddenly it seemed as if the entire room was waiting to hear my answer.

I looked at her and simply said, "Some families have lots of people — three or four, even five or six people. Sometimes even more. When they go out together, people always know they're a family because they walk together and laugh and talk with each other.

"Well, Danny and I do that also, but there is only him and me in our family, so we are a family of two. Sometimes God just plans it that way. Since we are a family of two, I get to be the mommy and the daddy — so I came to have lunch with Danny today."

I tried to sound as casual as possible so that the children, especially Danny, would know that being a family of two wasn't any different than being in a family of three or four or even six.

I heard several sighs let out and I slowly realized that several of the adults who were near us had been holding their breath while I explained about our family of two.

There may very well have been other mothers wearing the daddy shoes there at the school lunchroom that day, but I didn't see them. All I know is that when it was all said and done, my little boy was just fine with a mother at the father's day lunch. Which was all I was hoping for, really.

~Ginny Dubose

Chapter
11

Parenthood

Saying Thank You

Not what we give, but what we share,
For the gift without the giver is bare.

~James Russell Lowell

Making Friends with My Kitchen

Cooking is like love. It should be entered into with abandon or not at all.
~Harriet van Horne

I f you asked my son what his mom does best, you'd probably get an answer that relates to cooking. When his kindergarten teacher had the kids draw pictures of their moms as part of a Mother's Day gift, he drew me in the kitchen baking a birthday cake. For about six months, he kept inviting all of the neighborhood children over to sample my banana bread muffins—even on the days when I hadn't actually baked any muffins for breakfast! I have a note taped to my refrigerator that says, "Deer Mom. Yor fud is gud."

If you happened to ask me what I thought I did best, cooking would be pretty far down the list. Growing up, I viewed cooking as something hopelessly old-fashioned and not relevant to the life of the modern working woman. When I moved into my first apartment, I memorized the pizza delivery guy's phone number. Until we started having trouble coming up with money to pay all our bills, I figured restaurant meals were a well-deserved reward at the end of a long day. Why slave over a hot stove when Visa and MasterCard can come to your rescue?

Now, I cook from necessity. Hungry family + tight budget = being forced to become friends with my kitchen. When I made my son's birthday cake, it was because I didn't have the cash for a fancy bakery cake. When I made the muffins, it was because throwing away all the overripe bananas seemed like a ridiculous waste given our rather limited grocery budget. The meal that inspired the note on the refrigerator was actually an invented dish made from leftovers and random cans of stuff from my pantry.

One day, after getting particularly frustrated in the kitchen by a recipe that wouldn't turn out and a family that wanted food NOW, I decided to ask my son why he thought his mom was such a good cook. He thought about it for a while, furrowing his forehead as if I had asked him to find the solution to world peace. "Because you love us," he finally said as he reached over to give me a kiss on the cheek.

Yup. That works for me.

~Dana Hinders

89

The Day You Were Born

I would thank you from the bottom of my heart,
but for you my heart has no bottom.
~Author Unknown

"**W**here do you want to go to lunch today?" I asked our son Ben on his fourteenth birthday. He was seated at the kitchen table inhaling a second bowl of Frosted Flakes.

"How about Buffalo Wild Wings?" he responded between spoonfuls.

"Sounds good, do you want to take your presents with us?"

"Why can't I open them back here?" he asked.

"Because you're going to your mom's afterwards, remember?" I finished loading the dishwasher and sat down beside him as he drank the rest of the milk from the bowl, a habit I chose to ignore.

This sharing of birthdays and holidays was not unusual for him and his sister. Ben was just five years old when his father and I met. I can still recall his crooked little smile with several missing teeth. He was such a gentle soul and gave his love freely while his father and I were dating. Two years later, on our wedding day, he slid a heart shaped plastic ring under my bathroom door and shyly asked if I would wear it. This innocent gesture touched me so deeply that I nearly choked on grateful tears. A difficult medical history made it uncertain if I would ever have children but here I had been given the amazing opportunity to love and parent two children anyway. They were such wonderful little people and I knew that I was fortunate that they accepted me so quickly.

Bonding with Ben was not only easy, it was fun. We spent hours playing "Sardines," his favorite version of hide and seek, and his giggles upon finding him were contagious. He loved learning silly jokes and camp songs and I was thrilled to supply them. His creativity amazed me and his imaginative play always included wielding a sword or plastic gun as our faithful hero. But for as many times as he saved the universe on our behalf, it wasn't uncommon for him to sneak into our room during a thunderstorm or whisper quietly in my ear if he had wet the bed. He made me feel like a mother.

The boy that sat before me now was tall and thin with a hint of stubble appearing here and there on his chin, but his brown eyes were the same, and I knew if I looked deep enough I would see the little boy inside him.

When he returned from his mother's house he brought home a surprise. His mother had found the video of his birth and he wanted to share it with me. This may sound strange to others but his mom and I have a unique relationship. From the very beginning I respected her role as a mother and did all that I could to honor her position. It cannot be easy to share your kids with another woman but she was always gracious in doing so. The joint custody arrangement was a 50/50 schedule so communication was imperative. We frequently discussed issues regarding the kids and collaborated on decisions before taking action. Schedules were agreed upon in advance and we were mutually considerate regarding revisions. These things helped make our co-parenting relationship successful and allowed us to foster a friendship. But even still, this was a pretty private thing to share and I was torn between feeling honored and feeling intrusive.

My concern was alleviated as Ben shoved the old VHS tape into the player. He was excited to see it again and sat close to me on the couch. Soon images of my husband as a younger man appeared. At twenty-four he looked so young to be a father of two! Our sweet little Emily emerged at the scene as her two-year-old self and I marveled at recognizing expressions she still uses today. And when his mother filled the screen with her swollen belly I was reminded once again how the children began as a part of her.

I felt my admiration for her grow deeper as I realized that the life I live now, loving these children as my own, was in part made possible by her. Ben popped the video out once it was over and I gave him a long hug, whispering in his ear, "I'm so thankful for the day you were born." He returned my embrace with arms that were no longer a child's and I was grateful for who he was. Part of a man I loved and a woman I admired. While it wasn't my birthday, I knew that I was the one who had received a gift that day.

~Brenda Watterson

A Bad Hop

It's not whether you get knocked down, it's whether you get up.
~Vince Lombardi

I hit it easy on purpose. As both coach and father, I wanted my six-year-old's first ever Little League team practice to be a confidence builder, not a scary experience. Who would have guessed this simple father/son rite of passage would become so meaningful just five years later?

"Come on, Michael. Charge it! Get that glove down!"

My little tow-headed boy looked like a natural, running forward from second base, blue eyes beneath the bill of his too large baseball cap focused on the prize, bending his knees, making sure his glove was all the way down on the ground just like I taught him, his bare right hand ready to cover it when the ball entered his glove.

And then it happened....

As if in slow motion, that barely bouncing ball took a funny hop, jumped up, and popped Michael right in his cute little nose! I knew it wasn't moving fast enough to cause any real injury, but after a moment's surprise, the tears started to flow.

Think fast, Coach. Last year, Michael fell when trying to ride a two-wheeler. Now he's afraid to even get close to one. And all those six-year-old first time ballplayers were watching, traumatized that this could happen to them. The last thing we needed was fifteen kids afraid of the ball. It was time for some quick talking re-direction.

"That's why we always charge ground balls, guys. The fewer the bounces, the less chance of a bad hop. But by using his body to keep the ball in front of him, Michael still had time to throw that guy out at first! Way to go, Michael!"

I scanned the faces. Their attention was off my son and on me. Michael had even stopped crying, the praise heaped upon him in front of his peers perhaps eclipsing the shock of the baseball bopping him in the nose.

I handed the bat to another coach and went to check on him. "Great job, tough guy. Let's go take a look at that schnoz of yours."

We walked over to the fence with my arm around his shoulder. Kneeling down so we were eye-to-eye, I took off his baseball cap and dried his tears with my T-shirt. I could see a trace of blood in his nose. One of the moms watching practice from the bleachers handed me a tissue. "How cool is that?" I said as we stared at the tissue with a dot of red on it. "You got a bloody nose at your very first practice. You know how long it took me to get my first one? Years! And you played that ball perfectly. I'm so proud of you."

I gave him a big hug. I could feel his fear of facing another ground ball melt away. "You ready to get back out there and show those other kids how it's done, Tiger?" The corners of his lips curled into a smile. He nodded and I watched with pride as Michael charged back out to second base, fearlessly ready for more grounders.

Parking the car in the garage, we walked into the house. My wife, Diane, called out, "How was practice?"

Michael flew into the kitchen, sliding to a stop in his baseball socks and in his most excited voice said, "Guess what, Mom? Dad gave me a bloody nose!"

With a sheepish grin, I rounded the corner on cue, my eyes met with Diane's daggers. "What happened?" she said, as she examined his face.

"He's fine. And Michael made a great play on the ball, didn't you?"

"Yup. I'm okay, Mom. It was actually pretty cool." And off he went to share his tale of bravery with his twin sister, Danielle.

It was time for me to face the music.

"What the hell happened?"

"I hit it really slowly but the ball took a bad hop. I couldn't have aimed it any better if I tried."

"Well next time hit someone else's kid," she said, stomping away to check on her wounded cub more thoroughly.

•••

Michael's baseball skills improved consistently over the subsequent five years, while the marriage deteriorated just as consistently. Danielle and Michael lived in the same house with their mom, but now I drove over from my apartment to pick him up for practice.

This would be Michael's last year of Little League. He was the starting shortstop and would lead the team in hitting with better than a .500 average. At one of our final practices, we were scrimmaging amongst ourselves. There were seven kids in the field, with Coach Jim pitching and me catching. Three other kids were batting. When all three kids on the hitting team reached base, I dropped my glove to hit with the bases loaded.

I stepped into the batter's box and imitating Babe Ruth, pointed with the bat to the left field fence 250 feet away, saying "Grand Salami, here it comes!"

"No way!" the kids jeered. "You're gonna hit into a double play," Michael added from shortstop.

The pitch came in a little high on the outside part of the plate. I took an easy swing with my arms fully extended. The ball flew up high in the air to left field. Every head turned to watch its flight. The left and center fielders converged, and watched the ball drop out of reach over the wall. Grand Slam.

"Woo-hoo," I cheered as I took my homerun trot around the bases, making sure to stick my tongue out at Michael as I rounded second. My teammates met me at home plate with high-fives all around. I had ended practice in style.

I drove Michael home and walked him to the front door. This was always difficult for me, knowing I was no longer welcome in the home where we raised our children. Just five years ago I was wiping Michael's teary eyes, proud of him for facing and overcoming his fear. Now, I was the one with fear—fear of losing the close connection with my children.

As I turned to leave, Michael said, "You know Dad? That Grand Slam you hit was really cool!"

My eyes teared up as we hugged. I wonder if he knew how much his words of pride showed me I had nothing to worry about. I wonder if he could feel my fear evaporate in his embrace the way I felt his fear melt away five years earlier. We broke from our hug and the corners of my lips curled into a smile. "Thanks, Michael. I did it for you!"

And I charged back out into the single parent world, fearlessly ready for the next ball life would hit at me.

~Jonathan D. Katz

91

Lucky Pen

A hundred hearts would be too few
To carry all my love for you.
~Author Unknown

"Mommy, I got something for you!" Cody ran through the door after school. His face wore the biggest smile ever. He waved something above his head. "It's a pen. But not just any pen. It's a lucky pen!"

He handed me the pen proudly. He stood in front of me with his shoulders back and his chest puffed out, waiting for my reaction.

I looked at the pen in my hand. There was nothing special about it. It looked just like any other ballpoint pen. I had a drawer full of them. But oh, looks can be deceiving. I didn't realize how special it was at the time or how much I would come to treasure it.

I had made the decision to pursue a career in writing. A decision that was full of fear and anxiety for me. I had dreamed about it for a long time but I was afraid to take a chance. I was scared of rejection.

The night before, I had voiced those fears to my husband when I thought Cody wasn't listening. "What if everyone hates my writing and I fail miserably?"

But Cody always did hear more than he was supposed to. Now he stood in front of me, watching me examine the pen.

"You don't have to be scared now," he said. "This pen will make your stories great and everyone will love you."

Tears filled my eyes. I grabbed him and pulled him tight against me. I was afraid to speak. Afraid I would break down sobbing if I tried. With that pen, my six-year-old put everything in perspective.

Rejection didn't seem like such a big deal any more. Even if I never sold the first story, I had everything I could ever need. I knew that pen would bring me luck, though. How could it not? I felt lucky already, just by having Cody in my life.

I found out just how lucky when I heard what he did to get it. In the lunchroom, Cody heard an older boy talking about having a lucky pen. He had to get it for me. The boy was a tough negotiator but Cody didn't give up. In the end, he traded his lunch, his favorite Matchbox car, two army men his brother gave him, a crayon, and a piece of candy. He traded his most prized possessions for that pen. Just to make me feel better.

I still have that pen, though it's long out of ink, in a cup on my desk. When a rejection letter arrives and I start feeling sorry for myself, I look at it and remember just how lucky I am.

For while I treasure that pen, it's the little boy who gave it to me who's the real treasure.

~Kimber Krochmal

92

Somos Una Familia

*There is… nothing to suggest that mothering cannot be
shared by several people.*
~H. R. Schaffer

"Greetings from Honduras," the letter said. "You are the adoptive parents of a child you've named Maddy."

I froze right there beside the mailbox, one hand holding the letter. Two years before, we'd traveled to adopt newborn Maddy, whose brokenhearted birth mother, Sofia, had been unable to feed another mouth. At the time, Sofia had declined to meet us, probably because she felt she might not be able to follow through. All the same, I'd sent a few photos and a letter for her after our return home—something had told me a time would come when that link with her daughter would become desperately important.

Now, suddenly, after all this time, here was this letter. My first panicked thought was: She wants Maddy back.

The letter, written in English by a nun who worked in Sofia's community, told me Sofia was grateful Maddy was with us, "but her 'mother's heart' longs for her child."

My own heart thumped painfully.

Sister Elizabeth Ann told me what a good woman Sofia was, and how much my letter and photos had meant to her—that she carried them with her everywhere. Now she had come to a place in her life where she longed to know how Maddy was doing.

Strangely, I'd never felt any sense of competition with Maddy's birthmother. When we'd been going through the screening and placement processes, I'd had to realize my children would always have more than one mother; I could never completely supplant this very elemental relationship. Not that coming to grips with that had been easy. I often said, "The children have rights; the birthparents have rights; adoptive parents retain the right to sign checks."

As Ann Buchwald, wife of humorist Art Buchwald, wrote in her memoir, *Seems Like Yesterday*, she wanted to forget other arms had once held her adopted children. Now those other arms were front and center in our lives once again.

I didn't care—I was just relieved Sofia wasn't trying to reclaim Maddy. I'd welcomed Sofia into my heart long ago. In fact, I was happy Maddy would have this contact. Seeing her sunny disposition, bright curiosity, and tender heart, I figured these wonderful qualities very likely came from her birth mother, Sofia.

Long ago, I'd been humbled by Sofia's courage in trusting God with her child, letting her go to a place, and to people, she couldn't possibly begin to imagine. Deep in poverty, Sofia had known this was Maddy's best chance at survival. I knew that birthparents who made adoption plans for their children were subjected to enormous peer and family pressure not to follow through. Urban legends about adoptions solely in order to harvest organs for transplantation were rampant in Central America. Would I have had so much love, faith, and courage?

I also knew my own relationship with my children had to be based on transparency and trust. I could never sabotage their original, primary relationship, and hope to have their trust and respect. Of course, I wrote back. I sent photos and one of Maddy's scribbles.

Thus began a correspondence—first, through Sister Elizabeth Ann, and later directly, at Sofia's request, with my less-than-fluent Spanish. As this correspondence continued over time, Sofia and I got a real sense of each other's personalities. I genuinely liked her.

In 1998, Hurricane Mitch tore through Honduras. The destruction of this Third World country's fragile infrastructure wiped out one-third of its roads, as well as safe water supplies. Mudslides carried away houses—and people—even in middle-class neighborhoods, but especially in the hillside colonias of scrap-wood and cardboard houses. Over 5,000 people died; more than 8,000 were missing.

When I heard the news that morning, I woke Maddy, who was now twelve. "We must pray for the people of Honduras," I told her, with a hug. I assured her that her family was probably safe, but possibly in a shelter somewhere.

After I'd sent her off to school with this cheerful prognosis, I looked at the photos of Sofia and her children, and I prayed. Then, I cried. I cried all day, until it was time for the school bus to return, and I had to pull myself together. I did this every day for a week. While Maddy was at school, I scanned Internet reports and posted on websites devoted to missing persons. Our youth group worked to assemble relief packages. At least, we could help others—and who knows? Maybe one of them might reach some member of Maddy's family.

But Maddy's family had disappeared. My letters went unanswered. Finally, as days became years, we faced the likelihood that they hadn't survived. Surely, Sofia would have contacted us somehow if they had made it.

Middle school days ended and high school days began. Sofia's bittersweet smile, forever preserved in the framed photo on the wall, still followed me when I walked through Maddy's room, putting away laundry. We lived through boyfriend issues and broken hearts, musical dreams and crushing disappointments, college ambitions, silly laughter, misunderstandings. Sometimes I felt in over my head, and I talked to Sofia. "What are we going to do about this, Sofia?" When I made mistakes—did things or said things I thought Sofia might disapprove—I told her I was sorry; that I was trying my best. Sometimes, I avoided her eyes.

When Maddy did something especially wonderful, I'd ask, "What do you think of our girl, Sofia?"

Maddy and I sometimes talked about her. I knew she longed for some kind of contact from her mother, some connection with the world and the people she had come from. On a vacation trip to

Honduras when Maddy was sixteen, we visited the Junta de Bienestar, the welfare agency, to try to locate Sofia or other members of the family. They had no recent records. "Sorry" was the response we received.

Years passed. College. Grad school.

"She's doing well, Sofia. She's a good girl."

Maddy and I were extremely close. I was her mama, and she was my daughter. Nothing would, or could, ever change that. But Sofia was a part of us, too. I was grateful she had given birth to Maddy, and that she had given me the incredible privilege of these years with her. Every day, I prayed for her. It had taken both of us to bring Maddy to this point, and if I could've given Maddy anything in the world, it would have been the chance to know her mother.

A decade had gone by since the hurricane. One summer day, I returned from buying groceries, and there stood Maddy at the top of the stairs. She was sobbing so hard I could barely make out the words. "My sister found me on Facebook. My mother is alive—they lost our address, and they've been looking for us all these years."

"Somos una familia," Sofia had once written to Maddy—"We are one family." And so we are.

~Susan Kimmel Wright

93

Listen and Learn

Courage is what it takes to stand up and speak;
courage is also what it takes to sit down and listen.
~Winston Churchill

Last week my husband and I attended a gala. You know, the kind where you get all dressed up and have to mingle and feel totally uncomfortable.

I put on black pantyhose. I wasn't sure if it was still okay to wear pantyhose but a quick Google search informed me that bare legs are so 2010. Apparently Kate Middleton has been working sheer stockings all year. All right! Check me out dressing like royalty! Except that my hose are maybe a little too small and the crotch part has settled around my thighs and I am not accustomed to heels so I have this whole lurching, unsophisticated waddle going on.

Perhaps even more awkward than my drooping pantyhose is the conversation—the small talk at these gatherings—with women you're meeting for the first time. If they're mothers, of course you know what they'll do. They'll talk about the one thing that's always on their minds, the thing that makes their hearts beat with an incomparable passion: the rugrats at home. No matter the age, there's always talk of development—milestones reached and future plans. And then they'll ask you about yours.

And I never know quite where to begin.

I am a mother of a child with autism. Everything I see, experience and do in life is colored to some degree by that fact. I am blessed to know and walk with some incredible mothers of special needs children—there are not enough words to describe their courage, resilience, strength, get-it-done mama bear-ness, and compassion. They make me proud to be counted among the autism mamas.

But I'm learning that it does not define me, not in total.

So this particular night I challenged myself to a little test: How long can you go before dropping the word *autism*? Five minutes? Ten minutes? The whole night? Can you talk about anything else? Can you turn off the educator, advocator, blogger for one night and just listen? Can you listen, for once, without comparing? Can you genuinely smile because her daughter does ballet and made the honor roll? Can you understand that her concern is a valid one, her son talking *too much* in class? Can you listen to another mother's story and just appreciate her because she's a mother… with experiences so different and yet so similar to your own?

We sit around the table, passing the butter and rolls. Someone asks me the ages of my children. Seven and a half and almost five, I say. Oh, so you're past the hard stage, she says. I want to say, "Girl, lemme tell you," but I remember my little test. She goes on to detail the woes of toddlerhood. We laugh at the stories of her son's antics. I can totally relate because I can still totally relate. But I don't say that. Then she grows serious and tells us that even though she's exhausted she counts every day with her son a blessing. She tells of how he was born at twenty-seven weeks gestation, weighed less than two pounds and spent five months in the hospital. She named him Samuel, her long-awaited, prayed for, miracle baby.

I remember my friend Judith's wise words: human suffering is not a competitive sport.

And all of us mothers treasure our children, our gifts, with fierceness, and all of our children are miracles.

As I enjoy the anecdotes around the table I settle into a contentment I've not known before, like being in my skin is right where I am supposed to be, happy to be.

My own motherhood story is far different from the tale I would have crafted had I held the pen. But as my story unfolds, I realize it's wilder, tougher, sweeter, funnier, more poetic, more amazing than anything I could ever compose.

~Jeneil Palmer Russell

94

Home Safe

*Live so that when your children think of fairness and integrity,
they think of you.*

~H. Jackson Brown

O ne of the proudest moments of my life started with a question. The question came from our son Tim, who wanted to join the Army. Shortly after his nineteenth birthday, he asked if I would take him down to the recruiting office and drop him off, saying I could watch him being sworn in if I wanted. I told him, "I wouldn't miss that moment for anything in the world."

After we arrived at the recruiting station, we were led into a room for the swearing in. The Army commander explained the swearing in, and the oath the recruits were about to take, asking the soldiers if they were attending of their own free will. All answering, "Yes, Sir!" He then asked the group to hold up their right hands and follow him, repeating the vow to serve our country.

As I looked at the soldiers, it was obvious that every one of them meant every word. The service took my breath away. They all knew what they had just committed to do. I kept saying to myself, "Dear Lord, give them strength!"

The ride home was one of the longest of my life. I felt like I had just given my son away. Questions filled my mind. "Had we taught him all he needed to know? Did he listen? What would he be like when he was done? Did he know how much his mom and I loved him?" This was my little boy! We watched him grow up, and now he belonged to America.

Fast forward to Tim's second tour of duty in Iraq. He called and asked if we would mind if he came home on leave for Christmas. Just the thought of our family being together for Christmas took my breath away. Waiting for the day we could pick up our son from the airport seemed to take forever.

When the day finally arrived, many people at the airport asked us if the welcome home sign (our daughter Natalie proudly displayed) was for a soldier. We said yes, it was for our son Tim and we were there to welcome him home from a year in Iraq. All of the people we talked to made us feel so proud with their words of thanks. Most everyone asked us to thank Tim for serving our country. We said we would do our best to let him know.

I could hear people in the terminal clapping as Tim passed by them on his way to us. I stood there speechless, listening to all the questions and words of thanks from people like us who were calling my son a hero.

After picking up his bags we made our way to the parking lot and were loading his things into our trunk. Tim said, "Oh, I almost forgot! Here, Dad," as he pulled out a box from his duffle bag. "Sorry about the box, Dad. I think it got flattened on the trip!" he said.

As I looked at the red, white and blue box, trying to figure out what it was, I pulled the end open to reveal an American flag. Tim said, "Happy Birthday Dad!" He then asked if I remembered the phone call a few months before, on my birthday, when he had told me that he had a present for me but he couldn't give it to me yet. Tim then reached in his jacket, pulling out a pristine piece of paper in a clear plastic protector. "Dad this letter goes with your flag."

Certificate of Recognition

These colors were proudly flown in the face of the enemy, in continuing effort to ensure democracy for the people of Iraq and forever erase the scars of tyranny created by years of oppression by terrorist forces threatening the freedom of the United States of America and the World on August 30 in Kirkuk, Iraq.

They are now most respectfully retired and entrusted to the care of William Garvey recognizing his support for Soldiers fighting the War on Terror.

His First Sergeant and the Battery Commander had signed the certificate at the bottom.

I stood there speechless, with tears in my eyes. Now I knew why Tim had called a few months before, saying he couldn't send my present yet. It was because that flag was flying over his camp on my birthday.

The flag and certificate were the second best birthday present I had ever received—the first was the soldier who brought it safely home to me.

~William Garvey

Chapter 12

Parenthood

Giving Them Wings to Fly

If you raise your children to feel that they can accomplish any goal or task they decide upon, you will have succeeded as a parent and you will have given your children the greatest of all blessings.

~Brian Tracy

95

Wonderful Noise

*A daughter is the happy memories of the past,
the joyful moments of the present, and the hope and promise of the future.*
~Author Unknown

T
he camera panning across the seniors performing their graduation theme song stopped on my daughter. Her smiling face
showed on the huge screen as she played the marimba, her
favorite instrument. It seemed to me they stayed with her
for longer than the others but perhaps it was just my inability to let
go of the image of her as a graduate—white gown, newly short hair,
smiling face and marimba mallets.

She was always beating on something for as long as I could
remember—from the pots and pans in the kitchen to empty garbage
cans while she waited for the bus. It was no surprise when the third
graders chose musical instruments and she went for percussion along
with half the class.

Since so many kids wanted to try percussion, the music teacher
did a brief tryout with the kids to see if they had potential. My daughter was nervous but followed his lead and performed well enough
that he asked her if she had played before. No, not officially. She had
natural talent then, but we already knew that.

I still remember the night she brought home her drum kit. Most
kids started with just a snare drum, but we knew somebody who
knew somebody who set her up with a complete kit for about the
same price. It was set up in our basement in front of the water tank

and she, wearing her pajamas, tried her first tentative swipes with the drumsticks on the snare and cymbals. Little did I know how many private concerts I'd get over the next eight years.

School lessons, private lessons, school band, county band, indoor percussion all followed in succession once she picked up the sticks. There were hours of practice, bus trips, visits to the drum shop for replacement sticks, uniform fittings and concerts.

Day after day, sometimes far into the night, I heard the sounds from the basement. Often the cat ran and hid and the house shook, but it always made me smile to hear her play. You always know where your child is when you have a drummer. They are never still and they are never quiet.

All through the middle school years I thought we were busy, but then when she started high school I knew what it really meant to be busy. In the summer before her freshman year she started marching band.

I had no idea what it meant to be a marching band parent, so when the e-mails and phone calls started coming about volunteer opportunities, bake sales, fundraisers and trips to Florida I was a little overwhelmed. I baked dozens of cookies, hung signs, drove miles to and from school, fitted uniforms, sewed flags and signed check after check for all the things a band kid needs.

But that first night football game when I saw her in her uniform playing with the drum line leading the rest of the band onto the field, I knew why everyone did it. Seeing the band filing out there on the field filled me with pride for her and all that she had accomplished. These kids work so hard to get their music and drill right that nobody can deny they deserve every bit of help we can give them.

So for four years I was a band parent and I did what I could to keep those kids making music. I baked macaroni and cheese, sold candy, supplied drinks and food and muscle for all kinds of events. The entire family pitched in to help as much as we could. And though it was physically and financially draining, I wouldn't trade it for the world.

But on this night I saw it all ending and I felt a deep sense of loss for the child she was and the musician she had become. I knew that most likely this would be the last time I'd ever see her play, or at least it would be a very long time before it happened again.

Rather than study music, my daughter had decided to lay down her drum sticks and join the armed forces as a Marine recruit. We thought perhaps she'd try for the band, but no, she wanted something different, to be of service in another way. I am so proud of her and I know it was her years of commitment and hard work as a drummer and band member that have prepared her to contribute as a member of our military.

A few weeks from now, before she leaves for boot camp, we will pack up the drum kit and store it until she returns home from her service. The house will be empty of her music for the first time in nearly a decade.

Everyone always asks if it was hard to have a drummer in the house, considering all the noise they make. I always enjoyed hearing her play. I truly did and nobody knows just how much I'll miss her wonderful noise.

~Shawn Marie Mann

Reprinted by permission of Mark Parisi
and Off the Mark ©2011.

96

More to Life than Basketball

Figuring out who you are is the whole point of the human experience.
~Anna Quindlen

y sixteen-year-old son came home from school. Eric threw his gym bag into the laundry room, walked into the kitchen, and lifted the lid of a pot of simmering spaghetti sauce.

"Ah, onions, garlic. Where's Dad?" He hoisted his six-foot seven-inch frame onto the kitchen counter and wiggled into his favorite spot. A corner. Since he was five years old, he'd sat cross-legged in that corner. Now, he held his crossed knees with his hands.

"Dad's at work," I said, washing lettuce in the kitchen sink. "You're early. It's only 4:00. No basketball practice today?" He shrugged. "So, how was your day?"

"Great! The best day of my life!" Such jubilation was unexpected. In recent years, the corner seat had been reserved for days when Eric wanted money or had a problem.

"What happened?"

"I quit basketball." If my son had sung "The Star-Spangled Banner" while standing on his head, I wouldn't have been as shocked. Quit basketball? He was two weeks into eleventh grade. The year before he had played behind the star center on the varsity team. This was his year to shine and I had assumed he would play in college. He'd received letters from college coaches. Mechanically, I stirred the red sauce.

"You what?"

He flicked his fingertips on his knees. "I talked to Coach. I quit basketball." Questions swirled in my head. What happened? What did Coach say? Did you talk to your dad about this?

Finally, one word escaped. "Why?"

"Hmmmm, there's got to be more to life than basketball." His fingers played a fast rhythm on his knees.

I breathed deeply. My brain couldn't wrap around his decision or his happiness. "There's a 'rest of the story,' right?" He nodded. "We'll talk when Dad gets home." I couldn't listen to more.

Allen got home an hour later. I gave him time to change out of his office clothes. "Eric quit basketball. He seems happy. He's going to tell us the whole story together." Allen's face froze in a confused frown. "He's sitting at the kitchen table."

"Hey, Dad. How was your day?" Eric greeted Allen.

"So far, so good. What's going on?" said Allen.

Eric stretched his legs under the table. "I told Mom. I quit basketball. I talked to Coach."

"And you didn't tell your mother and me first? Or even talk to us about it?" Allen crossed his arms over his chest.

"No. I didn't want anyone to talk me out of it. I figured it was my decision."

"So you just decided? When?" I asked.

"Not just decided. Like you both always said—I listed the pros and cons. I've been thinking about it since we got back from summer basketball camp last month."

"And what caused your decision?" Allen asked. He poured a glass of tea.

I wanted to scream, "Show me the list!"

Eric looked out the window. Right at the basketball goal. "I just don't want to graduate from high school and the only thing I've done is play basketball. There's got to be more to life than basketball. I want to do some other stuff."

The three of us sat silently for a few minutes. Eric drummed his fingers on the wooden table. Allen sipped his tea. I stared at Eric and remembered how he'd dribbled a red playground ball as a toddler, dunked a basketball through a pint-size goal at age five, and excelled in organized team games at age seven. He'd been the center and often the top scorer. And now he was quitting? With just two more years in high school?

I didn't say what I was thinking. "So what's more to life than basketball? What do you want to do?"

"I don't know. I can lifeguard more at the Y." Eric worked as a lifeguard four hours on Sundays at the YMCA.

It was Allen's turn to ask a question. He didn't. "Well, Son. I'm shocked. I guess I always thought you liked basketball."

"I do. I just want to do some other stuff. And I don't want to play ball in college."

I couldn't control the tears that ran down my cheeks. I cry when I'm sad. Or mad. Or upset. Or frustrated. And I was all of these. Had Eric felt that we forced him to play ball just because he was tall? Did we make a mistake encouraging him to play when he was too young? Allen and I had saved for his college education, but we welcomed the possibility of an athletic college scholarship. Did Eric feel pressure to play for money? Guilt questions.

The next few days were strained in our home. Neither Allen nor I slept well. We wondered what we should have done differently and we struggled to truly support Eric's decision.

How many hours had Allen and I spent taking Eric to practice and to games? Eric's high school ballgames were written in ink on my calendar. Those games came before any other family plans. I liked being a basketball mother. Was I angry that Eric had taken something from me?

When I was in high school, I was the tallest player on the team. I was also the least competitive and least coordinated, with no natural athletic ability. But I like basketball. For two years I tried and my coach was encouraging, but by my junior year, Coach and I agreed that I'd be the team manager. I was sad, and maybe a little mad, that Eric had given up playing the sport that I'd wanted to play.

During supper about a week later, Eric said, "Hey, I'll be home late tomorrow afternoon. I'm the girls' new volleyball manager." That fall and winter Allen and I went to every high school basketball game and most of the volleyball games. Eric was a supportive fan. He cheered. He stood and encouraged other spectators to stand and cheer. He was happy. I liked seeing my son relaxed and smiling and having a good time.

Eric found more than basketball. He helped organize and swam on his school's swim team, and he taught Red Cross swim lessons. His classmates elected him senior class president. During the summer, he lifeguarded at a camp for children with special needs. He sang in our church youth choir. I was proud of him.

One afternoon during the first week of Eric's senior year, he sat cross-legged in the corner of the kitchen counter. "Hey, Mom. The principal's going to call you or Dad." His chin touched his chest. I couldn't see his eyes. I waited, breathing slowly. He jerked his head up. Big grin. Eyes dancing. "Gotcha! He said he wants me to be on a leadership committee that'll involve travel and overnight trips. He wants to be sure it's okay with you and Dad."

Yes, Eric got me! And he taught me. I learned to trust my son to live his life. Not an easy lesson for this parent.

~Susan R. Ray

97

Going Gluten-Free

If you break your neck, if you have nothing to eat, if your house is on fire,
then you got a problem. Everything else is inconvenience.
~Robert Fulghum

Imagine this, tasty pasta cooked *al dente* in a hearty marinara sauce with one plump meatball on the side of your plate. Add in some fresh-baked crusty bread and a Caesar salad tossed with croutons. And if you are lucky, a decadent multi-layered dark chocolate cake for dessert. But then in the blink of an eye, these foods are yanked away from you, forever.

"No more wheat," said the doctor to my nine-year-old daughter a few months ago. "You have been diagnosed with celiac disease, a severe form of a gluten allergy." I was shocked. We had been concerned about Taylor's growth and had decided to meet with a doctor specializing in pediatric growth issues. The doctor explained to me that Taylor's growth was being stunted due to the damage that gluten, a simple protein found in wheat and other grains, caused in her small intestines.

"She will have to start a gluten-free diet immediately," he calmly stated. Tears welled up in my eyes as I received this life-changing directive. I looked over at my sweet daughter innocently listening to her iPod, not understanding that her little world was about to come crashing down around her. The pizza and cake shared at birthday parties, the treats given at school, hot lunch, and even those addictive Goldfish crackers were off limits to her now.

The doctor cautioned me about cross-contamination by trace elements of wheat in our old pots and pans at home. We would need a brand new saucepan and toaster in which to make Taylor's gluten-free food. There was so much to process and consider. I worried about fitting additional food preparation into our busy lifestyle. I didn't want to cook two meals, I didn't want to shop at the fancy organic stores, and I didn't want to rearrange my life for this. We both held it together while in the doctor's office, but once we reached the car, the tears came. It broke my heart to watch her sob as she grasped the implications of avoiding gluten.

The hardest part initially was the change in the taste and variety of her food. Instead of selecting any snack food in the pantry, Taylor now finds herself limited to a few products made from nuts, popcorn and rice. We bought hundreds of dollars in gluten-free products and sampled them. Some we spit out, a few tasted liked pressed cardboard, and others were actually quite delicious.

Besides the food, Taylor has experienced a roller coaster of emotions. She doesn't understand why she has been singled out and she doesn't like being different from her friends at school. She used to love school lunch and now that is no longer an option most days. She treasures the few days when she can order the school lunch. Something as simple as handing the cafeteria worker your lunch ticket, taking the tray and eating from it feels normal. And, that is exactly what she wants to feel again.

My daughter is still young and doesn't see any health benefits from avoiding gluten in her diet. But my husband and I see an increase in her energy level. She plays recreation soccer and is a different player this year. Last year, she could barely run the field for ten minutes before asking to come out and sit down. This year, she is the leading goal scorer and a powerhouse on the field. Her little motor doesn't stop and she has gained a new confidence in her abilities. Is this due to going gluten-free? We can't be sure, but it is the only variable that has changed in her life and diet.

Going gluten-free has not been cheap. Each product labeled *GF* is going to be at least five dollars. And for this reason, the entire family has not made the switch to being completely gluten-free. Taylor eats her own breakfast and lunch foods, and then I try to cook a gluten-free dinner for the entire family. We have found a way to compromise that doesn't break the bank, but also brings us together each night around the dinner table.

Over the course of a few months, we have altered our lifestyle, not to be trendy, but to help Taylor realize her full potential. As parents, you never know what changes you will have to make—diagnoses like celiac disease are so unexpected.

But that mouthwatering pasta can still be made with a corn-based spaghetti noodle, the meatball made with gluten-free bread crumbs, the Caesar salad with a gluten-free dressing and gluten-free croutons, and the decadent chocolate cake can be found gluten-free at Whole Foods in the freezer section. Luckily for us, going gluten-free hasn't been bad!

~Karen C. Talcott

98

On Her Own Terms

Any man can be a father, but it takes a special person to be a dad.
~Proverb

As a parent, I was hoping that Valerie would not be interested in Barbie dolls. It seemed obvious to me that any young girl who played with them would grow up to be deranged. After all, Barbie is completely unrepresentative of the female population. Studies have shown that, were she a real woman, she'd be something like five feet ten inches with a twenty-two-inch waist. Also, her breasts are unduly large, so she would have trouble supporting their weight.

Maybe you can understand my concern when one day I came home and my daughter was playing with two Barbies that she had received as gifts from her mother. I initiated my usual lamenting, but it was to no avail. The Barbies were going to stay.

Over time, I realized that Barbie's world is colossal. There were skating Barbies, motorcycle Barbies, Olympic Barbies, wheelchair Barbies, nurse Barbies, and Barbies of all races. I once encountered what I could have sworn was a Marilyn Manson Barbie, and I'm eternally thankful that Valerie never asked for that version. As a birthday present, she received Barbie's Fold 'n Fun House in which all the Barbies could live, hang out on the roof, or do whatever Barbies do at night.

When her collection reached fifteen Barbies, I asked Valerie if she thought the group was large enough, and she said, "Yeah, probably."

One day, Val asked me for two boxes. I didn't ask why and handed her two packing boxes. Later, when I went downstairs, to my utter amazement I saw her carefully putting her Barbies into the boxes. I was curious about this development and said, "Val, what are you up to?"

"I'm packing them up," she said.

"Why?" I asked.

"Well, I'm not going to play with them anymore," she explained.

"Val," I said, "you've been playing with your Barbies for years, and you've got it set up — you've got the skating rink, the house, and everything else the Barbies could need. What's going on?"

She wouldn't say.

When I spoke to her mother, I found out that someone at school had made fun of her because she played with Barbies. I remembered how originally I had disliked those Barbies, but they were a good pastime for her. She's an only child, so it's important that she engages in creative fantasy. While she's still young, if she lets somebody taunt her out of something she enjoys doing, where's the end to it? I want her to grow up to be confident of her individuality. I don't want her to give in to peer pressure now.

Rather than offering her a heavy-duty fatherly lecture, I said, "Well, I'll tell you what, Val. Instead of packing all of them up right now, why don't you leave most of them out? Then maybe after Easter we'll put the rest of them away." Valerie agreed, so most of the Barbies stayed out of the box, and she continued to play with them. I hoped that she had forgotten the words of the kid from school.

I realized that I had now come full circle. I felt terrible when I saw the Barbies being packed up. Regardless of the reason, I felt as if it was another episode in my little girl's life that was over, and I found it hard to accept. Then, when I found out from her mother that she was packing them up because a classmate had negatively influenced her, I felt doubly bad.

When Val accepted my idea of waiting until Easter, I was overjoyed because now she would be playing with the Barbies again, which was her wish all along. That Easter came and went, and she still played with them, decreasingly so, but it was her call.

Then, over time, on her own terms, she chose to pack them up.

~Jeff Davidson

Skid Marks
and Screeching Rubber

Never lend your car to anyone to whom you have given birth.
~Erma Bombeck

"Wanna take me driving?" my daughter asked, while jangling the keys in front of my face. As if to sweeten the offer she used the same singsong voice she uses when coaxing the dogs to go for a walk.

Little did she know, jangling the keys was far from enticing. My stomach knotted up, my shoulders stiffened, my neck tightened and my heart began a little afib action. At fifty-five, I'd come to terms with my strengths and weaknesses. I knew some people were good at jobs like transporting plutonium or teaching their children to drive. I was not.

When Zoe got her "learner's permit" I dubbed it my "license to drink." Not because she could become my designated driver when we went out together, but because when she drove, I needed a drink.

It's not that she was a bad driver; it's just that I feel things deeply even before they happen.

All I had to do was look at our steep, short driveway with the sudden sharp left turn, the dinged plaster wall and the skid marks on the concrete, made by people who already knew how to drive, and my heart would pound as I'd imagine the air bag exploding into my face. We had begun and ended all of our practice driving sessions at the foot of the driveway.

"Watch me honey," I'd say, narrating the blow-by-blow execution of the turn over and over. "You have to approach the driveway at the correct angle, get a little speed and head for the wall, but at the last second lay off the gas and make a sharp left turn."

Around the sixth demonstration I decided to switch places with her. *This is insane*, I thought. *I am instructing my daughter to aim for the wall with my side of the car.* I lurched left, clutched the center console, and braced for air bag deployment while my daughter laid a smoking strip of rubber on the ground with full audio accompaniment.

"That was pretty good, honey," I coughed out, attempting to be supportive.

She rolled her eyes. "You know that's not helping."

But that little shot of vodka will, I thought, as I closed the car door and headed for the kitchen.

Like I said, I feel things deeply even before they happen, so even though I start out all centered and calm, muttering my "I-will-be-patient" mantra, I can get pretty jumpy and lose my Zen.

My last Zen-less escapade occurred at a tricky five-way stop sign. "STOP! STOP! STOP!" I screamed while slamming my foot on my imaginary brakes to avoid hitting the pedestrian who'd wandered into our path.

During the excruciating six months of required road time, we practiced night driving, rush-hour driving, complicated-intersection driving, and rain driving. Who thought up this government-sanc-tioned activity? A Darwinian theorist? A sadist? Seriously, who puts someone who still sleeps with stuffed animals, and has a frontal lobe resembling Swiss cheese, behind the wheel of a two-ton vehicle, gas-ses it up and watches what happens?

Zoe claimed she'd been ready to drive since she was eight. She pointed to episodes when she was three and my brother let her sit in his lap and steer in a parking lot. She reminded me that my sister-in-law let her hold the wheel, when legally she should've been strapped into a car seat, and she ratted out her dad, who took her for a few spins months before she even had a permit, yet seemed to be mostly MIA on our legal outings.

"I'm more like Dad when it comes to driving," Zoe said coolly, as she whizzed along with one hand on the steering wheel.

"Dad got two tickets last month," I reminded her, noting that she was doing forty-five in a thirty-five mile per hour zone.

I knew being Zoe's driving coach would test me, but I didn't expect the one-two sucker punch that lay in store.

For years I'd doused her with the pearls of wisdom I thought would guide her through life's toughest circumstances, things like, "Manners cost nothing, but their value is priceless," "Stand for something or you'll fall for everything," "Don't wish it were easier, wish you were better," and the gold standard, "Always wear clean underwear."

But what did she remember? Dad's one and only tip for life: "Avoid a ticket: never be the first one down the hill."

From where I sit it feels exactly as if she is careening down that hill and plowing straight into this milestone of independence and separation. My precious daughter, my one and only, has just taken the test that grants her permission to drive out of my life.

It's the test my daughter claims she's waited for her "whole life." The test she claims will "lift a burden" from my shoulders. A milestone that has aged me visibly. Speaking of which, in general, I am not a milestone wimp; I am a hurdler. I have embraced all the notable ones: applauding when she toddled off to preschool alone, or wandered into the wilderness of her summer camp adventure, even when she flipped her tassel in elementary school and sauntered off to middle school. But now I am futilely pumping the brakes, trying desperately to make everything stop or at least slow down.

Yet I know it won't. She is racing through her childhood at a NASCAR clip and all I can do is cheer from the stands.

Zoe passed the test and obtained her coveted license. In fact, the examiner proclaimed her a "really good driver." Yet, this did not stop me from reciting a long list of safety rules as I handed over the keys for her first solo drive at night.

"Text me when you get there, and before you leave, but not while you're driving. Watch your speed. Pull over and call me if you have any problems. Be home by eleven. Drive safely. I love you."

She forgot to text me when she arrived at her destination, but was exuberant and apologetic on the phone, exclaiming how "amazing" it was to drive by herself and how she was "so, so, so sorry" that she forgot to text me. She remembered to text me before she returned home.

I know there will be many sleepless nights ahead, but for tonight at least, at 10:55 p.m., it's the sweet sound of screeching rubber skidding up our driveway that lulls me to sleep.

~Tsgoyna Tanzman

Reprinted by permission of Mark Parisi
and Off the Mark ©2009.

Swing with Me

Childhood is a short season.
~Helen Hayes

"**S**wing with me." The neglected swing set calls me. Gritty, squeaky, and booby-trapped — the girls don't play here anymore, and the spiders know it. They've claimed the play set's tree house as their own no-girls-allowed zone, planting their flag of gossamer threads across the threshold. Two arachnophobic girls would never invade their fortress now, though it once hosted daily clubhouse meetings, filled with plastic teacups, Barbie dolls, and hushed giggles. Pastel, chalk-etched promises of BFF-4E have long been washed away by the rain.

"Swing with me."

How long has it been since either of them begged me to swing with them? How is it that I can still see it so perfectly, my selective photographic memory recalling the sentimental, but not always the most useful, information. Their matching, lopsided ponytails on top of their shining, golden heads. Their blue eyes, so different from each other — one pair Irish sky, the other Aegean Sea — squinting in the sun as they looked up at me with those similar, expectant looks.

"Swing with me."

I joined them on the swing set, even if I had to squeeze into the deceptively small hammock of a seat with a shoehorn. Because I had an inkling, even then, that they wouldn't always ask me. That if I said "No" too many times, the invitations would stop coming. So I pumped my feet back and forth and watched their faces burst with rapture. Mommy can swing! It must have seemed aerodynamically impossible to their young eyes, but there I was, defying gravity right beside them. They tried to catch up and I let them. It was a race, until they flew so high my stomach would cramp with worry. I'd make them slow down with that shrill voice all mothers find right after we pass the placenta.

In the beginning, it was just Maggie and me on the swings. Shy with even the closest of friends and relatives, she was my magpie, especially during those moments. I was honored that she trusted me with her thoughts. I was never one of those mothers who took those moments for granted or couldn't wait for them to move on to the next stage of development: to feed themselves, be potty trained, or stop chewing crayons. I needed to bank those moments to draw on during the teen years, when I was bound to be crowned the most imperfect creature on the planet.

Then came Julia. We bought a baby swing just for her and struggled to thread her two squirming legs into the foot holes, a feat not unlike trying to wrestle an octopus into a pair of pantyhose. She howled, she cried. She did not care for the motion of the swing, or the confinement of the swing, for a very long time. And when she finally did, it became obvious that there were cavernous differences between my two golden-haired girls. The swing became a vehicle to take her somewhere, elsewhere, internally deeper, farther away from us. There wasn't as much talking as with Maggie. Or eye contact. It would be a few years before we knew. Before we understood. But eventually, she too asked.

"Swing with me."

Now, the kitchen wall is etched with pencil marks that celebrate each inch of growth and serve as a daily reminder of the years that have passed. But the real mark of time is where my babies fit against my body. Where once they rested their tired heads against my ample hips, Julia now fits comfortably under my chin, and Maggie is eye to eye with me. Within the year she will tower over me. My firstborn, my Yin, has blossomed from a shy toddler into a graceful, mature, and confident young woman, still selectively quiet but wet-your-pants funny when her guard is down. She defied her parents' genes by excelling at math and being more organized than all of us combined. Julia, my Yang, is creative and funny, mercurial and sensitive, intelligent and inquisitive. She has developed from a nonverbal toddler to a ten-year-old who scores in the superior range in her language testing. As a family, we have grown from a diagnosis of despair to celebrating a child with Asperger's.

The days are almost painfully longer and emptier now. The girls are either at school, music lessons, chorus, or "hangouts," formerly known as "play dates." Their lopsided ponytails have been replaced by elaborately coiffed French braids. Chubby arms have slimmed down to showcase stacks of friendship bracelets. We've also reached a new demographic: instead of toy catalogs and diaper coupons, now teen fashion catalogs clog my mailbox.

I have always resented the housework, the endless surfaces and crevices that need constant sponging or sweeping and sometimes even bleaching. But the house gets dirty from living, from happiness. Blankets and linens that need to be folded after an impromptu tent is constructed in the den should be a mother's celebration of a childhood well lived. This dirty swing set entombed in spider webs taunts me as it collects layers of grime from lack of use. I want to bring all of my cleaners, sponges, and sprays, and peel away the layers, the years. I want to reverse time and go back to who we were, when my babies still looked at me with that hopeful, expectant look. When my only failure in their eyes would be to not accept their invitation to swing.

I glare at the passive-aggressive swing set defiantly. I'm angry at this filthy, firmly planted inanimate object for making me weepy with nostalgia for the essence of its being, for no longer swooping my babies into the air. Today, at this moment when I'm feeling so vulnerable, I cannot see the swing set for what it truly represents: the foundation of a healthy mother-daughter relationship.

~Amy Giles

Something Bigger

We may not be able to prepare the future for our children,
but we can at least prepare our children for the future.
~Franklin D. Roosevelt

Today I realized, as I stooped down to pick up my sons' dirty laundry, that I must be doing something right as a mother. Now I may be avoiding the obvious fact that I have yet to teach my children to hit the hamper with their dirty clothes one hundred percent of the time, but instead I focus on the more important fact at hand and that is that the clothes I am picking up are more than just plain street clothes. The clothes I'm picking up are uniforms — dirty, sweaty, stinky, and sometimes bloody, uniforms.

Come to think of it, I've been picking up these uniforms for years. I've even gotten to a point where I don't mind the smell of those mangy practice jerseys that went an entire season without being washed and those sweat-soaked socks that endured robust practices beneath the hot desert sun. To be perfectly honest with you, picking up my boys' dirty laundry is just another day at the office for me.

The truth is, as I toss my firstborn son's McDonald's uniform into the washer, along with his brother's grass-stained junior varsity game jersey, I feel like I have accomplished something rather extraordinary in my life. As I wash away the harsh stench of French-fry grease from my older son's first work uniform and the foul scent of football from my younger son's early sports career, I realize that I have raised my children to respect the uniform, and all that goes with it, regardless of which uniform it may be. I think it's an important rite of passage to be a part of something bigger than you are.

What I want, more than anything, is for my boys to appreciate the hard work that comes with being a part of that "something bigger." And this can be accomplished brilliantly by throwing on a uniform, by stepping onto a team and working toward a common goal. I don't care if you're sacking the quarterback or slinging burgers. Wearing a uniform is an experience every kid should have.

After five years of high school football and as many years of baseball, I can clearly see how those years of uniforms have shaped my boys into extraordinary young men of discipline, integrity and confidence. They know what it means to sweat, bruise, break and even bleed for causes bigger than they are. It has defined them.

It's an important life lesson for children. I believe that in my heart. Sure it's not always great for the nose, these soiled uniforms that lie on my wood floors, but it sure is good for a mother's ego to see that her children are in many ways better prepared for the world because of a few dirty, sweaty, stinky, and sometimes bloody, uniforms.

All you need to do is to look as far as our military, our firefighters, our police officers and the good-looking, green-eyed guy handing out hamburgers, fries and milkshakes through the drive-thru window. There's just something about a uniform that makes people part of something bigger than they are, and thus makes them better people themselves.

~Natalie June Reilly

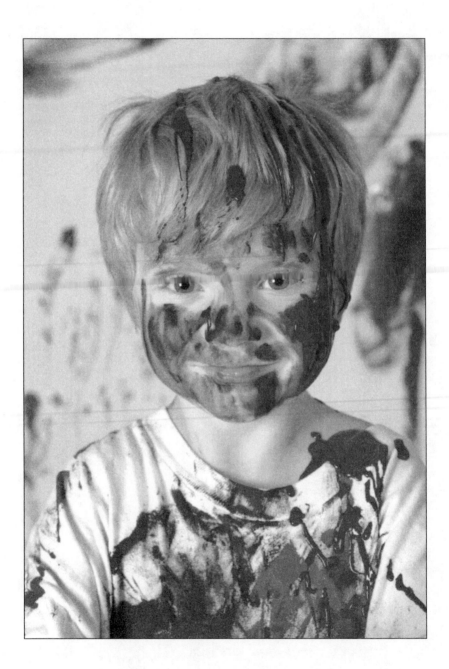

Parenthood

Meet Our Contributors
Meet Our Authors
Thank You
About Chicken Soup for the Soul

Meet Our Contributors

Rachel Allison is associate editor of *Bible Advocate* magazine. Her writing has appeared in such publications as *Focus on the Family*, *In Touch*, and *Today's Christian Woman*, as well as *Chicken Soup for the Soul in Menopause*. She enjoys playing drums, swimming, and walking.

Elisabeth Bailey believes that sharing our stories is critically important to our life purpose of serving one another. She has a PR firm in New York, and works with clients on all aspects of effective communications. Central to her joy are her husband and two children.

Susan Barclay is a librarian and writer. She has published short stories for adults and is actively seeking a publisher for her children's picture books. Susan lives in Ontario, Canada with her husband, teenaged children, and the family's beautiful Boston Terrier. E-mail her at author@susan-barclay.ca.

Rob L. Berry resides in Bakersfield, CA with his wife and two sons. Rob is a member of Writers of Kern and has previously appeared in *Chicken Soup for the Soul: Count Your Blessings* and *Chicken Soup for the Soul: Hooked on Hockey*. E-mail him at robberry74@gmail.com.

Jack Blandford is a commercial film producer, living in Connecticut with his wife Jeanne and their two kids. When he's not shooting TV commercials for Fortune 500 companies, he and Jeanne can be found cruising the country on their Harley Road King.

Stu Blandford earned business degrees from Emory and Vanderbilt, and then decided he'd rather be a writer. His first novel, *Bottle of Red* (under the name Stuart Clarke), was published in 2012. He's currently working on a children's book called *Seizures Can't Stop You* for children who suffer from epilepsy. E-mail him at stublandford@att.net.

Michele Boom turned in her teacher chalkboard to be an at-home mom. While juggling two toddlers and a traveling husband, she began to write. Her work appears in regional magazines across the U.S. and Canada. She's now working towards the publication of her first novel. Visit her at www.mammatalk.blogspot.com.

Melanie N. Brasher is a full-time mother to three boys and wife to an incredible husband who understands her bicultural background. She moonlights as an inspirational fiction and freelance writer and dreams of inspiring change one story at a time. To learn more about her writing visit www.melaniebrasher.com.

Barbara Burris studied creative writing at University of Wisconsin-Madison. She loves to read, paint and take endless photographs of the countryside around her. She is currently at work on her mother-in-law's biography and a series of autobiographical essays about cottage life.

Jane McBride Choate received her Bachelor of Science degree from Brigham Young University. Writing is a dream come true for her, especially appearing in the *Chicken Soup for the Soul* series.

D'ette Corona is the Assistant Publisher of Chicken Soup for the Soul Publishing, LLC. She received her Bachelor of Science degree in business management. D'ette has been happily married for twenty years and has a sixteen-year-old son whom she adores.

Jeff Davidson, of Raleigh, NC, holds the trademark "The Work-Life

Balance Expert." His fifty-sixth book, *Simpler Living*, was selected by four book clubs. His books, *The 60 Second Organizer*, *The 60 Second Self-Starter*, and *The 60 Second Innovator*, are popular in China, Japan, Malaysia, Indonesia, Russia, and twelve other countries. Learn more at www.BreathingSpace.com.

Heather Davis has a finely tuned snarky side that she uses to save her sanity. *Oversharing My Life*, a collection of humorous essays, is due to be released in April 2013. She and her family live in Oklahoma, where she chronicles her life at www.Minivan-Momma.com. Yes, she drives a minivan. Really.

Lynn Dove is a Christ-follower, a wife, a mom, a grandmother, a teacher and a writer (in that order). She is the author of the award-winning *Wounded* trilogy and won a Canadian Christian Writing Award for her blog, Journey Thoughts. Connect with Lynn on Twitter, Facebook and lynndove.wordpress.com.

Drema Drudge is an MFA student at Spalding University, and has recently completed her first novella. She teaches GED classes in Indiana, where she lives with her husband, Barry. They have two children. Her blog can be found at dremadrudge.wordpress.com.

Ginny Dubose is an avid writer of short stories. She credits her mother for her love of reading. A Florida Southern College graduate, Ginny lives in Florida with her husband Ray and sons, Danny and Alex. She hopes to write a book on landmark Supreme Court cases for use in middle school classrooms.

Laura Guman Fabiani lives in Pennsylvania with her husband and three children. She graduated from Douglass College with a degree in English and continues her education as a forever student in the School of Special Needs Parenting. E-mail her at LGF8998@gmail.com.

Melissa Face lives in Virginia with her husband and son. She teaches eleventh grade English and writes as often as possible. E-mail Melissa at writermsface@yahoo.com.

Victoria Fedden received her MFA degree in creative writing from Florida Atlantic University in 2009. She is a stay-at-home mom who enjoys writing, cooking and reading. She has just completed a memoir about life in South Florida. E-mail her at victoriafedden@gmail.com.

Karen Filek enjoys spending time with her husband, four children and animals on the family farm in Indiana. Her hobbies include photography, reading, and genealogy. She works as a legal assistant and is currently earning her Bachelor of Science degree in anthropology at Northern Kentucky University. E-mail her at karen_filek@yahoo.com.

David Fillingim is an award-winning author and editor whose books include *Georgia Cowboy Poets*, *Redneck Liberation: Country Music as Theology*, *Extreme Virtues: Living on the Prophetic Edge*, and *More Than Precious Memories: The Rhetoric of Southern Gospel Music*. He teaches at Cape Fear Community College in Wilmington, NC.

Christa Gala received a Bachelor of Arts degree in journalism from UNC-Chapel Hill and a Master of Arts degree in English from North Carolina State University. A freelance writer, she lives in North Carolina with her husband and nine-year-old son. E-mail her at writer@christagala.com.

William Garvey lives in Michigan with his wife Lorraine and family. He enjoys writing, photography and his family. William has had several stories published in *Chicken Soup for the Soul* books as well as other venues.

Amy Giles received her Bachelor of Arts degree in English Literature from the State University of New York College at Oneonta. She has worked in publishing for many years and is a freelance copywriter. She lives on Long Island, NY with her husband, daughters, and new muttigree pup. E-mail her at amygiles1066@verizon.net.

Tiffany Doerr Guerzon is a freelance essayist who writes about parenting, family and home life. She tries to highlight the inevitable humor in the life of a mom, as well as the tougher moments. You can read more of her writing at www.TDGuerzon.com.

Cynthia Hamond, S.F.O. is in over 110 publications including *Chicken Soup for the Soul* books. Two of her stories appear on television and as audiobooks. She received two writing awards and was featured in *Anthology Today*. She founded Joyful M.O.M. and Grandmas in Pajamas. E-mail her at Cynthiahamond@aol.com.

Carol Hartsoe writes from her home in Bear Creek, NC. A former newspaper columnist and retired teaching assistant, she now devotes her time to writing for children. E-mail her at chartsoe@ec.rr.com.

Jonny Hawkins lives in Sherwood, MI, with his wife, Carissa, and their three children. His cartoons have appeared in *Parade* magazine, *Reader's Digest* and in over 600 other publications. He creates six *Cartoon-a-Day* calendars and his recent books, *Amusing Grace* and *The Awesome Book of Hilarious and Heavenly Cartoons*, are currently available.

Susan M. Heim is a writer, editor and blogger, specializing in parenting, publishing, Christian and women's issues. She is a longtime editor for the *Chicken Soup for the Soul* series. Susan is married to Mike and has four sons: two college students and nine-year-old twins. E-mail her at susan@susanheim.com.

Christy Heitger-Ewing is a freelance writer living in Avon, IN. She is a columnist for *Cabin Life* magazine and also writes regularly for

Christian teen publications. She warns family and friends: "Anything you say or do may be used in a future story of mine." E-mail her at christy414@live.com.

Diane Helbig is an internationally recognized business and leadership development coach, author, speaker, and radio show host. As a certified professional coach, president of Seize This Day Coaching, and co-founder of Vision 21, Diane helps businesses and organizations operate more constructively and profitably.

Dana Hinders has been a freelance writer since her son was born in 2004. She frequently writes about parenting, crafts, and creative ways to save money. E-mail her at danahinders@butler-bremer.com.

Erika Hoffman often writes nonfiction narratives for the *Chicken Soup for the Soul* series, *Not Your Mother's Book*, and other anthologies. She used to teach school; she used to raise kids; and she even used to cook dinner. But now, she bangs the keys and pretends she's Erma Bombeck!

Christina Hunt is a single mother of seven children. She works as a crisis counselor. She loves to write to inspire, move, and uplift. She writes poetry and short stories for all ages about many difficult to discuss topics. E-mail her at christinahunt7@yahoo.com.

Theresa Hupp has previously published short stories and essays, including earlier pieces in the *Chicken Soup for the Soul* series. She has an anthology, *Family Recipe*, available through Amazon and Barnes & Noble. Theresa works with Whispering Prairie Press, publisher of *Kansas City Voices* magazine. Follow her blog at mthupp.wordpress.com.

Barbara Hussey retired from teaching English to pursue a career in clinical research. Combining interests, she is currently employed as an editorial consultant in a medical school. She lives in Louisiana where she enjoys gardening, reading, writing, and preserving memories from the past.

Craig Idlebrook is a journalist and editor whose essays have appeared in several anthologies, including *Chicken Soup for the Soul: Grieving and Recovery*. He regularly writes for *AAA*, *The Working Waterfront* and the *Hill Country Observer*. He lives in Massachusetts with his wife and daughter. E-mail him at craigidlebrook2@yahoo.com.

Deanna Ingalls teaches kindergarten in Alabama. She would like to thank her husband for encouraging her to follow her dreams and her three children for being the inspiration for her writing. This is her second story published in the *Chicken Soup for the Soul* series. E-mail her at teachingauthor@gmail.com.

Suzan L. Jackson is a freelance writer specializing in topics related to family, travel, books, and chronic illness and lives with her family in Delaware. She also publishes book reviews at her two blogs, bookbybook.blogspot.com and greatbooksforkidsandteens.com. For more information, visit her at www.suzanjackson.com.

Joelle Jarvis's passion has always been personal development. She has worked with many of the world's most inspirational names, including Tony Robbins, and now has her dream job as marketing director for Chicken Soup for the Soul. Her greatest love is her son Jackson. E-mail her at joellejarvis@mac.com.

Ron Kaiser is an unusually lucky writer from New Hampshire, who managed to convince a staggeringly beautiful woman to marry him. Astonishingly, her beauty grows as she ages, and if not for her, Ron Kaiser would likely live in a ditch, somewhere cold. They also have an awesome little boy together, named William.

Jonathan Katz is a recovering attorney, receiving his B.A. degree from Emory University (1981), his JD from the University of San Diego

(1984), and his MBA from Thunderbird (1986). He enjoys speaking French, exploring new worlds, rafting, tennis and especially his twins, Danielle and Michael. E-mail him at jkstrategy@aol.com.

Mimi Greenwood Knight is a "Luzianna" mother of four and freelance writer specializing in humorous essays on motherhood. Her collection, *Mom, You're Not Going to WRITE About This, Are You?*, is currently in search of a publisher. (Hello out there!) Mimi has essays in two-dozen *Chicken Soup for the Soul* books.

Kimber Krochmal lives in a small town in North Carolina. When not writing she enjoys drawing, painting, and spending time with her large family. Her children are a constant source of inspiration for her art and storytelling.

Cathi LaMarche is a novelist, essayist, and short story writer. Her work appears in numerous anthologies. Living in Missouri with her husband, two children, and three spoiled dogs, Cathi enjoys reading, gardening, and cooking. Every so often, she dares to venture forth into the wild.

Lynne Leite is proof that it is never too late to pursue your dreams. Now an empty nester, she is pursuing her dream of being a storyteller through the written and spoken word. She is thankful to God for the opportunity and to her husband, son, daughter and son-in-law for being the world's best cheerleaders.

Janeen Lewis is a writer living in Kentucky with her husband, Jesse, and two children, Andrew and Gracie. She has been published in several *Chicken Soup for the Soul* anthologies. When she isn't refereeing her kids, she loves reading and knitting. E-mail her at jlewis0402@ netzero.net.

Jaye Lewis is an award-winning inspirational writer and frequent contributing author to *Chicken Soup for the Soul* and other anthologies. She lives with her family in the Appalachian Mountains of Virginia. Follow her on Twitter @encouragingjaye or her blog at entertainingangelsencouragingwords.blogspot.com.

Barbara LoMonaco has worked for Chicken Soup for the Soul as an editor and webmaster since 1998. She has co-authored two *Chicken Soup for the Soul* book titles and has had stories published in various other titles. Barbara is a graduate of the University of Southern California and has a teaching credential.

Shawn Marie Mann is a writer and geographer who enjoys learning about her home state of Pennsylvania while traveling with her family. She can be reached through her website at www.shawnmariemann. com.

Erin Mantz is a writer and communications professional in the Washington, D.C. area. She is a graduate of Ithaca College in Ithaca, NY. She is the mom of two adventurous boys, ages eight and eleven, and weaves many real-life experiences and humor into her writing. E-mail her at ELMTree1@gmail.com.

Tim Martin is a contributing author to over a dozen *Chicken Soup for the Soul* books. He has four books due out in 2013: *Fast Pitch* and *Don the Dull-Shelled Turtle* (Cedar Grove Books), and *Lil' Wog the Hip Hop Frog* and *Somewhere Down the Line* (Neverland Publishing).

Tina Wagner Mattern is a Portland, OR writer/hairstylist. She's the wife of an awesome husband and the mother of two great kids. This is her sixth story in the *Chicken Soup for the Soul* anthologies. She is blessed beyond measure. E-mail her at tinamattern@earthlink.net.

Shannon McCarty writes humor articles to keep sane. She is a software trainer and part-time fitness instructor. She has three lovely and spirited children: Tess, Tabitha, and Riley. Shannon and her family live in Austin, TX. E-mail her at smccarty@austin.rr.com.

Dean K Miller is a freelance writer and member of Northern Colorado Writers. His work has appeared in *Trout* magazine, *Torrid Literature Journal Volume IV: The D.N.A. of the Poet* and online. Employed as an air traffic controller, Dean volunteers for PHWFF, enjoys family and fly fishing. Learn more at www.deankmiller.com.

Tracy Minor is a single parent of six children and grandparent of two. She works as an accountant full-time and does some freelance writing in her spare time. Her love for writing developed at an early age. This is her tenth story to be published. Her writing is dedicated to the memory of her son Eric, who passed away at age eleven.

Krisan Murphy received her B.A. degree in English from UT Arlington. After years of traveling, Krisan and her extraordinary family call coastal North Carolina their home. Besides reviewing books and writing for a city guide, Krisan serves young families in the church. E-mail her at krisanmurphy@gmail.com.

Judy O'Kelley's stories have appeared in the *Chicago Tribune* and *Country Woman* magazine, and her poetry featured in musical lyrics and greeting cards. A passionate parent and private tutor, Judy finds endless inspiration in her own talented children and her many spirited students. E-mail her at judyokelleycards@gmail.com.

Kim Ozment-Gold is a transplanted California native living in Texas with her husband of twenty-five years. She has had several articles and poetry published. Her writing reflects her life experiences with her greatest inspirations being her two grown children. E-mail her at mozart02_99@yahoo.com.

Mark Parisi's award-winning "off the mark" cartoon appears in newspapers worldwide. His work also appears on calendars, cards, books, T-shirts and more. Visit www.offthemark.com to view 7000+ cartoons. Mark resides in Massachusetts with his wife and business partner Lynn along with their daughter Jen, three cats and a dog.

Donna R. Paulson likes writing stories about her life with her four children on the island of Martha's Vineyard. She enjoys walking on the beach and looking for sea glass and appreciates a good laugh. She has written a novel and is currently working on her memoir.

Andrea Peebles lives with her husband of thirty-five years in Rockmart, GA. She is a frequent contributor to the *Chicken Soup for the Soul* anthologies and enjoys reading, writing, travel, photography and spending time with family. E-mail her at aanddpeebles@aol.com.

Novelist, blogger, and award-winning food writer, **Perry P. Perkins** is a work-at-home dad, and the owner of hautemealz.com. Perry has written for hundreds of magazines and his inspirational stories have been included in many *Chicken Soup for the Soul* anthologies. You can find Perry on Facebook at www.facebook.com/hautemealz.

Jennifer Quasha is a freelance writer and editor who is the co-author of *Chicken Soup for the Soul: My Dog's Life, Chicken Soup for the Soul: My Cat's Life, Chicken Soup for the Soul: I Can't Believe My Dog Did That!* and *Chicken Soup for the Soul: I Can't Believe My Cat Did That!* Learn more at www.jenniferquasha.com.

Susan R. Ray is a retired elementary school teacher who writes a weekly column entitled "Where We Are" for her hometown newspaper. She likes to play with her Grands (grandchildren), visit friends, bake bread, play *Scrabble*, knit, exercise, read, and write—columns, memoirs, and stories about her Grands.

Carol McAdoo Rehme made four trips along the parenting journey and some of the roads weren't paved! She is a widely published editor, author, and ghostwriter whose recent releases include a biography, *Finding the Pearl*, and a coffee table book, *Fundamentally Female*. She has also coauthored seven books.

Natalie June Reilly, communication major at ASU, is a proud football and Navy mom. Since T-ball, her time has been spent raising two young men in uniform, and laundering the blood, sweat and tears out of said uniforms. She's the author of *My Stick Family: Helping Children Cope with Divorce*.

Dan Reynolds' cartoons are seen in every city in the country via greeting cards (from American Greetings, Papyrus, NobleWorks, and others) and nationally in *Reader's Digest*.

Bruce Robinson is an award-winning published cartoonist whose work has appeared in the *National Enquirer*, *The Saturday Evening Post*, *Woman's World* and many other magazines. He is also the author of the cartoon books *Good Medicine* and *Bow Wows & Meows*. Contact him at CartoonsByBruceRobinson@hotmail.com

M. Cristina Ruiz is enjoying a second career as a new wife and born again mother. She shares her time with her grown kids and grandchildren. She was an elementary school teacher for twenty-five years and now spends her days reading, writing, and keeping up with her three dogs.

Jeneil Palmer Russell blogs at rhemashope.wordpress.com about life with her Army husband Brandon and their daughters Rhema, who is nine, autistic, epileptic, beautiful, brilliant, funny and gentle-hearted, and Hope, who is six, silly, joyful, imaginative, kind, and full of all of the best of childhood. Jeneil is author of *Sunburned Faces*.

Donna Finlay Savage is a pastor's wife who loves encouraging women. When she isn't writing or teaching, she's trying to simplify her life, see more joy, and conquer her addiction to chocolate. Her phone contains 100 photos of her grandson. You can reach Donna at donnasavagelv@cox.net or www.donnasavage.blogspot.com.

Denise Seagren-Peterson received her bachelor's degree in human relations at the University of Pittsburgh at Bradford and a master's degree in counseling psychology at St. Bonaventure University. Denise enjoys music, genealogy, history and spending time with her family. She plans to write historical fiction for young adults.

Ritu Shannon is originally from Victoria, BC, where she graduated from the University of Victoria with a Bachelor of Commerce. She now lives in Surrey, BC with her husband Jamie and two children, Priya and Keegan. She is a working professional who enjoys spending her spare time travelling with her family.

Tanya Shearer lives in Alabama with her husband, Clay. Their family includes a wonderful son, daughter and son-in-law. She enjoys taking her dog Cornbread for walks and writing children's stories and devotions. She is also a contributor to *Chicken Soup for the Soul: Here Comes the Bride.*

Deborah Shouse is a speaker, writer, and editor. She loves helping people write and edit books and she enjoys facilitating creativity and storytelling workshops. Deborah donates all proceeds from her book *Love in the Land of Dementia: Finding Hope in the Caregiver's Journey* to Alzheimer's. Visit her at www.thecreativityconnection.com.

Lori Slaton is originally from Long Island, NY. She is the mother of two teenagers and currently lives near Atlanta, GA. Lori enjoys writing as a hobby and hopes to fulfill her goal of completing the novel she began writing years ago. E-mail her at lori_slaton@bellsouth.net.

Rosemary Smiarowski has been happily married to her husband Greg for twenty-six years and together they have raised two great children: Matthew, twenty, and Cristina, eighteen. After choosing to remain at home for the past twenty years to raise her children, Rosemary now has some time to focus on one of her passions… writing!

Christine M. Smith is mother to three, grandmother to fourteen, great-grandmother to five and former foster mother to many. Her faith in God and family is her passion and spending time with God and family is her favorite joy. Writing about those experiences has become her greatest hobby. E-mail her at iluvmyfamilyxxx000@ yahoo.com.

Jean Sorensen's cartoons have been published in numerous national magazines, including *Good Housekeeping*, *The Saturday Evening Post*, *The Lutheran*, and *Funny Times*. Her work also appears in greeting cards (Oatmeal Studios), the *Chicken Soup for the Soul* series and the book *Laughing with Lutherans*.

Marcelle Soviero is the Editor-in-Chief of *Brain, Child: The Magazine for Thinking Mothers*. Her award-winning essays have been published in numerous publications including *The New York Times*, Salon.com, *Eating Well* and heard on *The Story* on National Public Radio. She lives in Wilton, CT with her husband and five children.

Julie Speece graduated college with honors in December 2011, while her husband and seventeen-year-old triplet daughters looked on. She lives in West Virginia, currently works as a substitute teacher, and plans to begin work on her master's degree in special education. She hopes to write a book someday.

Diane Stark is a former teacher turned stay-at-home mom and freelance writer. She loves to write about the important things in life: her family and her faith. E-mail Diane at DianeStark19@yahoo.com.

Julie Stephenson (B.A., M.A.T.) is a teacher and writer. In addition to reading and writing, she enjoys collecting antiques, watching college sports, and spending time with family and friends. Julie lives in coastal South Carolina with her husband, son, and crazy Boykin Spaniel.

Sue Summer writes for *The Newberry Observer* and *Newberry Magazine*, co-hosts a radio show for WKDK-AM, and is artist-in-residence with the S.C. Arts Commission. She graduated from USC and is author of the most widely read unpublished novel in history. She and her husband Henry have three children and one adored grandchild.

Karen C. Talcott is the co-author of three devotional books published by Chicken Soup for the Soul. When not writing, she loves spending time with her three children and husband. Going gluten-free this year has been a challenge, but if you need more information or support, e-mail Karen at Kartalcott@aol.com.

Tsgoyna Tanzman's career spans from fitness trainer to speech pathologist, to memoir teacher to life coach. Writing is the ultimate "therapy" for raising her daughter. Published in ten *Chicken Soup for the Soul* books, her essays and poems can be read online at More.com and mothering.com. E-mail her at coaching@changeitup.me.

Andrew Toos is the cartoon pen name of Andrew Grossman. His cartoons appear in textbooks, trade paperbacks and one-of-a-kind books published by Cambridge University Press, Simon & Schuster and many others. His business cartoons are consistently rated the most popular in surveys of speakers, authors and presenters.

Ginger Truitt is a columnist, speaker, and mother of five. Her award-winning column appears weekly in Midwest newspapers. Ginger enjoys tagging along on her husband's international business trips, and remodeling their 100-year-old farmhouse. She is working on her first book, *International Adventures of a Midwest Housewife*. E-mail her at ginger@gingertruitt.com.

Samantha Ducloux Waltz is an award-winning freelance writer in Portland, OR. Her personal stories appear in the *Chicken Soup for the Soul* series, numerous other anthologies, *The Christian Science Monitor* and *Redbook*. She has also written fiction and nonfiction under the name Samellyn Wood. Learn more at www.pathsofthought.com.

David Warren is the Vice President of Lutz Americas and attended Eastern Illinois University. He just turned fifty and is devoting more time to his love of writing. David is working on a novel and several children's stories. E-mail him at dwentwar@sbcglobal.net.

Brenda Watterson grew up in Ohio and graduated from Ashland University in 1991. She has enjoyed a successful career in human resources and sales development in both the retail and event technology industries. Brenda lives in Algonquin, IL, with her husband Billy and four children. E-mail her at brendah2oson@gmail.com.

Beth M. Wood is a mom of three, marketing professional and freelance writer. Her work can be found in both regional and national magazines, and in various *Chicken Soup for the Soul* anthologies. She is a devout reader, semi-fanatic editor and not-so-great golfer. Follow along at bethmwood.blogspot.com.

Susan Kimmel Wright lives in a western Pennsylvania farmhouse with her husband and an ever-changing assortment of animals and adult children. She has authored three children's mystery novels and many Chicken Soup for the Soul stories. Follow her on Twitter @ alphamomma or floatingagainstthecurrent.blogspot.com.

D.B. Zane is an educator, writer, and mother of three. While not an artist, she likes to do crafts with her kids and students. Her stories have appeared in other *Chicken Soup for the Soul* books. E-mail her at dbzanewriter@gmail.com.

Helen Zanone lives in Pittsburgh, PA, with her husband and three children. She is on the board of St. Davids Christian Writers' Conference. Helen is active in her writers' group and in fulfilling her love for writing. She has multiple stories published in the *Chicken Soup for the Soul* series. E-mail her at hzanone@yahoo.com.

Meet Our Authors

Jack Canfield is the co-creator of the *Chicken Soup for the Soul* series, which *Time* magazine has called "the publishing phenomenon of the decade." Jack is also the co-author of many other bestselling books.

Jack is the CEO of the Canfield Training Group in Santa Barbara, California, and founder of the Foundation for Self-Esteem in Culver City, California. He has conducted intensive personal and professional development seminars on the principles of success for more than a million people in twenty-three countries, has spoken to hundreds of thousands of people at more than 1,000 corporations, universities, professional conferences and conventions, and has been seen by millions more on national television shows.

Jack has received many awards and honors, including three honorary doctorates and a Guinness World Records Certificate for having seven books from the *Chicken Soup for the Soul* series appearing on the New York Times bestseller list on May 24, 1998.

You can reach Jack at www.jackcanfield.com.

Mark Victor Hansen is the co-founder of Chicken Soup for the Soul, along with Jack Canfield. He is a sought-after keynote speaker, bestselling author, and marketing maven. Mark's powerful messages of possibility, opportunity, and action have created powerful change in thousands of organizations and millions of individuals worldwide.

Mark is a prolific writer with many bestselling books in addition to the *Chicken Soup for the Soul* series. Mark has had a profound influence in the field of human potential through his library of audios, videos, and articles in the areas of big thinking, sales achievement, wealth building, publishing success, and personal and professional development. He is also the founder of the MEGA Seminar Series.

Mark has received numerous awards that honor his entrepreneurial spirit, philanthropic heart, and business acumen. He is a lifetime member of the Horatio Alger Association of Distinguished Americans.

You can reach Mark at www.markvictorhansen.com.

Amy Newmark is Chicken Soup for the Soul's publisher and editor-in-chief, after a thirty-year career as a writer, speaker, financial analyst, and business executive in the worlds of finance and telecommunications. Amy is a *magna cum laude* graduate of Harvard College, where she majored in Portuguese, minored in French, and traveled extensively. She and her husband have four grown children.

After a long career writing books on telecommunications, voluminous financial reports, business plans, and corporate press releases, Chicken Soup for the Soul is a breath of fresh air for Amy. She has fallen in love with Chicken Soup for the Soul and its life-changing books, and really enjoys putting these books together for Chicken Soup for the Soul's wonderful readers. She has co-authored more than four dozen *Chicken Soup for the Soul* books and has edited another three dozen.

You can reach Amy with any questions or comments through webmaster@chickensoupforthesoul.com and you can follow her on Twitter @amynewmark.

Thank You

We owe huge thanks to all of our contributors. We know that you poured your hearts and souls into the thousands of stories that you shared with us. We appreciate your willingness to open up your lives to other Chicken Soup for the Soul readers and share your own experiences, no matter how personal. As I read and edited these entertaining and inspirational stories, I was excited by the potential of this book to inspire parents, to give them a fun break during their busy days, to remind them why they have undertaken the huge job of raising children. This was a fun project for our assistant publisher D'ette Corona and me and I was almost sorry when we finished it!

We could only publish a small percentage of the stories that were submitted, but every single one was read and even the ones that do not appear in the book had an influence on us and on the final manuscript. Our editor Jeanne Blandford read many of the early submissions and helped us figure out the focus of the book. D'ette Corona read all the submissions and developed the chapter ideas. And Barbara LoMonaco and Madeline Clapps performed their normal masterful proofreading jobs while Kristiana Glavin Pastir made sure we got to the printer on time.

We also owe a very special thanks to our creative director and book producer, Brian Taylor at Pneuma Books, for his brilliant vision for our covers and interiors.

~Amy Newmark

Improving Your Life Every Day

R eal people sharing real stories—for twenty years. Now, Chicken Soup for the Soul has gone beyond the bookstore to become a world leader in life improvement. Through books, movies, DVDs, online resources and other partnerships, we bring hope, courage, inspiration and love to hundreds of millions of people around the world. Chicken Soup for the Soul's writers and readers belong to a one-of-a-kind global community, sharing advice, support, guidance, comfort, and knowledge.

Chicken Soup for the Soul stories have been translated into more than forty languages and can be found in more than one hundred countries. Every day, millions of people experience a Chicken Soup for the Soul story in a book, magazine, newspaper or online. As we share our life experiences through these stories, we offer hope, comfort and inspiration to one another. The stories travel from person to person, and from country to country, helping to improve lives everywhere.

Share with Us

We all have had Chicken Soup for the Soul moments in our lives. If you would like to share your story or poem with millions of people around the world, go to chickensoup.com and click on "Submit Your Story." You may be able to help another reader, and become a published author at the same time. Some of our past contributors have launched writing and speaking careers from the publication of their stories in our books!

Our submission volume has been increasing steadily—the quality and quantity of your submissions has been fabulous. We only accept story submissions via our website. They are no longer accepted via mail or fax.

To contact us regarding other matters, please send us an e-mail through webmaster@chickensoupforthesoul.com, or fax or write us at:

Chicken Soup for the Soul
P.O. Box 700
Cos Cob, CT 06807-0700
Fax: 203-861-7194

One more note from your friends at Chicken Soup for the Soul: Occasionally, we receive an unsolicited book manuscript from one of our readers, and we would like to respectfully inform you that we do not accept unsolicited manuscripts and we must discard the ones that appear.

Chicken Soup for the Soul®

Thanks Mom

101 Stories of Gratitude, Love, and Good Times

Jack Canfield,
Mark Victor Hansen & Wendy Walker
Foreword by Joan Lunden

A mother's job is never done, but in this great gift book she gets the praise she deserves. Daughters and sons share their words of thanks in this new collection of stories for moms. Stories of special memories, loving and hard lessons, support and encouragement will bring any mom joy, inspiration, and amusement. Mothers of all ages and stages will feel good about the recognition they receive. Includes foreword with special story by Joan Lunden!

978-1-935096-45-0

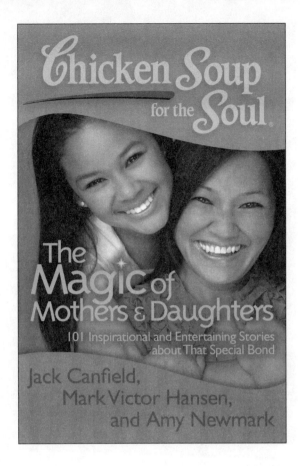

Chicken Soup for the Soul

The Magic of Mothers & Daughters

101 Inspirational and Entertaining Stories about That Special Bond

Jack Canfield, Mark Victor Hansen, and Amy Newmark

Mothers and daughters. They are, at the same time, very similar and completely unique. This relationship—through birth, childhood, teen years, adulthood, grandchildren, aging, and every step in between—can be the best, the hardest, and the sweetest. Mothers and daughters will laugh, cry, and find inspiration in this collection of stories that remind them of their shared love, appreciation and special bond.

978-1-935096-81-8

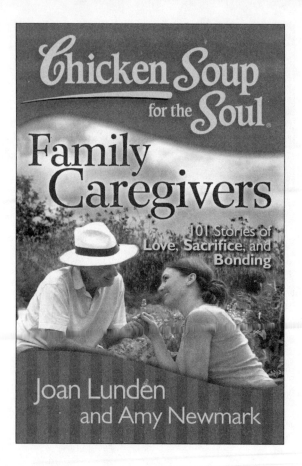

Chicken Soup for the Soul

Family Caregivers

101 Stories of Love, Sacrifice, and Bonding

Joan Lunden and Amy Newmark

Do you have a family member who requires constant care? You are not alone. This collection offers support and encouragement in its 101 stories for family caregivers of all ages, including the "sandwich" generation caring for a family member while raising their children. With stories by those on the receiving end of the care too. These stories of love, sacrifice, and lessons will inspire and uplift family members making sacrifices to make sure their loved ones are well cared for, whether in their own homes or elsewhere.

978-1-935096-83-2

Nearly everyone thinks their own family is "nutty" or has at least one or two nuts. With 101 stories of wacky yet lovable relatives, funny foibles, and holiday meltdowns, this book is usually hilarious and occasionally poignant. This book shows readers that we all have the same family matters and what really matters is families. It is a quirky and fun holiday book, and a great bridal shower or wedding gift!

978-1-935096-55-9

Chicken Soup for the Soul
for the Soul.

Think Positive

101 Inspirational Stories about Counting Your Blessings and Having a Positive Attitude

Jack Canfield,
Mark Victor Hansen & Amy Newmark
Foreword by Deborah Norville

Every cloud has a silver lining. Readers will be inspired by these 101 real-life stories from people just like them, taking a positive attitude to the ups and downs of life, and remembering to be grateful and count their blessings. This book continues Chicken Soup for the Soul's focus on inspiration and hope, and its stories of optimism and faith will encourage readers to stay positive during challenging times and in their everyday lives.

978-1-935096-56-6

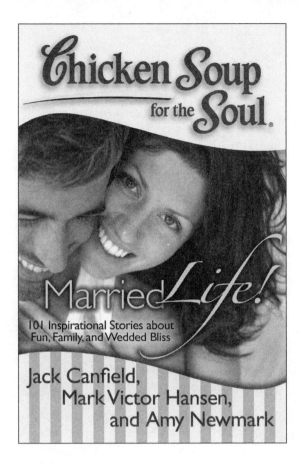

Marriage is a wonderful institution, and in this fresh collection of stories, husbands and wives share their personal, funny, and quirky stories from the trenches. This book will inspire and delight readers with its entertaining and heartwarming stories about fun, family, and wedded bliss. Whether newly married or married for years and years, readers will find laughter and inspiration in these 101 stories of love, romance, fun, and making it work.

978-1-935096-85-6

Chicken Soup for the Soul

www.chickensoup.com